HOW WE CAME BACK

HOW WE CAME BACK

Voices from Post-Katrina New Orleans

Nona Martin Storr,
Emily Chamlee-Wright
& Virgil Henry Storr

MERCATUS CENTER
George Mason University

Arlington, Virginia

Book cover and interior design by Joanna Andreasson
Typesetting by Thomas J. Piwowar & Associates, Inc.
Editorial services by Publications Professionals LLC

Mercatus Center at George Mason University
3434 Washington Blvd., 4th Floor
Arlington, VA 22201
(703) 993-4930
mercatus.org

Library of Congress Cataloging-in-Publication Data

Storr, Nona Martin.
     How we came back : voices from post-Katrina New Orleans / by Nona Martin Storr, Emily Chamlee-Wright, and Virgil Henry Storr.
        pages cm
     ISBN 978-1-942951-14-8 (paperback) -- ISBN 978-1-942951-15-5 (kindle ebook)
     1. Neighborhoods--Louisiana--New Orleans--History--21st century. 2. Hurricane Katrina, 2005--Social aspects--Louisiana--New Orleans. 3. Urban renewal--Louisiana--New Orleans--History--21st century. 4. Disaster relief--Louisiana--New Orleans--History--21st century. 5. Community life--Louisiana--New Orleans--History--21st century. 6. Disaster victims--Louisiana--New Orleans--Biography. 7. New Orleans (La.)--Biography. 8. New Orleans (La.)--Social conditions--21st century. 9. New Orleans (La.)--Social life and customs--21st century. I. Chamlee-Wright, Emily, 1966- II. Storr, Virgil Henry, 1975- III. Title.
     F379.N56A276 2015
     976.3'35064--dc23
                                                    2015009192

Printed in the United States of America

Contents

Foreword
THE ANATOMY
OF RECOVERY

Nona Martin Storr, Emily Chamlee-Wright, and Virgil Henry Storr have compiled an intimate and detailed account of the trials and tribulations the people of New Orleans encountered in trying to rebuild their businesses, their churches, their communities, their families, and ultimately their lives after Hurricane Katrina. *How We Came Back* is a collection of oral histories that explores how individuals strive to resume "normal" life after a disaster.

As the principal investor of the broader project of which this volume is a part, I could not be prouder. When I started my social science career as an economist in the field of Sovietology, one of my strongest influences methodologically was Alain Besançon's essay "Anatomy of a Spectre." As he argued,

> The Soviet economy is the subject of a considerable volume of scholarly work which occupies numerous study centers in Europe and the United States and which provides material for a vast literature and various academic journals. *But those born in the Soviet Union or those who approach Soviet society through history, literature, travel or through listening to what the émigrés have to say, find that they cannot*

recognize what the economists describe. There seems to be an unbridgeable gap between this system, conceived through measurements and figures, and the other system, without measurements or figures, which they have come to know through intuition and their own actual experience.*

With the encouragement of my advisor at George Mason University, economist Don Lavoie, I started to think of ways to analytically combine a form of rational choice institutionalism (praxeology broadly understood) with more narrative and interpretative empirical work (*Verstehen* broadly understood). This approach to understanding social phenomena respects the past and recognizes the value of listening to the stories people tell themselves and tell others about themselves. It also recognizes the importance of economic ethnography, which is critical to pursuing what economist and historian Deirdre McCloskey has described as an "empirical yet Austrian economics." This approach maintains the argumentative structure of rational choice institutionalism, but it uses that analytical framework to interpret human action from the purposes, plans, and understanding of the actors themselves in their unique circumstances. We must listen and learn from those on the ground.

In addition to Besançon's work in Sovietology, which suggested ethnography as a viable empirical strategy, I was also deeply influenced by the work of Nobel Prize–winning economist Elinor Ostrom on the nature of the rules in use as opposed to the stated, formal rules that constitute the working institutions in the rational choice institutionalism framework. She, too, focused on the informal sector on the ground.

The informal economy became a major theme of my research on the workings of the Soviet-type economy as well as the starting point for the analysis of that system's reform

---

*   Alain Besançon, "Anatomy of a Spectre," *Survey* (October 1980): 143–59, emphasis added.

that occupied my research efforts for much of the 1990s. The lessons from the Soviet experience expand beyond the fields of Sovietology and comparative economic systems. They lead to radically rethinking the entire project of political economy and the economics of everyday life.

Virgil Storr and I wrote a paper about what we called at the time "post-classical political economy." We emphasized the triple embeddedness of social action, in which the economic and financial aspects of human action overlap with the political and legal aspects as well as the social and cultural aspects. A proper political economy analysis, we argued, cannot ignore the embeddedness of human action and the pattern of exchange and production relationships that emerges in that context. Outcomes, in short, are context dependent. Like Ostrom, we don't deny that we can learn from more formal structures in theory, or from more controlled settings in our empirics, but we insist, like Besançon and Ostrom, that a lot can be learned from the folks on the ground. Indeed, we need to listen and learn from the voices on the ground before we analyze and diagnose their situations with the aid of our theoretical framework, and we need to evaluate the analytic narratives we construct against this ultimate empirical check: the beliefs, thoughts, aspirations, and meanings of those living the experience we are trying to analyze.

Influenced by this perspective, shortly after 2000, the Mercatus Center at George Mason University formed a research team to examine the role of institutions in economic development and the political economy of transitioning economies. For several years, we had research teams in less developed countries and in transitioning economies. Members of the research team published journal articles, dissertations, and books addressing issues in countries from the Czech Republic to China, from emerging markets to failed and weak states. From 2000 through 2005, this group was very productive, and we learned a lot from our on-the-ground research about the political economy of everyday life and the prospects and perils of economic reform efforts.

The critical next move was to examine disasters and disaster recovery using the tools of economics. "Disaster economics" is a sub-branch of development economics. In August 2005, as we saw the horrific events caused by Hurricane Katrina's landfall on the Gulf Coast, we committed to studying the recovery process over the next five years to learn what we could about how resilient communities were, how they rebuild social relationships that have literally washed away, and how this rebuilding occurs at the intersection of economic and financial institutions, political and legal institutions, and social and cultural institutions. The paper that Storr and I published in 2002 in the *American Journal of Economics and Sociology*, "Post-classical Political Economy," created the intellectual framework that guided our studies from 2005 through 2010 dealing with the post-Katrina shuffling and reshuffling of the economic, political, and social spaces in New Orleans.

Like our earlier work, we had teams in the Greater New Orleans region focusing on various aspects of the recovery. Some focused on the interaction of the political and legal systems in the economic recovery. Others studied the interaction between private-sector commerce and the economic recovery, including the role of big-box stores such as Wal-Mart. Still others studied the way communities work to get the population to move back, as in Chamlee-Wright's examination of the leadership exhibited in the schools and churches.

Again, our research effort produced published journal articles, some that employ a conventional economics form and others that depart radically from the mainstream methodology. But all our studies challenged the conventional wisdom about "right action" in the wake of the storm.

The received wisdom, as embodied in the mainstream media coverage in the months following Hurricane Katrina, was that the Gulf Coast had only just began to recover. This proclamation was not based on a fair assessment of the facts. Hard-hit communities faced serious problems, no doubt. But recovery was occurring at the neighborhood level early on; views of recovery based on political jurisdictions did not reflect accurately the quality or sustainability of the recovery. We discovered that the ability of disaster victims to leverage social capital as well as the leadership emanating from the voluntary sector was critical to promoting community recovery. Our desire to study the recovery process in an intimate and in-depth manner led us to create this oral history.

Across the Gulf Coast, people affected by Katrina have shown us how people acquire knowledge and how people perceive government, businesses, and community efforts. Our social scientific research, based on more than 450 hours of interviews with people from the Gulf Coast, is critical to better understanding how people, businesses, and communities prepare for and rebuild after disasters and to better understanding the role that the for-profit, nonprofit, and public sectors play in everyday social and economic interactions.

Community organizations, businesses, nonprofit groups, and religious institutions help families make informed decisions about rebuilding. Reopened businesses, resumed church services, and similar phenomena send positive signals that communities are coming back. Residents making decisions about returning rely heavily on these signals in the face of conflicting or incorrect signals from authorities.

Despite the immense scope of this disaster, individuals and communities found hope and help in the immensely generous philanthropic contributions of informal networks of voluntary social action, such as religious organizations, as well as in established nonprofits. Social entrepreneurs play a vital role in disaster recovery efforts, providing the materials, services, and information that people need to rebuild their lives and filling in the frequently immense gaps left by government-provided services. The centralization of compassion, more often than not, distorts or even displaces the self-governing properties of civil society.

In *Democracy in America,* sociologist and political theorist Alexis de Tocqueville writes,

> There is nothing, in my opinion, that merits our attention more than the intellectual and moral associations of America. The political and industrial associations of the Americans easily fall within our grasp, but the others escape us; and, if we discover them, we understand them badly, because we have hardly ever seen anything analogous. You must recognize, however, that the intellectual and moral associations are as necessary as the political and industrial ones to the American people, and perhaps more. In democratic countries, the science of association is the mother science; the progress of all the others depends on the progress of the former.[†]

Tocqueville's observation holds true today. Real, democratic self-governance resides in the communities where citizens are willing and capable co-producers of civil society. The face-to-face forces of reputation and community membership not only coordinate highly effective small-scale projects that support those in need, they also provide a sense of community and identity to us all.

How We Came Back is a testament to the resilience and power of a self-governing citizenry and the trials and tribulations they endure in dealing with the "cares of thinking and all the troubles of living," as Tocqueville put it. Its stories offer a fascinating window into the self-governing capacity of a people and the truly democratic way of life, even in the aftermath of

---

[†]   Alexis de Tocqueville, *Democracy in America: Historical-Critical Edition of De la démocratie en Amérique,* ed. Eduardo Nolla, trans. James T. Schleifer, vol. 3 (Indianapolis: Liberty Fund, 2010).

horrific devastation. Acts of courage, acts of compassion, and acts of cooperation are all required to rebuild a community and the lives that constitute that community.

Listen and learn.

Peter Boettke

University Professor of Economics and Philosophy, George Mason University

Vice President of Academic Research, Mercatus Center at George Mason University

Introduction
WHAT STORIES OF
RETURN CAN TEACH US

This volume presents 17 oral histories of Hurricane Katrina survivors from four very different communities in New Orleans, namely, the Ninth Ward; Central City; the Gentilly Woods, Gentilly Terrace, and Pontchartrain Park neighborhoods; and the Mary Queen of Vietnam (MQVN) community in Village de l'Est. These survivors and their neighborhoods had dissimilar pre-Katrina, Katrina, and post-Katrina experiences. And their oral histories speak to the dissimilarities and offer rich descriptions of what these communities were like before Katrina; how these individuals and their families survived Katrina; and most important, how these individuals, their families, and their communities came back after the devastation of Katrina. Collectively, they show that individuals and communities can be surprisingly resilient in the wake of disaster.

At five in the morning on August 29, 2005, Hurricane Katrina, one of the strongest and costliest hurricanes in the United States' history, made landfall in southern Louisiana. The storm and the storm-related flooding that followed it displaced half a million people and caused more than $100 billion in damage in the Greater New Orleans region. Recovering from a disaster of this magnitude would be a daunting challenge. Still, within a few years after Katrina, hundreds of thousands had returned and were rebuilding their homes. How they came back is, to say the least, something of a puzzle.

The oral histories of Katrina survivors presented here were collected as part of a multiyear investigation of community rebound in the Greater New Orleans region after Katrina. That investigation resulted in several efforts to find answers to the questions posed by this post-disaster environment.[1] Why, for example, do we observe some communities rebounding quickly and others lagging? Even after we accounted for obvious factors, such as degree of damage, median income, flood insurance, and other standard explanations of recovery, we found that much of the variance remains unexplained. Why, despite overwhelming obstacles, are some residents, even in the most impoverished and severely damaged areas, exhibiting robust signs of individual and community rebound? What are the socially embedded resources that communities are drawing on to develop effective recovery strategies? Recovering from a disaster almost always requires individuals to tap their social networks for material and emotional support. Why, despite the commitment of significant government resources, have many of the official forms of assistance been met with such disappointing results?

Although we have drawn on social scientific theory and analysis to address these questions, we knew that only by talking with people who were experiencing the challenges of post-disaster recovery firsthand would we be able to address these questions adequately. But, somewhat ironically, much of our work that addresses such questions abstracts the fullness and continuity of individual narratives to identify patterns that extend across neighborhoods and communities. The present volume has afforded the opportunity to swing the pendulum in the other direction and to focus on the individual narrative in greater detail.

This volume, thus, makes a deliberate attempt to let the Katrina survivors that we met speak for themselves. Their stories are sometimes sad, sometimes horrific, sometimes surreal, occasionally funny, and almost always uplifting as they catalogue people overcoming tremendous odds to rebuild their lives and their communities. They often speak about loss (their loss of property and their loss of neighbors, friends, and loved ones); about their hopes and fears before, during, and after the storm; and about the difficulties of returning and rebuilding.

Although we made every effort in this volume to put the voices of those who have returned to post-Katrina New Orleans at the center, we are mindful that framing is an inevitable part of what we do as narrators, no matter how light-handed that narration might be. The fact, for instance, that we have bundled particular individual stories within community-based chapters asserts that physical place, neighborhood, and community are part of the story. Although we have reason to believe that this is indeed the case generally,[2] we recognize that individual lives are rarely, if ever, perfect and unqualified demonstrations of such patterns. As important as it is to identify patterns that help us understand the process of post-disaster recovery, social scientific explanations also tend to direct attention away from the tension, contradiction, and messiness that exist at the individual level. For example, though Richard and April, whose oral histories appear in the Ninth Ward chapter, are staking their personal and financial futures on the New Orleans recovery, they are deeply skeptical about the political and cultural health of the city. Similarly, as you will read in the Gentilly Woods, Gentilly Terrace, and Pontchartrain Park chapter, Easton's return to New Orleans had more to do with his wife's sense that there is no other place as good as New Orleans than his sense of belonging. Likewise, Joyce, a Central City resident, admitted that she will stay in the city, not because it is what she would prefer, but because she knows her husband and her mother would feel lost in any other place. While sense of place is an important pattern that helps explain community rebound in New Orleans, individual narratives remind us to recognize the tensions within and around such patterns.

Further, though this collection of oral histories places first-hand accounts at the center, there is no escaping the perspectives we as editors bring to this project. The perspective of the oral historian cannot help but privilege certain voices over others; in this case, we have privileged the voices of those who experienced the calamities of disaster firsthand. Surely in this privileging we gain certain kinds of insight that would otherwise be closed off. But, by doing so, we reduce the emphasis on other kinds of insight, such as the insights drawn from, say, experts trained in post-disaster recovery. Moreover, the perspective of the social scientist is surely at work whenever we direct attention to clues within firsthand accounts that suggest a causal connection—in particular, a connection between individual behavior and broader social patterns.

Rather than defend ourselves against harboring such biases, or make an attempt to minimize the importance of such biases, we think it more productive (and more honest) to admit them freely. Doing so gives us an opportunity to explore some of the lessons that surface when we are able to (a) present fuller and more detailed personal narratives, as opposed to the snippets of narrative customarily featured in qualitative social scientific research, and (b) view these narratives from the perspectives that have informed the larger project.

One of the advantages fuller, more detailed narratives afford is the opportunity to see that an event such as Hurricane Katrina, even for all its significance, represents continuity as much as discontinuity in the lives and histories of individuals and communities. In the absence of a fuller story, it is easy to forget that people caught in the throes of Katrina and post-Katrina recovery had lives—sometimes idyllic lives, sometimes deeply troubled lives; more often than not, complicated lives—before the storm. And though Katrina has loomed large in the years since the storm, many of those complicating factors—young children, aging parents, a new marriage, health problems, career ambitions, the death of a loved one, marital strain, and so on—have mixed with, shaped, and colored post-Katrina life.

Individual narratives enable us to see better the ways in which pre-Katrina life set the stage for how people responded in the aftermath of the storm. For example, Elizabeth and Ervin's story (in the Ninth Ward chapter) and Saundra's story (in the Central City chapter) enable us to see how their attachment to New Orleans made their return all but inevitable. Further, fuller narratives allow us to see not only that people move on with the business of ordinary life in the midst of chaos, but how they move on: Richard and April quit their jobs to focus their effort on rebuilding rental properties; Mary (in the MQVN chapter) suddenly finds herself leading a community development corporation as its executive director; Melvin (in the Ninth Ward chapter) recognizes that the first order of business in making his life whole is to be reunited with his dog, Bandit. In one sense, how people move forward in the wake of disaster is something of a mystery. But their narratives help us lift the shroud by allowing us to see how a person's past sets the stage for effective and meaningful action.

Having access to fuller, more detailed narratives also gives us a window into the personal resilience that is at the heart of successful rebound and recovery. Examples of such personal resilience and clues to its source can certainly be found in the narratives presented in this volume. The fact that Miriam (in the Ninth Ward chapter), a woman with few financial resources, was able to survive the storm, the chaos of the convention center, and evacuation, and to move back and rebuild her life and home in the city she loves is noteworthy by any standard. But when viewed in the broader context of a life history that includes the loss of three children, two at the hands of another son, Miriam's actions appear nothing less than heroic. Gentilly Woods resident Lydia's positive outlook about the prospects for her community is heartening given the devastation it has endured. But again, viewed from the broader perspective of a woman who has lost her closest friend and her husband since the storm and is left to care for an adult child with significant disabilities, such positivity seems worthy of our attention if we are to understand the connection between personal resilience and post-disaster recovery. In Miriam's case, resilience is born of an ability to adapt her behavior to any new set of circumstances in which she finds herself, whether it is becoming an Indian runner in the convention center or finding a way to set fear aside and protect herself and her property in the first harrowing days of returning to her home. For Lydia, the ability to see almost any setback as an opportunity and a blessing—a torn-up house is the vehicle for connecting to good-hearted people she would otherwise never meet (and acquiring hardwood floors she would otherwise never have)—seems to be at least part of her foundation for resilience.

Just as individual narratives can shed light on personal qualities of resilience at the individual level, personal narratives can also shed light on potential sources of community resilience. For example, able-bodied retirees like Elizabeth and Ervin played a vital (though mostly unsung) role in the recovery process by devoting full-time effort, pensions, and any accumulated assets to the task of rebuilding, often at the critical early stage of the recovery process in which people waiting on the sidelines were looking for concrete signs that normal life was returning to the neighborhood. Similarly, mutual support offered within families, such as the roving gutting brigade Pontchartrain Park resident Michael, his cousins, and his siblings assembled, filled a critical logistical need they and members of their family were facing and injected forward momentum into, not one, but seven neighborhoods within a brief span of time. Father Vien's use of the church facilities, personnel, and volunteers to orchestrate supply distribution, communication within the community, and negotiation with service providers beyond the community enabled a swift recovery within the MQVN neighborhood. As our broader research confirms, early and disproportionately large effects of individual efforts such as these were often critical to the recovery process.[3]

Clarity of purpose is another element that helps explain the connection between individual resilience and community resilience—and again, one that is best revealed through personal narrative. If neighborhoods are to rebound, at least some within the community must possess a certainty that taking on the hardships of rebuilding is worthwhile. Without at least a few stakeholders possessing this level of certainty, no one ever takes the first critical steps that signal the future viability of the community. But what gives rise to this kind of certainty in a context that seems to conspire against it at every turn? The personal narratives that connect past and present help us understand at least some of the sources of this kind of deep confidence. For example, Kim's narrative (presented in the Ninth Ward chapter) reveals a continuous thread that connects her sense of purpose in the community pre-Katrina, her ability to withstand the uncertainty of her husband's fate immediately following the storm, and her husband's determination to rebuild their business after the storm. This thread was the belief that divine intent was guiding her steps at every juncture. She believes she is playing a critical part in God's plan to restore a neighborhood in which the good life can once again be found. Similarly, even with the many obstacles and frustrations they faced, April and Richard were certain of the correctness of their decision to return, or in April's words, "We both feel like this is where God wants us to be right now and we wouldn't feel comfortable going somewhere else just because it seems easier."

The oral histories presented here teach us about what Katrina victims have had to overcome and how they and their communities have rebounded after the storm. They remind us that though disaster tears the social fabric, the threads can often be used in new ways that meet immediate needs, rebuild homes, and restore communities.

1
NINTH WARD

Before Hurricane Katrina, it is fair to say that most of America had never heard of the Ninth Ward of New Orleans. After the storm, for most Americans, Katrina and the Ninth Ward were almost interchangeable. The pictures of people trudging through chest-high water; the images of collapsed structures and cars through the walls of houses; the scenes of victims dehydrated and suffering from almost interminable heat on rooftops hoping to be rescued; the stories of the despair that occurred in the Superdome—many of these were images from the Ninth Ward or of displaced Ninth Ward residents. When Kanye West proclaimed that the President of the United States did not care about black people, he likely believed that he was speaking on behalf of the people in the Ninth Ward. Spike Lee's *When the Levees Broke* was largely a story of the Ninth Ward and Ninth Ward residents. The images of blighted and desolate neighborhoods one, two, and even five years after Katrina that became the emblematic images of the slowness of community recovery in New Orleans are also pictures of the Ninth Ward. The Ninth Ward, however, is more than just the stock photo or a symbol of despair. It is a real community with its own history and character.

The Lower Ninth Ward is the most famous subdivision of the Ninth Ward. The Lower Ninth Ward can be divided into two distinct neighborhoods, Holy Cross and the Lower Ninth. Holy Cross is across from the Lower Ninth on the other side of St. Claude Avenue. Both communities are separated from Bywater (the adjacent neighborhood) by the Industrial Canal, which was built in 1923 and added to the isolation of the Holy Cross and the Lower Ninth neighborhoods.[1] The area above the canal is called the Upper Ninth Ward.

The entire Ninth Ward was once an environment where human inhabitation was not possible. It was not until the latter part of the 19th century that the Ninth Ward became a place where people could settle. Before then, much of the Ninth Ward was a thick bald cypress swamp. The real change, however, came in 1910 when New Orleans started a large-scale pumping program and made this area much more livable. Still, it was prone to flooding, which was likely the reason it was among the last areas of the city to be settled. The people who eventually settled there were those who could not afford housing anywhere else in the city: mostly poor immigrants and African Americans.

In the 1930s, building lots in the Ninth Ward sold for as little as $250 each. People who moved into the Holy Cross and the Lower Ninth neighborhoods tended to build shotgun-style houses similar to those that are popular in Central City. The layout of these houses, which allows breezes to blow through the structure, is perfect for the stifling Louisiana summer heat. An African/New World hybrid, there is little wonder that the shotgun house became the style of choice, because so many of the residents were of African descent and the humid climate in New Orleans made the style a sensible one.[2]

Even as the rest of the city changed and modernized, the Ninth Ward appeared a perfect snapshot of a place stuck in time. As historian Sarah Searight observes, if one wanted to see what New Orleans looked like in the 18th century to early 19th century, one simply needed to "turn off the main roads dissecting the city's impoverished Ninth Ward." As she writes, looking at the Ninth Ward, it would "not require much imagination to visualize early conditions."[3]

The physical conditions in the Ninth Ward certainly were in need of improvements by 1955, when members of the Ninth Ward Civic and Improvement League sent a letter to their representative, bringing to his attention some of the most bothersome issues in the ward. As the letter described, the neighborhood suffered from "poor housing and overcrowded conditions of [the] schools, the disease-breeding septic tanks, cesspool, outdoor toilets, stagnant water and the gutters; the flooded and muddy streets; the uncontrolled trash and garbage and the foul odor in the air."[4]

By the end of the 20th century, the Ninth Ward was over 95 percent African American and still suffering from the problems of concentrated poverty. Thirty-nine percent of the population in the Lower Ninth (the area excluding Holy Cross) lived below the poverty line. Sixty percent of these households were led by a female head of family in whose home there was at least one child under 18 years of age.[5] Additionally, the homicide rate in the Ninth Ward was among the highest in the city.[6]

Even in the face of such social concerns, many residents of the Ninth Ward held their community in high regard. It had, as the preceding request for assistance demonstrates, concerned and involved citizens. Arguably, this has a lot to do with the relatively high rates of homeownership in the Ninth Ward. Homeownership in the Lower Ninth Ward was particularly strong, with close to 60 percent of residents owning their homes.[7] Before Katrina, in fact, the Lower Ninth Ward had the highest rate of homeownership of all New Orleans. These homes were more often than not passed down through family from the original occupants. Because the homeowners did not have the disposable income necessary for their upkeep, many properties were not always in the best physical condition. As Dessauer and Armstrong describe, "the median home value of the Lower Ninth Ward was significantly lower than that of Orleans Parish at $52,420 versus $88,100, a reflection of the depreciation in home values from lack of upkeep and investments."[8] Consequently, the high rate of homeownership did not equal prosperity.[9]

This image of Lower Ninth Ward poverty is not the full story, however. Though not affluent, the neighborhood is home to small businesses, little eateries, salons and barbershops, churches, schools, and other social and commercial spaces that transform a collection of houses into a community. The strong attachment many residents have to this neighborhood is driven in part by the specific amenities they find within it.[10]

This community also has a rich history of survival that was in evidence long before Hurricane Katrina made landfall. The Ninth Ward was the site where some of the most important desegregation battles in New Orleans were fought. The first New Orleans schools ordered to desegregate were the two white elementary schools in the Ninth Ward. With the aid of the federal marshals, four black girls were escorted to their classrooms in the face of busloads of angry whites, many of whom rode daily from Plaquemines Parish to taunt these students.[11] Many residents still recall this history as a point of Ninth Ward pride. Hurricane Betsy, which made landfall on September 9, 1965, serves as another touchstone of community survival and resilience.[12] Betsy's 110 to 140 mile per hour winds caused massive structural damage and power outages. But much worse, the storm surges caused severe flooding along Lake Pontchartrain. The walls of both sides of the Industrial Canal levees failed. As the water continued to rise, many Ninth Ward residents sought refuge in their attics and on their roofs.

The Lower Ninth Ward boasts architectural and cultural significance as well. Though today shotgun houses connote poverty, it is worth noting that they are environmentally appropriate New World architectural creations. The Lower Ninth Ward is home to "steamboat houses," which, with their encircling decks, narrow interior halls, and open views, speak of the city's river culture.[13] It is also the neighborhood that gave the city many famous musicians. For instance, Fats Domino still maintains a residence there. Also, Kermit Ruffins hails from this neighborhood.

Moreover, the neighborhood has gained a distinct sense of place through multiple generations of New Orleanians living on the same block or in the very same houses. Sheila J., for instance, lived in the same house all her life. It belonged to her grand-parents. "First," she explains, "it was my nanny. I lived with my nanny here, and when she passed away, I just kept staying here. We own it."[14] This owning and intergenerational living rooted Ninth Ward residents in place and culture, making it a community that has strong generational ties. It was a porch-sitting community where no one on the block was a stranger.

When Lower Ninth Ward residents describe their neighborhood, it is often with a block-by-block level of detail, revealing islands of tranquility and hospitality in an environment that outsiders may see only as violent. Most of the residents spoke fondly of their neighborhood, their particular block, or the two-block radius around their houses. Sheila J., a woman who spent her entire life in the Lower Ninth Ward, reminisced about her neighborhood before Katrina. "It was different," she describes. "They always barbecued next door. The little guy in that white house over there across from us used to barbecue a lot. It was totally different. Everybody used to hang out. It was fun. Still right now, I can go off, and I don't lock my door. This neighborhood—this block here's real quiet."[15]

Unlocked doors do not fit the picture of crime and desperation that broad-brush descriptions of this community present. There may have been only one gas station that serviced the areas (because most residents didn't have cars), but there were corner stores aplenty, where a grandmother could send her grandson to get milk, bread, and a homemade po'boy. On his way back, the boy might purchase a huckabuck from the lady who lived two houses down.[16] This was a neighborhood with a particular character and appeal that cannot be captured by demographic statistics and crime indexes. Indeed, the Ninth

Ward was a "community where family potlucks and poverty coexisted."[17] Residents are quick to reject the negative views of the Ninth Ward as "stereotypes, insisting that portrayals of the Ninth Ward as isolated and dangerous failed to capture what it meant to the people who lived there: family, friends, and neighborhood. Indeed, soon after Hurricane Katrina forced them out, many residents were lobbying to return home."[18]

It is also from this neighborhood that one of the city's main industries—tourism—drew many of its workers. Not only have famous and struggling musicians made their home in the Ninth Ward, but so too have the busboys, janitors, maids, cooks, clerks, and so many others who staff the city's bars, restaurants, and hotels.[19]

The damage caused by the storm and the flooding that followed was arguably among the worst of any neighborhood in Orleans Parish, with houses lifted off their foundations and dropped down on houses across the street. Vehicles were tossed about as though a giant angry child had thrown his Tonka toys across the playground. Although some homes were left standing, no other area had been issued more demolition permits post-Katrina than the Lower Ninth Ward. Those houses that were not slated for demolition required gutting, mold remediation, and rewiring before rebuilding could begin.[20]

The level of devastation and the pre-Katrina levels of poverty meant that the displaced residents were often not in a financial position to rebuild their lives and homes, and many decided to wait on the slow-in-coming government assistance before beginning the rebuilding proces. Therefore, neighborhood residents were slow to return and rebuild. Not surprisingly, the vacant buildings and blighted neighborhoods have attracted criminal activity. As scholar Marline Otte notes, "No other part of town suffered the same irreversible destruction [although] residents remember it as a tightly knit community of working-class extended families. Drug trafficking had also turned it into one of the most crime-ridden neighborhoods in the city."[21]

Before Katrina hit, concerns that the Ninth Ward was particularly vulnerable were already heightened. The day before Katrina struck, for instance, the *Times-Picayune* reported that the Ninth Ward was in danger of flooding.[22] Still, on August 29, 2005, at about 3:00 a.m., when Hurricane Katrina made landfall and the Ninth Ward was experiencing 105–135 mile per hour winds and heavy rainfall, residents who had not evacuated reported that they were not worried. After all, many of the older residents who had experienced Hurricane Betsy, and younger ones who had heard the stories knew of that storm's fury and knew that the neighborhood survived. Though Betsy served as a touchstone for the community, as the *Times-Picayune* reported, "Hurricane Katrina struck metropolitan New Orleans on Monday with a staggering blow, far surpassing Hurricane Betsy, the landmark disaster of an earlier generation."[23]

Like Betsy, Katrina sent a surge of water into the Lower Ninth Ward at around 7:00 a.m. As with Betsy, the waters topped the Lakeview levees. By 8:45 a.m., residents of the Lower Ninth Ward were reporting six to eight inches of floodwaters in their homes. At 11:00 a.m., the National Weather Service confirmed that the Industrial Canal levee had indeed been breached, essentially emptying Lake Pontchartrain into the Lower Ninth, among other eastern New Orleans neighborhoods and St. Bernard Parish. Floodwaters continued to rise for two days in some neighborhoods, reaching depths of nearly 20 feet.[24] As Bruce Nolan reported, "the effect of the breach was instantly devastating to residents who had survived . . . Katrina's winds and storm surge intact, only to be taken by surprise by the sudden deluge. And it added a vast swath of central New Orleans to those already flooded in . . . the Lower 9th Ward."[25]

Those who chose not to evacuate, and there were many, sought refuge by escaping to their attics and climbing onto their rooftops as they did when they survived Betsy. But, unlike Hurricane Betsy, the water kept coming, rising higher and higher. Most were lucky enough to be rescued. For instance, Rita, an

African American woman in her 40s, sat in her Federal Emergency Management Agency (FEMA) trailer and recounted her uncle's story: "[T]hey heard a loud boom. They say they thought it was a transformer blowing. Then, another boom. They heard about three booms. And next thing you know, water started bubbling under the floor. My Uncle Dan lived in [the] attic for three days with the cat. He had to eat the cat food until the water receded. [When] he got on top [of the roof], he said all he did was watch bodies float down. Nothing he could do but watch the bodies decompose."[26] Those who were rescued were taken to higher ground on highway overpasses or were taken to the Superdome, which turned out to have a tragic tale of its own.

Most of the evacuees thought that their evacuation would be short-lived, as with so many other hurricane warnings they experienced in years past. They assumed and thus prepared for an evacuation that would last a couple of days, a week at the most, after which they expected to return. Eighty-one percent of the homes in the Lower Ninth Ward, however, suffered extensive damage, and by July 2007, almost two years after the storm, only 7 percent of the pre-Katrina population had returned to the Lower Ninth Ward. Four and a half years after Katrina, less than 20 percent of the Lower Ninth Ward residents had returned.[27]

When asked, Ninth Ward residents explain their community's slow rates of return, especially compared to other New Orleans communities, as having less to do with any of the social ills that affected their neighborhoods pre-Katrina and more to do with government inaction and even malfeasance. Residents point to mismanagement and corruption of the Levee Board, failure to maintain the integrity of the levees, a botched federal disaster response, delays in post-disaster government relief, and interests (some said conspiracies) of local elites to displace poor black communities for private gain.[28] It appears to them that, rather than helping return, official forms of relief represented further barriers that either were—or at least appeared to be—designed to inhibit recovery. Even 18 months after Katrina, for instance, many neighborhoods in the Lower Ninth Ward were still without the basic utilities of water or electricity. Not only did this situation mean that property owners could not begin the rebuilding process, but FEMA also refused delivery of FEMA trailers, leaving the neighborhood empty and increasingly vulnerable to crime and further decay.[29] As Pastor Willis, who leads a congregation in the Ninth Ward, asserts, "The government simply has not facilitated return or rebuilding of lives or communities."[30]

MIRIAM

"Ms. Miriam," which is how she referred to herself, is an African American woman whose age is indiscernible. At the time of her interview, approximately 18 months after the storm, she was residing in Bywater, in the Upper Ninth Ward, and is a lifelong resident of the Ninth Ward.

> I've been in this house about three years. We moved in this house a week before Katrina. I was living one block down the street, though. I lived there for about two years. I've been in the area all my life. My parents lived across in the Ninth Ward, the Lower Ninth Ward. I have always been in this neighborhood, though. Well we are in the process of buying this house. But we was renting the one down the street. But we own this one.

Buying a house was not always something that blacks could do in this area.[31] Ms. Miriam recalls the changes that occurred in this community after the civil rights movement of the 1960s:

> After . . . civil rights . . . we were able to purchase homes anywhere we wanted to because it would be biased if you wouldn't sell it to me. That's why . . . the poor whites that got trapped here—they changed the name. The minute the white folks move over on that side, they didn't want to say they was living in the Ninth Ward anymore.[32] They said, "Oh, we in the

Bywater District. They didn't want to say, "I'm living in the Ninth Ward." So they say, Upper Nine. So they changed it.

In the face of the storm and its aftermath, many Ninth Ward residents survived devastating hardships—some because they were no strangers to storms in their own lives. When reminiscing about life before Katrina, Ms. Miriam showed that she was all too familiar with grief. She spoke of it with a strength that would also come through as she shared her Katrina experience.

> My son—he's living with his father because he set—set the house on fire, which killed my other two kids. And I can't live with that, every time I look at him—so I gave [him] to his father who relocated in Texas with him because of Katrina, and he hasn't come back. But my oldest living boy, the one I got living here with me now—he came back post-Katrina—he came back that Thursday. . . . My other son that got work—him and his seven kids there—they relocated because of Katrina. And they're not coming back. And then the other children, they're dead: two in a fire, one by gunshot, in six months' time.

Although she was not always an active participant, Ms. Miriam recalls that before Katrina there was always a lot going on in her neighborhood.

> Oh, yeah. We used to have that festival back there on Pie and King where we would get together to sell little wares like the handmade blankets and the—what you call it—potluck things. They used to have—see, last week, they had the St. Patrick's Day parade. Well, normally, we start right here. So they would start here, then they would march all the way to the [French] Quarter, and they would pick up people.

No one in her neighborhood was a stranger to her.

> I know everybody in the neighborhood. Before Katrina the neighborhood was bustling. It had people . . . like this old lady across the street [we] used to look out for each other. She's 89

years old. Wow. She's 90 now. She would ask, "Miriam, what you doing?" "Nothing. What you want? You want something from the store?" "If you're going that way." And we used to sit out on the porch, and we was talking through the whole thing. I wasn't scared none.

She watched as her other neighbors evacuated as Katrina approached but felt no need to do so herself. She thought of the evacuees as cowards, and instead she stayed in her house during the entire storm.[33]

My neighbor—she's an attorney and her husband is an accountant, and we sit on the porch. We laughed about them because they were evacuating; we said, "Where all you all going?" "Ms. Miriam, we going." And I said, "Cowards."

Well, we didn't expect for it to flood up here. My son—the one that's staying with me now—him and his girlfriend were hit. They went to Atlanta, Georgia. I wind up staying here. I slept through the storm. I took two Xanax that night [and was out].

[Then] we was over at the tire shop over on Louisa and St. Claude so my fiancé could be at the tire shop. . . . Well you probably see him on CNN.[34] They just did a report on him because he stayed. He helped the policemen fix their tires. He helped the National Guard; well they [say] because of what he was doing for them, they brought him two generators . . . so he could have the air to fix their flats.

My sister came the day after, and when they came by me, I walked them to the convention center. And they said, "Why you going to the convention center?"

Miriam chose the convention center over the Superdome because she had been part of an evacuation to the Superdome during a past hurricane and remembered the tension and violence that built up there. At the convention center after Katrina, however, she had a different experience. She became the linchpin in the system of bartering for and sometimes commandeering required materials that emerged within the convention center following Katrina.

I was in the convention center for about three or four days. And I was the Indian runner. Yeah, I was the Indian; like, say you had pepper and you had milk [or] you needed milk and you needed pepper. People thought I worked there. They would come, "Miss, do you have any water [or] wait we're missing an egg." See [there were] these bad ass, wannabe gangsters strutting up and down the convention center [who] were scared to go in the icebox.

And see with the military . . . right across the street from us at this hotel. They had a water tank that they had hooked up to behind the convention center where they were getting their water from. And I discovered it. I discovered the icemaker because I was moseying around. I wasn't afraid.

We was cooking out. I went in there and got in the kitchen, me and my cousin Claudia. When the military left that hotel, I think, "They got 29 floors over there." I said, "Somebody gonna let us up. They got blankets and shit up in there. Let's go get them."

I even . . . told them how to steal. I said, "You put the TV and whatever radio—whatever you're stealing—under the bottom and put [blankets] and the food on top." So they did that. So every night they would go out raiding, and the food that they would come back with—they would put it at the foot of my cot. And I'd get up in the morning, and I'd give them to the old folks or the young people, the women with children that I knew couldn't go out looting. I gave it to them.

After the convention center, Ms. Miriam evacuated to Austin, Texas. Although she was impressed by how well the city of Austin responded, like many that we interviewed, she hated it there and wanted to be back home. She stayed there, however, until she could track down her mother. They then stayed in an apartment in Vicksburg, Mississippi, for seven months with help from United Way and FEMA. When she finally came back home, it was to a deserted neighborhood.

Well, anyway, it was kinda hectic, but I got through it. So, anyway, I got my house together, move in here and chain that generator up through that porch. Got me some cords to watch

TV, put my air mattress right there in the middle of that floor.
Took one dog, put him outside, took two dogs, put them inside.
I can hear him outside, but you can [also] hear [people] running
from the [police]. See, they was up to no good. They were stealing people's things [from] their houses . . . [taking] the mantel-
pieces and going and taking people['s] baths.

After Katrina, Ms. Miriam's Bywater neighborhood is still bustling, but things are different. The older folks of the community
have not returned.

But on this side, it's still a bustling neighborhood. It still have a
lot of white houses to it, but a lot of the older people, from 60
on up, they don't wanna come back. It's too hard for them to
rebuild, and some of them don't have any of the kids to help
them. And those that do have the kids . . . [the kids] are stealing
what they got. Or they stole whatever little money that they
got, so they can't come home, so they're stuck where ever.
That's my point.

A number of people we talked to described Katrina as a mixed
blessing. One woman was able to build a "mansion" in place
of the shack that was destroyed by the storm. Another person
described the storm as a great big washing machine that cleaned
up the city. Of course, not everyone saw it that way. But Ms.
Miriam does see some good coming out of Katrina. When asked
if she feels safe in her home on a mostly deserted street, she
replied that not only does she feel safe but she also highlighted
some other positive results of the storm.

A lot of people saying that a lot of criminal elements is coming back. Yes, they are, but you gotta understand, they are
only going to survive once they are allowed to go there. But
oh yeah [I feel safe] and then I'm not doing nothing that
I have to be worried about. And New Orleans ain't never
looked better. Let me tell you, people had trash under their
house. [It's] been under their house for almost 50–60 years.

> Katrina blew all that shit out there. She cleaned up all that.
> Stuff people needed to do . . . it's finally getting it done.

New Orleanians, particularly in the Ninth Ward, have a strong place attachment.[35] Ms. Miriam with all her trouble and heartache summed up what a lot of other New Orleanians feel about their home:

> New Orleans is a beautiful place, even in the storm.

KIM

Kim and her husband, Calvin, own a grocery store called "We Got It" and a diner called "The Spot" located in the Ninth Ward. She's an African American, likely in her mid-40s. She works with her husband, and they are very much involved in their community in an informal but active way. Eighteen months after Katrina, when we interviewed Kim, only the diner had reopened.

> [The store has been here] since '99, but we've lived in the area since '79. We married in '79, and we bought a house together in the 3300 block of North Robertson. We've lived around the corner since '94. We had the store right here, and it was convenient [to live here]. And then we had the house in Kenner that didn't get any water, so good thing we had a backup.

Kim believed that she was called to do more than just sell the residents of her community groceries and serve them food. She believed that she could minister to the community through small acts of care, one person at a time, day in and day out.

> Before [Katrina], the community was like, very poor, but there were a lot of people around here, and they were making it, but it's a poor community.
> Everybody around here—if you ever walk up and down the street and ask them about Mrs. Kim—they all will have something good to say because they all know me, and they all

know I work in the community. I always made sure the kids had shoes. If I saw one without a coat, I'd go get a coat. And around Christmas, I made sure every child in the neighborhood got a toy. Anybody could come and say they were hungry, [and] they were gonna eat. So those kinds of things. And that's when I realized this is where God wanted me, outside of church. I [used to] go to church on Tuesday night, Wednesday night, Saturday morning, and Sunday. When I opened this grocery store, I wasn't able to do that. But I then kind of felt like I'd [been] given my own little ministry right here on this corner.

So I was unable to attend church regular, like I said, but I had so much to do here, so much more. Mostly young students, and that again was God using me in their lives. [I] had a lot of youngsters come work for me from ages 16 to maybe 25.

I kept them under my wing for at least a year or two; if they moved on it was always [to] a better thing. I've had to take in some off the street that have gotten put out. And, mostly young ladies, I don't take any of the young men. Especially one—her and her two-year-old daughter got put out. They didn't have nowhere to go. Her mother's deceased. I had a daughter at home already. My son was gone off to college. So I took her in and helped her get on her feet. And she has a success story now.

Kim and her husband hired their employees from the neighborhood as well.

Most of our employees are from this neighborhood. I wouldn't hire anybody else, because there's so much needed in this neighborhood, why would I look anywhere else? And I have some that come in and try to do the wrong thing at first, and I just continue to work with them, pray with them, and talk to them. And, eventually, I think they get the message— eventually they go ahead and go back to school, get a GED, get registered in community college. There were some that went to regular college.

Like other small business owners, Kim spent a great deal of time on her business, and the ties that she had to the community were strengthened by it.[36]

> Basically the office—the business was my life. When you have a small business, you don't have a life other than that. Outside of the business and the ministry that I've done on this corner, I don't have time for anything else. I'd be lucky if I got a little sleep in. But yes, it really, really was demanding a lot of the time, but I loved it.
>
> Like I said, some of the parents would actually come here. They would have teenaged sons that'd be into [trouble] and they couldn't get them to stop. They would come get me and I could break—I could call them and just calm them down right quick. I don't know. God just blessed me with that, and I'm just glad he's using me. There was a lot to do here. There was, always.

Kim's mother has had to live with her because of the slow recovery of her mother's neighborhood after Katrina.

> My mom used to live in the neighborhood. She's living with me still after Katrina. My dad is deceased. But my mom's been with me since November after Katrina. And she's still with me, but she's lived around the corner up until then. We're still rebuilding . . . her house. As a matter of fact, we've just really gotten to where she could move back in, but we're trying to delay that a little bit because there's not a lot of people back in the area yet.

Like many people, Kim's family has not all returned. Some are still staying in trailers in other parts of the city. Others are out of state, waiting for the right time to return.

> [My mom's] alone and so much has been happening, so I'm just trying to get her to stay with me a little while longer until we get more people back in the area, or one of my sisters that's in Texas is maybe gonna come down and maybe live with her because we don't want her living on her own right now.

She's used to being independent and being on her own, so no, really she's not [okay with that plan], but we keep on pursuing it, so—and just taking it one day at a time. I called some other sisters and get them to talk to her. She said, "Well, okay because I really don't like staying in the house at night by myself." [I got worried because] I know they had a lot of thefts going on, like breaking into the homes. And as people begin to rebuild, they've been stealing the materials.[37] Even the house that I'm talking about, they went under the house and stole the copper piping. They stole the hot water heater. So yeah, I'm afraid for her to come down here right now.

I have five sisters. Three of them are out of town. One of them was in the Ninth Ward before Katrina, but she's in Texas now. Two of them are here (over in the Gentilly area), and they're rebuilding. They're staying in trailers. They all were living with me after Katrina, the ones that lost their homes here. I had at least about 20 people living in Kenner with me. The one in Texas, she's undecided right now. She said that she's gonna come back but she wanna wait a little while longer. So if she does then I'm trying to get her to come and stay with my mom for a little while.

To rebuild her business, even to the point where it is now, Kim and Calvin have had to rely mostly on their savings because they did not receive much in the way of government assistance. At the time of the interview, they were pursuing litigation with their insurance company rather than accept what they thought to be an unfair settlement.[38]

We haven't been able to get our grocery store back open yet. We're about 50 percent finished. We're still waiting on our insurance company to pay us money. And we didn't get any help from the government. We redid this out of pocket from savings.

The government gave us $2,000 initially, and then $2,300 and that was it. Our insurance offered us a little bit of money. They know you're not going to accept it because then it goes to court and it's tied up in litigations for—see, I guess they're hoping two or three years until they can get the money to pay you or whatever.

The stories that Kim had heard about Hurricane Betsy and the possible explosions of the levee influence what she thought of the levee breaches during Hurricane Katrina.

Actually, I remember stories about the Ninth Ward when Betsy came through because I had a lot of family members down here. My godmother was down here. The Ninth Ward over the bridge, the lower canal, what they call the Industrial Canal, it flooded and the water was up to the rooftops back then because they blew up the levee to keep the water from going downtown. And a lot of people drowned then and lost everything they had, just as they did this time.

Actually, that's what I think was intended this time, but it didn't quite happen that way. A lot of other people were affected as well. I don't think they meant for it to be as widespread as it was, but several people, including my brother [heard], there was a boom and another boom, and after that the water came. They heard some dynamite. This is Katrina that I am talking about. My brother stayed in the Ninth Ward, throughout the whole thing. Throughout the storm over the lower canal, and he told us, he said, "It was definitely something blew up." He said, "Everybody was like, 'What was that?'" And then a few minutes later they heard it again, [and] they were like, "And what was that?" And then he said, "A little while after that, here comes the water." He said, "And the water came so quick."

When Kim evacuated, her husband Calvin stayed behind to watch the store and protect it. In the meantime, she and a friend found refuge through a friend's religious network.

Another of my brothers stayed here with my husband in the store. And me and my kids, we left. My daughter left that Saturday and went to Texas with some of her friends. I was supposed to go with her, but I wasn't sure if I was gonna leave or not. So I told her, I said, "Well, you go ahead, and I'll meet y'all if I decide to leave." Then I decided to do something different after talking to a friend of mine. She was going to Eunice, Louisiana, to a retreat center where her church used to go and have their retreats. And they had little cottages. And they told her she could have as many of them as she needed, so she reserved like 20 of them.

She was telling me about it; she said, "Why don't you come and go with us? It's so nice out there." So I said, "Well, my son needs to come—go with me, so he's gonna need a place to stay too." She said, "Well, there's only about 12 of us, and there's 20 cabins, four to a room to stay, so why don't y'all come with us?"

So we did. I went with her. I left Sunday morning and my son left at noon with the directions, and he met with us out there as well. It was . . . it was very nice. It was—they had swimming pools. We were having a good time. We didn't know what was going on back here. They opened the doors, and everything was free. They told everybody, "We'll feed y'all and put y'all up."

And I was able to talk back and forth to my husband. Everything was fine here up until like midnight Sunday night. That was the 28th of August. The last time I called him I could barely understand him, and the last thing I said, "Well, just promise me after this passes you're gonna give me a call." And I didn't hear from him until—exactly one week after Katrina, I was able to see him but couldn't speak to him. And I'll have to explain that to you.

Our cell phones stopped working immediately after Katrina. So we had no contact with nobody. They didn't have any power or anything down here. And the only word I had gotten was from people saying that the water was over the rooftops down here, everybody drowned.

Although her children were worried about their father, Kim had faith that he was okay. That faith would be rewarded time and time again.

And so, of course, my kids were upset. So my daughter [who] was in Texas got that news, then she drove to Eunice to be with us. And she was crying constantly and really upset because she couldn't hear from her dad. And our son was real—just quiet. "Mom, you think he's okay?" I was like, "Of course he's okay." I said, "Because if 999 drowned, your daddy would be up at the top of the light pole saying, 'I'm up here!'" I kept cracking all these jokes, and they just kept looking at me like I was crazy.

And I told them, I said, "If Tarzan survived in the jungle, your daddy will survive in the Ninth Ward, because he's a black Tarzan." And I was just saying all these kind of crazy things. But I knew that he was okay, so I was trying to cheer them up.

But we kept trying to get word down here, and we were unable to do so. So I prayed about it and asked God to let us get word. So a young man came from this neighborhood to that center [in Eunice], which was kind of bizarre. That was kind of like God answered the prayer because this place was way back off the interstate in the woods. You really had to know somebody to know about this place.

And he came, and I was asking him, "So how did you get to come here?" And he explained to me that he had went to LSU and they sent him over here—that was on a Saturday. But he told me he left New Orleans on Thursday, and he said, "When I left on Thursday your husband was okay." So that was the first word I got. My son was with me when I was talking with him. So I told my daughter, I said, "So you see, your daddy's okay."

He also told us that—"Mr. Calvin was in there firing rounds inside the store"—because somebody was trying to break in. I said, "Okay, that sounds like him." So we knew he was okay. My daughter still wasn't satisfied. She was just crying and upset.

People chose to weather Katrina for many reasons. The memories of previous hurricanes heavily influenced their behavior. Kim's husband was aware that looting usually takes place after a hurricane, and he stayed behind to protect the store.[39]

One reason he stayed down here is to protect the store from looters, because that happens a lot after storms and he knows that, so he said he was not leaving. And he didn't think it was gonna be nearly as bad. He just thought that the storm was gonna come through, you know, knock a couple of trees down, do whatever, and then they was gonna start breaking into everything. And so he stayed—because the power would be out, and we don't have any alarm system, and the police are not available. So he said, "I'm not going anywhere. I'm gonna be right here."

When she did come back to find her husband, Kim had a difficult time getting back to see her house. The police and Coast Guard were concerned about safety, but residents often saw the presence of these forces as an inconvenience: an inconvenience that some people were able to get around.

So that Saturday [after Katrina] we left Eunice, Louisiana, and drove to Laplace, which is about 40 minutes from Kenner where we were living at. We were trying to get in Kenner to see what shape our house was in. Initially, we were told the house had flooded because they said the levee in the back of our house had broken. A lot of homes around there did, but the water stopped like one block from our house, so we were blessed.

And when we drove to Laplace, and we stayed there overnight with our friend to get up the next morning and drive to Kenner. The police wouldn't let us in. And I had already spoken and told them that we were gonna get in. My son said, "We're not gonna be able to get in Kenner." I said, "Yes, we are." He said, "How do you know?" I said, "I just prayed on it." We went Airline [Highway], and we were able to get in.[40] So we drove all the way in and were able to make it all the way to our house and see that we hadn't gotten any water. But there was a lot of cleaning up that needed to be done because our neighbor, all of his shingles were in our front yard and our backyard. And the refrigerators, of course, needed to be cleaned; that was awful.

So we decided, okay, we're gonna go back and—they had already said on TV that weekend, that same weekend we heard that the mayor was gonna let everybody come in on Labor Day and just look at the damages and then we had to leave back out. And he promised us to be back home within two to three weeks [so] we have like some warning. But he said he was gonna let everybody come in that Monday. We said we'll just come back then and clean up, and we did. We came back; we cleaned out the refrigerators; we cleaned up the front yard. We had wheelbarrows toting shingles and putting them in piles. There were so many shingles.

When they got back, they expected to find many like them returning to check on their property. This would not be the case.

It was me, my son, my daughter, and my son's girlfriend. At that time when I got back, I thought we were gonna see a lot of our neighbors, a lot of people trying to come back in and see about their property. We saw one other person who was a fireman who was forced to stay. His family was gone. But we saw no other neighbors or anything. It was like a little deserted town really.

So we went in, and I told [my children] that day, I said, "Well, we're gonna hear from your daddy today." They thought I had talked to somebody. I was like, "No, I prayed on it." And they looked at me crazy again, but they said, "Okay." I think they were getting a little faith because we did get in Kenner.

Kim was determined to get news of her husband and went to great lengths to do so.

After we finished cleaning up, we went to the Kenner Police, we went to the State Police, [and we] went to the National Guard. We flagged a rescue team down. I followed them for 10 minutes on the interstate blowing and trying to get them to pull over. And when they finally pulled over, and I pulled behind him, the guy said, "Only one of y'all come and come with your hands up." Because people were afraid because they were doing so much, and he didn't know who I was.

And when I got to him, I just told him, "I'm sorry." And I told him my husband was trapped down here because he stayed down here to protect the store from looters, and I was afraid for his safety [because] I'm hearing about the contaminated water. I know that he's alive and well because the guy came to the center and told me. I said, "I just need to find a way to get down there to get him out of there."

And he said, "Well, where is he?" I gave him the address. He said, "Well, I've been down there. I rescued like 50 people today." He said, "I'm not going back until tomorrow morning, but I promise you I'll go down there and look for your husband." So I said, "Okay."

But in [the] meantime, we were talking about all kinds of things we could do. I told my son, I said, "We can make it to where the water is." So I had like $5,000. I had went and gotten money out the bank just to have cash money on me because

I didn't know what we were gonna face next. I said, "I got like $5,000 on me, and we can possibly pay somebody to bring us down there or either find somebody with a helicopter, because I know there are a lot of helicopters flying down there. I'll be willing to pay them." So we were talking about all or our options.

We got to the New Orleans and Metairie line, and there was a police officer there. I got out and talked to him. I said, "Officer, you have to let us through." And he said, "I can't." So as he was saying, "No," I saw a helicopter on the other side of the bridge.

So I got in a hurry to get over there before [the helicopter] leaves. I was just like, "Okay, officer. Thank you." And I shot over there and I went up to him, and I was talking so fast telling the man the story. The man said, "Wait a minute. Calm down. Wait, wait, wait." He said, "Who's with you?" I said, "My son, my daughter, and my daughter-in-law." He was like, "Y'all pull over and come on." He brought us. I was so focused on the helicopter and intent on wanting to pay him to bring us down there [that] I never saw the big old trailer. It was a big long trailer. And he brought us in that trailer. And he said, "We're channel 39." And then they had all these TV screens set up.

He started telling the guy who was sitting at the computer with all these screens the story. "She says her husband is trapped down there in her store in New Orleans." And then when he got like right over the store—we have a red roof so it stands out. So I was like, "That's it! That's it! Pull this up." And then he—when he pulled up you could see the whole big store. He had—the whole area, but then when he zoomed in right on the store I was like, "That's it! That's it! We got it!" And so I was like, "That's where he's at! That's where he's at!" And he was on the phone telling them where to go and that they needed to be down there within an hour. They were down there within 30 minutes.

And the good thing about it, he sent the camera man down here by the rescue teams and had the camera on it the whole time. We were able to watch it. They dropped a man on the roof. The man slid down back, walked around knocking on the building.

These people were helping me to rescue my husband. I was so grateful. And I started crying. They said, "He's not answering. Nobody's in there." I was like, "Yes, he's there.

I know he's there." They said, "Well, maybe he's hurt." And
the cameraman said, "Well, there's a man across the street
waving at me. Maybe he wants to be rescued." And he put
the camera on the man who was waving, and that was my
husband saying, "I'm over here!"

He was standing on the porch where he had been going
every day to bring food, water, and medicine. From my understanding, he was the cook, the doctor, and the provider. He was
everything down here. He provided the food and the water, he
nursed the sick, he helped the injured, he fed the animals, and
he cooked beans and stuff every day—on a grill over there—and
fed the people.

Like so many, Kim's husband provided assistance to others even
when he himself was not in an ideal situation. Sometime after
the storm, Kim would learn of her husband's efforts.

I refused to come in the store because it was in such bad shape.
And a news lady from Dallas got out [of a car] and she came
and looked. She said, "Oh, I thought you were the man who
owned the store." I said, "I'm his wife." She said, "Oh," and she
started telling me about how he was doctoring on everybody
and taking care of everybody down here; she said she came
down here in a boat every day.

And she said, "I tried so many times to call you for him. I'm
so sorry I was unable to reach you." My husband never told me
any of this stuff. She said, "Every day I would come down, he
was like, 'Were you able to get in touch with my wife?'" And she
said she would go back to the hotel and try to reach me, but
my cell phone wasn't taking any 504 numbers or any numbers
out of this area because they didn't have any transmitters—the
power was down.

So she said, "I tried so hard to get a message to you for
him." She said, "I really wanted to do it because he was so
dedicated to the people down here." And she started telling me all the things he was doing. She said, "Even a little
dog that they found; he found him floating in the water. He
took him out of the water and put him on the porch and was
feeding him." She took the dog home, and she had pictures to
show of how the dog looked now. She said, "I wanted to show

him these pictures." I was like, "Well, thank you so much for trying to get in touch with me." But he's kinda modest, so he didn't tell me anything about all the stuff that he was doing and all that down here.

And I learned a lot of stuff about what he did. It had gotten so hot in the store, after the water went down he came out and his truck was flooded. So he had some plastic upstairs. He brought the plastic and covered the seats in his truck, and so at night he would sleep on the seats in his truck with a little window open because it was dangerous down here. They were shooting and acting crazy. He had to sleep with his gun in the truck at night. And in the daytime he would go in and get the food and all the stuff that he had and then go over there and help the people.

Kim characterized the government's response to Katrina as too little too late. She blames the delays on politics as much as incompetence.

We probably had a couple of hundred thousand worth of damage . . . and that's just the store stuff; that's not the restaurant. And everything in the restaurant was brand new. We had just built it five months from the ground. This is the addition that was put on. It started back here at this lot out to the front, 1,500 square feet. They just finished it, like I said, everything brand new, five months before Katrina. That was like a $200,000 project.

When it calmed down, the military came in [and] took over with martial law. And I think that was about 10 days after the storm. Way too late. They should've been ready to roll in immediately, and they didn't. I think somebody dropped the ball there because usually when a storm of that category is gonna happen and they know about it ahead of time, the minute the storm rolls through, the military's waiting with ice, water, medicine, food. And it was days before these people got food, water, and medical attention.

I think the government failed the people because if you know ahead of time that a Category 5 storm is coming through, shouldn't somebody have been prepared? I don't care if they had to come by plane, boat, or how they had to get here. They should have been ready to get here hours after the storm rolled through. The military should've rolled in within hours. They do it in third world countries. They have done it in other states. So why didn't they do it this time? I really don't know the answer to that one. I just think it's politics. Maybe somebody didn't like somebody, or somebody couldn't agree with somebody. Whatever the reason was, I mean, it's just not acceptable.

I mean, you had to go through military, and they didn't want you here rebuilding. They wouldn't allow you. They didn't provide the things like—lights wasn't provided down here until like, at least about four or five months after Katrina.

Kim had hoped that by the time we spoke with her, 18 months after Katrina, that the convenience store adjacent to the diner would be up and running. She filed her insurance claim and put in for a Small Business Administration (SBA) loan, but she seemed to hit one roadblock after another.

People were saying, "They don't wanna let the people come back." Or, "They want to take over the people's land." You heard all kinds of rumors.[41]

The government was saying it wasn't safe, so they wasn't letting people down here. Like I said, we would get through sometimes because we'd show up in the store and say, "Well, we need to go check on our business." And sometimes they would let us in, and sometimes they wouldn't. Really it was like late December before they actually started letting us come in and really gut out our property.

We're really hoping within the next couple of months, we'll have everything up and running because everything on the outside has been done. The store area, all of this is finished. We have to do the bathroom, and two little rooms need to be redone in the store. But still we were hoping for money from the SBA for the restock because as you can see we lost everything.[42]

When I filled out the papers for this SBA loan, they told me that we didn't qualify because they told me my income tax wasn't [filed] in New Orleans. So I said, "Well, I know I'm gonna get this loan if that's [the] only problem." She said, "No, I'm looking at this income tax, and there's no way we can give this loan to you." I was like, "Okay, I have something for you."

I had a letter where I had been audited the year before from the government, and they had congratulated me for my business and all my paperwork being in order for a small business. I said, "So you're saying my paperwork is not in order, and then in this the government's congratulating me." I said, "Now somebody's lying. I hope it's not the SBA." I said, "Do I need to go public with this on channels 4, 6, and 8?" Then they wanted to look at it again.

So that's been tied up, too, because now they're waiting on another document that they need. They're always waiting on something. There's always something with them.

Personally, I think is everybody had some kinda game. Like the insurance company. They know you lost $100,000 or $200,000 worth of stuff. We're gonna offer you $15,000. And you don't take that. So then they know it's gonna go in litigations, and it's gonna be tied up for two or three years. And like I said, adjusters themselves have came and sit down up in here and even tell us. They know they owe these people, and eventually they'll probably get their money if they fight them. He said, "But they don't have the money, a lot of them, because there were so many claims." And they paid out so much, so they're trying to pay so much as they go.

Their business got an unexpected boon when the president and the governor ate at their restaurant. At least for a couple of months after that visit, business boomed. Now it is slow, and they have an entirely different clientele.

Well, we opened March 6th. We had a visit from the president on March 8th. The president, the governor, the mayor, and the president's wife ate lunch here on March 8, 2006. And after all the publicity from that, business was booming. The next day we sold out [of] everything. People just wanted a piece of bread. Some people came up to me talking about, "Can you just sell me some bread?" because we were out of everything. I'm like, "We're sold out of everything." "You don't have no bread or water, I could just say I had something where the president ate at." It was funny. And it was really booming during that time. Then things got slow in November, December, January. Things are starting to pick up a little bit now.

Kim believes that the government should have planned better (perhaps taking a cue from the volunteers) and believes that, if it had, the government would have spent its money more wisely.

The clientele is not the same. It looks like I hardly ever see the same people twice. It's like people just coming and going: tourists, volunteers mostly. A lot are here from Common Ground, coming in from college.[43] They come on their spring break to donate that week of time to clean up or do whatever they can. Only about 10 percent of our original customers [are back]. It used to be all community people. I knew them all by name.

They can't come back. Have you looked in these homes? I mean, they have nothing to come back to. They have no schools for the kids to go to; they have no hospitals. I see how these kids come in, these college students; they can come in and take a week of their time and gut out these houses, and they can come up with a plan to get something accomplished, and the government can't—I think if the government would've said, "Okay, we have all these billions of dollars." If the government would've said, "Okay, we're gonna take 1,000 soldiers and put them in New Orleans and let them build 100 houses—redo 100 houses a month." Just give them credit cards. They go to Lowes and charge everything to the government. The $10 billion they spent probably would've only cost them $1 billion. A whole lot less money and a whole lot more would've been accomplished. To me, they're not trying to do anything. They're not trying to come up with a plan of something that's gonna work.

Kim sees FEMA's solutions as terribly short-sighted and grossly inefficient.

I think the government could've did without the FEMA trailers had they just brought the people in and started rebuilding the homes. The trailers were a waste to me, to be honest. And the money they spent—they showed the trailers in the newspaper and said it cost the government at least $300,000 per trailer

with the upkeep. Because, you know, they've gotta pay maintenance on the trailer for every week . . . these trailer parks where
they've got security guards and all this, that was—each trailer
park cost them something like $1 million a week.

Like others, Kim suspects that corruption is behind the government's actions. She is not convinced that the government is
actually trying to help the residents return.

These boats they had the people living on that was costing
them something like $250 million. The Road Home money
that they sent in for the people—it's federal money, come from
the federal government. But then the state government was
responsible for getting it out to the people. And the governor,
the state governor, hired a company and paid them $750 mil-
lion—this is according to the news and the newspaper—to distribute the money. Now does that make any sense at all? I don't
know, but to me that doesn't make any sense. Why are you
gonna hire a company and pay a company $750 million unless
you're gonna get some money back under the table?
  The company who they hired and paid the $750 million has
only been able to put money in 2,000 people's hands within six
months—within almost six months. Okay. The government can
do anything they wanna do really. They are the government;
they make the rules. They break the rules.
  If they'd have got with the people, the government and the
military and different ones, if the material was provided, and at
100 homes per month, we would be just about finished here.
If they had to go from state to state doing that, they could get
something done. They're not trying to get anything done.

Kim is confident in her and her husband's ability to withstand
the financial pressures but worries about her more vulnerable
neighbors. The government's response, in her view, has been far
more disappointing than it had to be.

We weren't really worried about stuff ourselves because I just
feel that I know eventually things are gonna get better for us.

We're working towards a bigger goal and whatever. I got my kids through college.

I have a son that's graduated from college. He's an electrical engineer. And I also have a daughter that's graduated from college. She's a registered nurse.

They're both on their jobs doing good. We're making enough money to make it. I just feel that God's gonna always provide for me if I keep just working hard trying to do His will. And He does.

So I don't worry about that. But I'm more worried about the people. They're not doing anything for the people around here. And I see some of them breaking down, some of them having heart attacks, some of them having strokes.

They go rebuild those third world countries all the time. And who does it? The military. They bring skilled people over there and let them rebuild the third world countries. Why can't they rebuild their own?

Kim explains that unlike residents in more affluent communities, the residents of this community did not have savings to draw upon.

The people who've gotten some money, like from insurance or may have worked on a job, . . . they're doing a little work themselves. Some of them will hire contractors. Some of them are waiting to get money from Road Home so they can hire contractors. These were poor people around here.

Now I can go in other areas where people have more resources. They're doing more. Some of them have moved back into their homes. And I wouldn't expect that in the Ninth Ward because, like I said, this is what they call "the hood," the poor people. They didn't have money. They don't have resources.

They'll come to me, "Mrs. Kim, let me owe you for a loaf of bread. Mrs. Kim, can you read this letter to me?" So if you don't get that foundation to even know how to read or write your name. So they already feel threatened as far as going to a job or whatever. They feel they can't do anything. They can't get anywhere.

So that's why they're in the shape that they were in. Because some of them, like I said, I would give them a job just sweeping up around here. Good people. There were some bad ones; I'm not gonna lie. They have bad people everywhere you go. But they have a lot of good people. They wouldn't have as many bad kids if they had resources and things for them to do.

Kim credits both her positive attitude and her spiritual beliefs for keeping her optimistic through this tough time.

I'm just a person that—I don't let nothing get me down. No matter what, I'm always smiling. I never cried over anything that was lost because it's just material things. And I feel that I have something bigger and better that I'm working towards, you know.

I heard people crying over their house or whatever. I just always say, "Don't worry about that. God's got a mansion for us." And they always tell me that, "You're always smiling, and you're always cheerful. How can you be?" Even my sisters, my niece, when they came to the house after Katrina, they wanted to know. I said, "Well, God gave me this smile, and I ain't gonna let the devil steal it."

ELIZABETH AND ERVIN

Elizabeth and Ervin, a married African American couple, have lived in the Ninth Ward for about 40 years. They raised their children in the Ninth Ward and have seen this area change over the time. We interviewed Elizabeth and Ervin in the spring of 2007 in their home, which they were in the process of rebuilding. Elizabeth also speaks of a rental property, also in the Ninth Ward, that she was rebuilding.

Elizabeth: [Before the storm this community was] very quiet, very comfortable, very peaceful, very relaxed. Everyone on the block was just about elderly. Maybe had a couple of people up the street with children.

Ervin: This was a quiet block. When the children was small, it was still a quiet block even with the children. They all played

together and everything; [we] didn't have no kind of disturbance or nothing. As long as I been there, we never had no
disturbance or nothing.

We got some people that would sit out on the porch and
like me and Reece would be—me and my neighbor across the
street used to be out there, sit out there at night sometimes,
11:00 p.m., 12:00 p.m. at night.[44] We didn't do it every night.
Mostly weekends because we all was working. Couldn't sit out
every night.

That is the kind of neighborhood we had. You didn't even
have to lock your doors over here. Some warm nights, I have
left that front door open. Until those devils moved in up that
street up there. They got a bunch up there right now on the
corner, on this corner up—in the apartment building—here. I
don't trust them.

Ervin explained that the neighborhood was once full of young
families but had transitioned to being an older community over
time. Also, the neighborhood went from a racially integrated
community to a neighborhood filled with mostly black residents.

Ervin: I moved here August 11, 1966. I was looking for a house
and this was—this house here was—offered to me. I came to
look at it, and I liked the house when I looked at it. I bought
it. Well, it was an all-white neighborhood, and then the blacks
started moving in and the whites started moving out of the parish. When I moved here, they only had two, three white families
left in this neighborhood: one on the corner, one about three
houses down, and one across the street. It was still a good while
before they left. And the old man down the street, he died, and
I think the old lady on the corner died and her son sold the
house. And these people over here, they left.

I was renting at the time and I wanted to get off of rent.
That's what made me look for a house. [I had] two girls when
I moved into this house. All my kids grew up here. [There was]
a good amount [of kids on the block]. Let's see this family had
about—well, they had one daughter that was almost around
the same age as my oldest daughter. And then the next two
houses down here, I think she had about two or three girls, and
this house here, they had two boys and two girls. And the next

house had two girls. And the next house, I'm not sure how many
they had, about four or five. Let's see, they had two boys [and
two girls]. And the one on the corner, I think they had three
girls and two boys. When dusk came, dark came, you didn't
see them up in the street. They play together and with all those
children they had around here playing, none of them ever got in
a fight with each other.

None of the four children from Ervin's first marriage lived in
New Orleans proper. Three of Elizabeth's children from her first
marriage had remained in New Orleans.

Ervin: I have four children by my first wife. The youngest
should be about 37; one should be right at 40; the other ones
should be like 44 and 45. Two of them are in Atlanta, one is
on the West Bank, and one is in Thibodaux. I have two other
children: one is in Plaquemines, and I don't know where the
other one is, the oldest one. She's about—she's 47, and the
youngest one is 28.[45]

Elizabeth: I have six children. My oldest is 45. My youngest is 36
or 37. I have four boys and two girls. I have three sons here, one
daughter in Alexandria, one just left to go to [another city]. I've
got three sons here. And I got one son in North Carolina.

Elizabeth and Ervin explain that their church's location dic-
tates where they spend their time. Although they live in the
Ninth Ward, they spend their time in St. Bernard Parish where
the church that Ervin grew up in is located. As with so many in
the Ninth Ward, religion plays a significant role in their lives.[46]

Elizabeth: We go to church in Saint Bernard Parish, so we spend
our time back there. We go to First Baptist. It has maybe about
400, 470, 475 [congregants]. We attend every Sunday and
Wednesday nights for Bible study. But right now, the church is
being repaired, so we meet in another church. [We are] very
close [to the people in our church]. It's a family. We was just
like if we wasn't kin, we were kin. We're kin in Christ anyway,

so we're kin. Most of them [are] from the parish. Some of them came from up here. Most of them live down there.

Both Ervin and Elizabeth had transitioned through several jobs before they retired, and their network of friendships reflected this.

Ervin: Well, when I first moved [here], I was working for Higgins veneer plant, and I left from there. We used to make hardwood flooring and little block tiles and that isn't the name they call them now. We used to make that. And then I left from there, and I went to New Orleans Public Service and worked there till '75–'76. I did maintenance work then I was driving trucks all over. Then I got my own truck, and I started driving my own truck after that. I drive dump trucks. [I'd] pick up dirt and deliver it to different people. I was working for different contractors. I did that till '89, '75–'89. I worked for a hospital cleaning company for a while, for about 13 years, and then I went to Loyola University and worked there for a while.

I still go say hi to my friends up there [at Loyola]. They'll come by and stop and see how I'm doing and everything. In fact, one came last week, to see how I was making out. I see [my friends from the hospital] too. They come and see how I'm doing. None of them live around here.

Elizabeth: Before the storm, I wasn't working anymore. I quit working in '94, but before that I was employed as an insurance manager for a security insurance company and an agent and manager. I did that for about 14 years. And before that I had my own school bus. I drove a school bus. As a matter of fact, I had a school bus, two vans, and a—what do you call that wagon—it was like a station wagon. I took the children to school and back. Then I started taking the elderly to the prison, to Angola. I did that for 10 years. I got together with two other guys to go back and forth to the prison, but when I started out, I was doing it by myself. I was going to Angola, Hunt, three different prisons in one day.[47] Go and drop off here, leave them there, go drop off at the next one, and then go on to Angola. On my way back, I come back and pick up everybody. So I did that for about maybe about five or six years, and then I decided to get with these two guys. We decided to split them up. You go one place, I'll go to the next place, and you go to the other one. And we did that—we did that for about 10 years.

Like Kim and her store, Elizabeth's work was more to her than a way to earn a paycheck. Elizabeth's entrepreneurial spirit was awakened by a need she saw in her community.

Elizabeth: Well, one morning, I was on my way to pick up my school kids, and it was about 4:30 a.m., and this elderly lady— lived in the project over here, Desire Project—she was on her way to catch that bus that would bring them to the prison. And on my way up the street, I saw this little guy. He run up to her and grabbed her pocketbook and knocked her down. And she was elderly, and I just stopped. I just stopped. When I got her off the ground, and I asked her where was she going out there this time of morning, she said she was going to catch the bus to go see her grandson in prison. My mind told me she had no business being out there [at this kind of time]. So I told her, the next time you want to go see your grandson, give me a call. And that's what she did. She called me. I got up that Saturday morning and took her out of there, but on my way out there, she said, "Oh, my friend might wanna go." So we picked up her friend, and then the friend said, "Oh, my daughter's going, too," and I went and picked up the daughter. So I had about three or four of them I took out there that day. And by me bringing them out there, that one time, they called everybody and told them that I said "don't go out there on that corner no more." It wasn't safe. It wasn't safe for them to be out there, not to catch no bus. Some of them were going to catch a bus. That was dangerous. At 4:00 a.m. And that old lady said she had been doing that for years. [I told them that] I'm gonna pick them up at their house, and that's what I did. I started picking them up at their house, 4:00 a.m. [and by] 5:00 a.m., I was on the highway. I hung in there with them. Me and them old folks, we were together. They ended up—look, they loved me so much, they wanted to buy me a van. I told them I do not want you on this highway out here.

So when I got started, that helped me out a lot, and I got started with my school kids during the week, and I had them on the weekends. I was rolling seven days a week. Sometimes I didn't sleep. I didn't sleep at all. I was going so many places. It was fun, though. I enjoyed it. It was really fun.

Ervin tells of his reactions when they heard of Hurricane Katrina's approach. He remembered Hurricane Betsy, and that memory influenced his decision to leave rather than ride out the storm.

> **Ervin:** [When the storm hit], we were in Alexandria. We left that Sunday morning. I always leave when I see a storm. Whether it's a little one or a big one, I leave. I don't take no chances. You see, I'd been through them and I know how they is. This part never did used to flood like down in the parish when they used to get bad weather. And, the night—when Betsy was coming—I was in the house and I got a phone call saying the levee was broke, and I got my wife, my children, and I put them in the car, and I had two old ladies standing next to me, put them in the car, and we left. And we left just in time. Because later than that, we would've got caught down there in that water.

Elizabeth also remembered Hurricane Betsy. Contrary to Ervin's response, Elizabeth's experience with Betsy left her with little fear in the face of Katrina's arrival.[48]

> **Elizabeth:** [When Betsy came] my mom and them was caught. They was caught in bed because they didn't go nowhere. My mom and dad was caught in the bed, and she said that she felt the water hit the mattress. She was deep asleep. And when the water hit the mattress, she hit my daddy and she told him, "Man, you're laying up here, wetting the bed!" And when she threw her hand, her hand hit that water, and she said, "It's not you," and she said, "Get up! Let's get out of here!" And they couldn't—they couldn't get out. They were stuck. So they wound up busting a hole through the ceiling and going up on the roof. We [all of the kids] were gone at the time, but I was living in the second Desire project with my children. And her and my father and her mother was living down the street down there, and I just knew they were gone

because the water had covered the house, but a boat came through and got them off the roof. That was during Betsy.

[My kids and I, however,] did fine [during Betsy] because where we [were] had five steps. We were five steps high. The water came up to the top step, and that's where it stopped at. We were in the projects, and that was the highest it got over in the projects. My kids know about it. They were here. Most of them were born, with the exception of my baby boy and my other son, Jimmy. They were the only two that weren't here during Betsy. Betsy never fazed me. But it fazed him [Ervin] because they were in it. See, I wasn't in it. I was in the project, and the water came up and stayed up for three, four days over there, and it went down. [He had to talk me into evacuating]. He kept telling me, "Are you gonna pack a suitcase so we can get out of here?" I had the suitcase packed, really I did. I had the suitcase packed, and I was running as if I wasn't going anywhere because I wasn't planning on going anywhere. And I said, "Oh, I'm gonna put these clothes in this suitcase." Then I decided I was gonna take the clothes out of the suitcase. I said, "We're not going nowhere and I'm not changing these clothes."

Like Elizabeth, not all of Ervin's family was as eager as he was to leave, and those who stayed behind found themselves in dangerous situations.

Ervin: I was gonna leave here because I know the danger of a storm. Down here when the storm came, you know how people got drowned in houses. I wasn't taking, I don't take no chances. My oldest brother, back in on Tennessee Street, about two blocks from that where that barge busted through the levees. I called him Sunday morning and I said, "I'm leaving. I'm going to Alexandria." "Oh, every time you see a storm, you gotta run." He left home and he came back, and he went back to his house and went to bed. I had left one of my brothers up there, my younger brother up there to help him drive, but he wouldn't leave. They had to get him out the roof. And his house completely floated off the pillars because his house was back there where the water hit first. He was staying by himself. He was in his own house. But my younger brother, Nathan, came from the Saint Bernard Parish to help him drive his car. But he stopped. See, he was gonna go get him some pork chops or something, and he went and got him some pork chops and he said, "Boy, I'm going home and frying me some pork chops and get in my bed." And that's what he did. He came right back home and went to bed. He would not follow them out of here. They got him out; somebody got him out, yeah. He almost killed himself, but he got out. If Nathan hadn't been there to help him get in the attic, he wouldn't have made it. The younger brother stayed there with him, and he was—he was in the part of the roof up there, hollering because they couldn't get out. They got in the attic. He finally got him in the attic because my older brother's six feet, two inches and he's a big man, and he couldn't hardly walk and he kept falling out of that attic, and my younger brother jumped down in that water and pushed him up there and he got in [the attic]. So he was hollering in [the attic] and the boat was passing by and he heard them. And that's how they got out. That's how they got them out of there. They got them out through the roof. Otherwise, if my younger brother hadn't been there, he would've drowned. He would've drowned in the house because he's 70-something; he's 77 years old now. My younger brother, Nathan, should be about 40 some years old.

Others in Elizabeth's family also went through traumatic situations.

Elizabeth: It was devastating. My oldest daughter and her daughter and her daughter's baby, the next-door neighbor and her baby, was in the apartment back there on Delery and Prieur, and I kept telling them to leave from back there. My granddaughter gets in these depression moods, and she got in one of those moods and she said, "I'm not going nowhere. I'm going to bed, Grandma." So my youngest daughter went to the house and told her, "I'm gonna take the children with me. If you wanna stay, let me take the children." She let her take the two biggest kids and left her with the baby, which was a year old. So my oldest daughter, her mama, was getting ready to leave with the friend. And when her daughter told her she wasn't going nowhere, she said, "Well, I'm gonna stick it out with my daughter."

So she went to the daughter's house and stayed there with her. And when the water came, when the water came up, my granddaughter called me on the phone and said, "Grandma, the water's coming in. What do we do?" But I had been telling them all the time, I don't care what happens, go in the attic. Bust a hole through the attic, get up there, and go out the roof. I kept telling them that. My granddaughter was 280 some pounds, she's big. And the baby, a year. I told her, I said, "I don't know what more to tell you. I told you to get up and go in the attic. Get in the attic." She said, "Uh oh, that's it." And I heard no more. She lost her phone in the water. She said that the water came, just busted open and just come on in. They sat there in that house looking at that water coming. My daughter, my granddaughter, the next-door neighbor, and her daughter. All of them, they got in one house, and then they tried to get in the attic from the water rolling, and she kept dropping that baby down in that water, pulling that baby back up. Then laying up on top of that roof out there, she said that water came and she said it looked like that baby was floating in that, was getting away from her, and she just reached over and pulled that baby up, [then] they saw a boat. That's how they got out.

A boat came and got them off that roof. I told them, I said, "You will leave from now on. You will not stay when a storm is coming no more. You will leave from now on." When she gets depressed, there's nothing nobody can do. She don't do nothing—it don't matter to her when she gets depressed. I was devastated that she had gotten that depressed at that point in time. She waited until everybody left here and then she said, "I'm not going nowhere. I'm going to bed. I don't care what happens. If I die, I die." That was that.

They wouldn't tell me anything at first because I didn't find them for a while. I didn't know where they was for a while, and then my son in North Carolina called and told me that he had heard that my granddaughter and the baby didn't make it. That upsetted them for a while. It took a couple of days before they told it to me. And it hit me and I started crying, but my intuition kept [telling me] didn't nothing happen. I just didn't feel it. You will feel it if somebody dies. I didn't feel it. I didn't feel like nothing had happened. I just told the Lord, whatever it is, bring them through this. And that was that. I left it at that. I gave it to the Lord, and I left her there.

And then when they did [initially] tell it to me [that she didn't make it], it hit me in a whip like that, and then all of a sudden, it dawned on me and I calmed myself. See, years ago when I was younger, the doctors said I was born with an enlarged heart. And I used to have these seizures and I would fall out. So this old doctor, he told me, he said, "Whenever you find yourself getting too hyped up, talk to yourself and bring yourself down because you can kill yourself. You get too hyped up, you don't calm yourself down, your blood is started flowing and it'll kill you." Every time I went to that clinic, he talked to me, and he told me, he'd say, "Now, remember, you're young. You got a long time yet. Calm yourself down. Like that, your heart won't beat or pump that blood so fast."

So when they told that to me, then I had to tell myself to calm myself down. And I told myself, I'm not gonna do this crying because I'm crying in vain. There is nothing wrong with my grandchildren. Nothing. After I found out [that they were all right], then that's when I really cried.

I was happy then. I walked away from them and I said, "Thank you, Jesus, yes, Lord," because—I gave her to Him when they called. I said there's nothing I can do about [it], Lord. If you don't take care of them, I can't take care of them because I'm gone.

Ervin and Elizabeth evacuated to Alexandria and stayed in a church where they knew the assistant pastor with other Katrina evacuees.

Ervin: We have friends up there in [Alexandria]. That young man I christened lives up there. And I went by his house, he's assistant pastor at a church up there, and they opened up the church and let everybody stay in their church. Oh, it was full. Four or five cars full, four cars of us going together. We stayed here together. But when we got here, the whole lot of people started coming. We were calling different ones to find out where they were. Some of them were stuck out there on the interstate, been out there for 17 hours. And we were telling them to get out, come to such and such a road and make a detour and come to Alexandria. Family and friends. We had people from different places. They came up there.

I think there were [eventually] around 400 people in that church. They opened the church. We were all over the place. We was in—we was in the bleachers of the church. We stayed on the floors. We was on the kitchen floors. We was everywhere. They gave us cots; they gave blankets. They gave us everything we needed. They had like about six classrooms in there, in that church, and we used all of them. They opened up the church like it was a house and let us in—we just moved in and we were just there. We were living four, five months at the church.

Every Sunday, we had to take all of our clothes and stuff out of the church parlor so they could have service. And then after service was over, we put it back. They took good care of us. They gave us everything we needed. Everything. I mean, when a truck rolled in there—with everything you needed. The pastor of that church, when he said he was gonna get something and he get on that phone and he would tell them what he needed and what he wanted, it was there. We didn't want for nothing.

Like so many others, Elizabeth and Ervin were the recipients of the generosity of countless strangers.

Ervin: When we first got there, I think they sent us a trailer load of used clothes. And he got on that phone and told them don't send another truckload of used clothes. He wanted everything with a tag on it, and you better believe everything came with a tag on it. We had so much food around there sometimes, we had to—when the truck was coming so regular, we had to call some of the people in the neighborhood to come and get it because we didn't have nowhere to stack it. We had nowhere to store it most of the time.

[The people of that church] gave us everything we needed. We didn't want for no food. We didn't want for no clothes. We didn't even want for washing powder or bleach. We didn't want for nothing. We didn't want for nothing. We had sheets, pillowcases, blankets, coats. See, when it would turn cold, we had all the coats and the jeans and stuff we needed. We had everything we needed. They gave us everything and anything that we thought we might have needed; they put it on the list and they got it. They got it for us. Two weeks, Red Cross came in and getting everybody together, and sent us to doctors that we needed to go to. Needed medicine? You had medicine right there, free. You got everything you needed.

Even within the ranks of the Red Cross, there were those who stood out as particularly gracious and attentive to the evacuees' needs. They were able to find a place to stay that was much better than the shelters in which many ended up.

Ervin: We had round-the-clock nurses at this place. Red Cross said all the nurses were supposed to leave at a certain point in time. We had one nurse, the day she came, she didn't leave for the five or six months we were there. She did not leave. Every time they said she had to go, she found another way to stay, and she stayed right there with us and took care of us. We had diabetics, we had [some with] high blood pressure, we had them all on—they had to go and get a dialysis machine. We had [those who needed] a wheelchair. We had all kinds of people.

If you didn't have a place to stay, you could stay there until you got somewhere to stay. See, [the government] started giving them vouchers for houses. We saw that they had an elderly home over there and, when we was up there, we just moved over to the elderly home. You had to have the age to move over there. It was walking distance from the church, and we worked in the church. We all had—little different things that we were doing. They started giving us little jobs to do to keep us occupied: painting and doing different other things, cleaning up around the yards. It wasn't nothing much, but we all made sure that we stayed busy, not just sit down and worry. They had just built the home. They had just finished building that apartment. Seventeen apartments and I think they had one or two rented, I think.

All the elderly people just took the apartments. We didn't have vouchers; we had to pay. We were getting a social security check. So that's how we were able to move in there and pay, and it was nice. It was really nice. It's still nice. It's still nice because we still have the apartment. We didn't give it up. Well, he had to go to the doctor out there a lot, and I had to come back here to go to the doctor because my insurance didn't work out there. But he had to go to the doctor out there, so he doesn't have a doctor here, so we have to keep going back. [It's about] two or three and a half hours. If we go out there and have to stay in a hotel, we're gonna spend some money because we're gonna have to stay overnight. So we may as well just keep the apartment.

Ervin decided that he would work on their house himself instead of trying to find a contractor.

Ervin: When we first came here, we couldn't stay down here because we didn't have nowhere to stay until we got a trailer. When we first came back—two months or better after the storm—they wouldn't even let us come this far. We got that trailer last year [2006] in July or something like that and then we started coming back and stay down here. Well, I'm down here staying now because I'm trying to finish my [rental] house up. I only go back when I have to go back now.

I've been working on the house. It's just that it's a whole process. Right now, I can't do the Sheetrock until my electrician and plumber finishes. If it wouldn't be for that, my house would have been completed. It's hard to find [contractors and workers], anybody, because when you get somebody—you gotta be careful who you let do your work—so I decided not to get no contractor. I did this all myself before.

Upon seeing the house after being allowed to return, Ervin and Elizabeth were confronted with the overwhelming scale of the damage their house and Elizabeth's rental property incurred and the work that rebuilding would require.

Elizabeth: We had just finished doing that addition [in this house] and [we] had to tear it all out. We had a lot of damage.

Ervin: I lost everything in the house. This house had seven feet of water in it. We lost all the cars, the truck, and that motor home you see sitting over there. When we came here, they wouldn't let us come down to see, until after the water had come down and kind of settled and dried up a little bit, because it took a while because the water stayed up about 18 days. The first time we seen it, when we came back here, the furniture was—that water had floated them all around. You couldn't get in. We cleaned it out and then we gutted it ourselves. Yeah, it took a little time to do it. We came in and moved stuff out, cleaned it out. We came down on the weekend, do so much, and then go back, come back again and do so much until we got it all up. We started that [in] 2006. [It was] in the summer.

Elizabeth: Oh, we had so much stuff up in here. That's a job when you've got a whole house full of stuff to actually shovel off the floor.

The timing of when people were allowed to return and begin the rebuilding process differed from one neighborhood to another, which seemed unfair to Ervin and Elizabeth.

Elizabeth: Saint Bernard Parish, they went back [immediately it seems]. They were gutting. They were able to do everything when they went back. We weren't able to do anything when we came back because they wouldn't let us in here. The Guards and things stopped us from coming in to our property every time we came back. They say a lot of looting was going on, but we had nothing to loot. And then again, they were finding a lot of dead bodies so they were really trying to keep the people out as much as possible until they could get some of those bodies and things out of here.

Although many New Orleanians have returned, some stayed in the cities and towns to which they evacuated. For some, the communities in which they found themselves following Katrina represented an improved quality of life relative to New Orleans.[49]

Elizabeth: My three sons are back. That's all. My daughter says she's not coming back. My youngest daughter, she's in Alexandria; her and her son they're in Alexandria. She says she's not coming back. She's gonna rebuild her house over there, but she says she's not gonna come back to stay in it. My granddaughter, she's in Dallas. Her and her children are in Dallas. She said when they went to Dallas, they gave her a house, they gave her a car, they gave her furniture, they gave her everything she needed. She's living there and she's working there. I say, "You're doing good. Stay where you at." I don't want her to be depressed no more. I think she will make it now. She [was just here for a] visit. She came in Friday and she left Sunday, her and the kid. I told her, I said, "Dallas is treating you nice. Stay where you at." She got a job and everything. She's doing good. She's really doing good, and she went back to school. She wanted to come back, but I told her don't come back to New Orleans. Just stay where you at. You sound like you're peaceful. Just stay there.

I told her when she misses us—just pack her little kids up and come on in. That's all. And stay for a few days and go back home. That's good for her. She don't need to be here. This is depressing here.

RICHARD AND APRIL

Richard and April, a young couple in their mid-20s to early 30s, were married after Katrina. Richard is a black New Orleans native who grew up in the Desire housing projects. April is a white Midwesterner who moved to New Orleans a year before Katrina.

April: Well, before the storm, we weren't married. I was actually renting, a little down closer to St. Claude in the Ninth Ward down on Alvar Street. I had actually just moved into that house about a week or two before the storm. Prior to that, I was living pretty much in the same neighborhood, just a little further across St. Claude and Bywater. I'm from Minnesota. I had just moved to New Orleans for a job almost exactly a year before Katrina. I was, basically, living up here before the storm. This was one of the pretty decent neighborhoods, kind of quiet. It was really quiet, nice neighbors. The most noise that bothered us was a little screeching on Main Street that everybody goes through because there's no cutting. This is the only way through the neighborhood so there was a lot of traffic noises.

I love New Orleans. I was excited to move here. I just really felt like this was where God was needing me to move. I had a job at the ministry, which is actually where we met each other.

The school and the church that I worked for . . . had a lot of different things going on. I ended up doing a lot of different things. I didn't really have a clear job description when I came down. But I was excited for the vision of where they were going. I ended up teaching in the high school when I first came down and then just different things, different community outreach stuff, and doing child care for a moms' group that met there once a week, coordinating different neighborhood activities and helping out with their summer programs. I was working with some similar programs in Minnesota. I went to a conference in Texas for kind of like-minded urban ministries, and I had met some people from New Orleans and that's how we got talking.

For both April and Richard, their life centered on the church organization where they worked. It was through this ministry and Katrina that they got together.

April: [We met at the ministry.] After he went to college, he came back and was working there too: coaching at the school where I came to teach. And that's actually the ministry he grew up with in high school. So that's where we met. We got married this past May.

Richard: The first day we actually hung out was the day we evacuated. We knew each other from working together, but we never really spent any time together outside of work. We were working up to it, just having difficulties. She just played hard to get.

Katrina changed many things. In April and Richard's life, they were fortunate enough to have the continuity of keeping their jobs even though they were moved to a different location.

April: Before the storm, the school was an all-boys school, and they had 140 students at school. It was 7th through 12th grade. Then, after Katrina, of course, it kind of took a crazy turn. The school actually stayed functioning and moved to Florida and became a boarding school. So we were in Florida for a few months with the school. I was teaching. He was staying in the cabins. They were living in a camp kind of thing. He was living in the cabins with the boys as a dorm dad. That was actually a pretty chaotic and crazy situation, too.

Richard explains how he got connected with this ministry. They helped him when he was a teenager, and now he finds himself on the other end.

Richard: Actually, initially, it was Bible study with the high school football team. In '91, we were sophomores in high school, that's when I met [the pastor]. Our high school coach allowed him to come and start doing Bible study, so it started in our locker room. Man, it was a nasty locker room. That's where God started His work in a locker room back in '91. It grew into a church, and then it grew into a tutoring program, and then it grew into a school. Now, the school is really the largest piece, but church is pretty much no longer really existent because people are scattered. It was a small church anyway.

So many people would just say we're part of [that church]. Maybe a hundred-some. It was a church that was dominated by youth, so they just grow up and go off to college, which is why it's hard to maintain after the storm, I guess. The facility is still there, but it's not really being used for that anymore. It's being used more to house volunteer groups. The school is actually down in Baton Rouge. But we don't have much connection with it anymore.

April and Richard believe that New Orleans was already going through a storm, a chaotic time, before Katrina hit and that Katrina simply magnified the chaos in the church, in the city, and in the city government. Richard speaks as a long-term New Orleans native and April as an outsider looking in.

Richard: A lot of people don't realize about our city, we was in the midst of a storm before Katrina came. It was just so chaotic. It was just like the hurricane hit before, every day of a New

Orleanian's life. Every day they woke up, it was like a hurricane [with the] crime [and] discombobulation: spiritually, mentally, physically. People was already just going through a lot even before the storm. The storm, to me, just magnified the problems that we already had in the churches, in the city, within the city government, all that kind of stuff. The storm just added to the brunt of all that.

In churches, people might disagree, but I think the church lost focus of being devoted to God. I think we, as a church, get so caught up in doing the things of God that we're not devoted to God.

You could be doing a lot of good deeds, but that don't mean God called you to do that deed. With churches, we don't have relationships with one another within churches. No relationship, no communication, there's no brotherly love. I think what Katrina did, especially, was expose our true relationship. When the time of chaos come, it's going to really show you who you are. We either going to bind together or you going to screw it up and just be at each other. I think that was the current situation with the city, with the churches, and with [the ministry we worked for]. Because right now, the government, the president, don't care; Governor Blanco don't care; the mayor don't care. Let's work together. Even before the storm, you could see it [the chaos of politics] in the news. You got some of them put in prison for stealing money. And all their friends [are] people just finding opportunities to make a little bit of extra money.

April: I was expecting some of the chaoticness, to a degree, [but] I'm still learning about it and still surprised by it. I could be fully immersed in the culture for the rest of my life and still not understand it to the degree Richard does because he's from here and he's grown up here. But some of it is specific to New Orleans, and some of it is just human nature; it's stuff everybody struggles with. When you have a situation like Katrina, it really magnifies everything that was already going on—good and bad. It just kind of brings a lot of clarity to stuff that was going on before, but you just might not have seen it until all this tension comes. Somebody might have been able to keep quiet about this before, but now they're under this level of stress, they're going to let it all come out. And I think some of this is specific to the situation, and some of it, I think, is just human nature.

Several of our interviewees point to the high levels of corruption that characterize New Orleans' bureaucracies.

April: That's one of the negative things I've noticed. It's really a system of who you know. Favors are expected. You can get by with this if you know such-and-such. And that was a brand-new thing to me. You can get by with traffic tickets. You can get by with breaking the law. You can get by with all the high-level government stuff, bribery and all that kind of stuff, if you know the person in the right place. I guess, to a degree, it happens all over, but it's really bad [here].

You see it. We have a friend—this is to the extreme—we have a friend whose husband was just killed in a motorcycle accident last summer. She had to get the police report. She couldn't locate the police report, and it turns out that the person who had the accident knew some judge or something and got the police report thrown out. I still don't even know if she resolved it. She wasn't going to be able to have access to insurance because someone's friend threw out the police report that people were racing and hit her husband and killed him. And they knew someone in the right place, so to speak. And that's just almost an expected thing here and that kind of blows my mind.

Richard agrees with April's assessment of the culture that she sees in New Orleans. He sees it as a place that lacks vision.

Richard: It's normal; it's every man for themselves. It's just like, hey, get it how you live. That's the saying in New Orleans. "You do you. I'm going to do me." There's no togetherness. People come together to fight to get back into the projects that's nasty and dirty, but the people won't stand together and fight for benefits or whatever in the neighborhood. They'd just rather come together for stuff that's just an easy road.

That's one thing I noticed about my city that's different from other cities. People in New Orleans really don't want to earn their way through things. They'd rather take a handout. "As long as you give it to me, I'm going to take it, because I'm not going to work for it." That kind of stuff.

But when you go to Arizona, you go to Minnesota, Chicago, and different places like that, people have goals. People have visions. People have 5-year plans, 10-year plans, and they're going on to accomplish them, and everybody that's around them are affected by it in a positive way. It's just like me and my wife. I have no doubt that when we have kids, our kids are going to graduate from college. That's because we graduated from college. And that works the other way. I mean, two parents together and not even married, don't have a degree, so their kid not going to have a degree. That's how it is down here in New Orleans.

Richard had initially thought to ride the storm out, but April convinced him otherwise. She persuaded him to go to Jackson, Mississippi.

April: The ministry we were working for was trying to get together whoever wanted to go. One of our coworkers, Daniel, used to be employed at this camp up in Jackson, Mississippi. And so he knew people up there, and he said they got cabins people can stay in, so they're just trying to round up as many people as wanted somewhere to go—people we worked with, kids in the school, and people in the neighborhood. Daniel was trying to organize it. I was getting ready to do that. I had packed my hurricane bag and everything. I didn't even know there was a storm coming that morning. My mom in Minnesota actually called me, "A hurricane is coming." "I didn't know that. Let me turn on the TV." We left on Saturday night. It kind of came at us a little by surprise, but I had already evacuated twice, and I had only been there a year. It was becoming a little more of a routine. So I packed up. And that was actually the first time we had hung out. [Richard] had borrowed his friend's motorcycle and called me, "You want to go for a motorcycle ride?" I was like, "Sure." So we went driving around, and I told him, "I really think you should get out of here." So that evening, we left, and he came later on in the evening with his mom and nephew and some other people. We had about 100 of us from around here at that camp in Jackson.

Like so many New Orleanians, they evacuated to a place that removed them from the direct path of the storm but was not far enough away to avoid feeling some of the effects of the hurricane.

April: When the storm actually hit—and it hit us there too, but it was just wind and rain and stuff—it knocked out power. It actually knocked the water out, too. I think maybe we spent two nights there or something. Eventually they were like, "We'd like to keep you all here, but we don't have enough supplies to keep this many people going." So everybody went their separate ways after that. Most people's phones weren't working, but some people were talking to kids who were still stuck in the city, trying to figure out what was going on. I think the morning after the levees broke, someone texted us from Florida and told me, "The levees broke and there's water all up in the Ninth Ward." But he still didn't know the extent of it. But then later that morning up at the camp, they were able to get a TV hooked up and so everybody kind of gathered around looking at the TV footage. It wasn't nice, it was raining and everything, but you could tell the whole city was underwater. But at that point still, we thought probably a week or two and we'd be probably be able to go back. We still didn't understand how extensive the damage was.

During the evacuation, Richard and his family separated, staying with different family members.

Richard: After leaving Jackson, Mississippi, I went by my dad's in Missouri. But my grandma went to Texas. I didn't want to go that far. I'm not a great Texas fan. One of my sisters was already living in Houston. During this whole situation, she was in the process of moving back down near Louisiana. So that was kind of the right timing, but I had some other relatives on my mom's side that was actually staying in San Antonio [who] invited my mom to come up there.

During her evacuation, April and others in her group experienced the generosity of people in Jackson, Mississippi. The school was able to relocate to Mississippi and continue operation.

April: The ministry actually set up a temporary office up in Jackson—which is where we both ended up; about a week later we was calling around and trying to locate people that were in shelters that were from the church or from [the] neighborhood trying to figure out where they were. Were they okay? Could we help get them into temporary housing? We were locating churches nearby where people were and trying to see if we could hook them up with clothes and furniture. Sort of the emergency response, I guess you could say.

So actually, they called us to see if we were willing to move to Jackson, indefinitely. That same day we got there, we had furnished apartments. People from the churches around there had furnished two apartments for us. Just with donations, spare stuff from their attics and garages and whatever. So we had everything: houses, coffee tables, pots and pans. The people were really great. And at that point, we still hadn't been able to be back in the city so we didn't know if our stuff was ruined, or when we'd be able to go back, or how long we'd be living in Mississippi. We ended up only being there for about a month.

There was maybe three or four students from the school staying up there as well. They had a girls' apartment and a guys' apartment. There actually was only two of us in the girls' apartment. The guys' apartment had people on the floors sleeping and everything. But they were there for a while, and I think they went to Atlanta after a couple of weeks. So we were just living there and working out of that office trying to locate people and trying to figure out what was going on. So we were having phone conferences almost nightly. And there'd be like 30 of us on the phone and someone leading a conference meeting. The president of the ministry would be like, "What do you all think about this?" He was in Atlanta. Essentially they ended up deciding on the campus in Florida for them to start the process of trying to figure out how to get all the kids who wanted to be reenrolled in the school and all that.

Maybe half of the kids ended up going to the Florida school. Maybe a little over half. Right about 80 kids. And other people started in public schools wherever they had evacuated, and some people were with extended family. But some parents chose to send their kids back, and they moved in. We were in Florida through February of 2006.

April's apartment did not sustain significant damage, but Richard's house would need to be gutted and rebuilt. The focus of their work changed as they helped coordinate the many volunteer groups that came to New Orleans.

April: Richard and I moved to back to New Orleans, and I was actually camping out at our friend's house, a friend who also worked for the ministry prior to the storm. Their house wasn't damaged, so they had people coming in and out of their house all the time. [The house was located] in the Seventh Ward. So I was staying with them, and Richard was actually in this. He had no hot water, no electricity or anything. He just had a mattress—basically, he was pretty much camping.

I was actually staying in the upper floor of the two-story. I was staying upstairs, so actually most of my stuff was okay, clothes and personal stuff. I didn't have a ton of stuff, but I had a couple couches that were messed up because the windows blew out and it rained in there. But other than that, I was able to recover my stuff.

Richard's stuff was pretty messed up in here. It didn't get a lot of water, but it got enough to get stuff moldy—for instance, the cabinets. We had to put new cabinets in because his refrigerator tipped over. The army busted all the doors in to check for people to make sure there was no survivors. The door was open and lots of people [were] vandalizing and looting. I think he had a TV stolen and maybe a couple of other things—but someone came in here and just turned dressers and stuff upside down. And knocked the refrigerator over and just crazy stuff like that. And the refrigerator, of course, was full of rotting food. So that was one of the most disgusting things I've seen in my life. It was just this black goo, smelling like death just all over the floor. When we came in to try to mop it up, some of it splashed on the cabinets, and nothing could get that smell out of the cabinets. And then when the weather started to be warm again . . . we had to get rid of these cabinets.

Soon after the storm, Richard and April began their courtship, which quickly led to engagement. Richard and April resigned from their positions with the ministry and focused full time on getting their rental property in shape to lease and their personal property in shape to occupy.

Richard: We got about six properties that we are presently working on right now. Trying to get some families back home. I owned all of them except one, the one we just bought this year. I was a landlord, father figure, Bible teacher, coach, exercising instructor. And recovering from all kinds of tragic things that went on in my life.

Let's see. We got here in mid-February probably. We were dating by then. We were engaged in Thanksgiving of 2005. So not that long after the storm we got engaged. And then we were married in May. And we resigned from the ministry in May right after the wedding. The houses was just getting to be a full-time job and [we were] kind of dissatisfied with the direction things were going there, so we just work on the houses full time because they were all in need of repairs, except one. That's what we've been doing ever since, full time, and it's been hard work and a long learning process.

Like many returnees, April and Richard had a hard time navigating the insurance companies, city permitting offices, SBA, and other organizations that they had to deal with after Katrina. They found persistence to be key.

April: [The insurance company has] been pretty responsive. We had some little hang-ups, like with repairs that they didn't want to cover. We had some plumbing pipes get rusted out from sitting in water. But the insurance company said, "We don't want to pay for that." Similar things with electrical. The city codes require you to rewire your house if it was flooded, and the insurance company says that's unnecessary. All you need to do is fix this, this, and this. Well, the city says it's necessary, so it's necessary. So there's some little things like that that have been frustrating, but some people who still haven't seen a penny from their insurance for whatever reason. A lot of people make the mistake of not calling. You have got to call them every day, that's something we really learned. And even though we have an SBA loan—two SBA loans, disaster loans—even with them, you really have to call them every day, every other day, because I'm sure they're just drowning in paperwork. And we're so thankful that we have this time because so many people those are working nine-to-five jobs. That's pretty much the only time you can get ahold of insurance companies or SBA or different things like that. [Other people] just don't have the time to be persistent with those issues. And a lot of people I just haven't had to deal with that kind of stuff in the past and just really aren't sure how to go about it. I think a lot of people are struggling with that. We just learned by trial and error.

It has been a challenge finding people to work on their houses.

Richard: We've went through about six electricians. We probably lost about $15,000 just from electricians. People are just shady. And in the beginning we were trying to save money, so we'd go with what seemed like the best price and then find out the person doesn't know what they're doing, or does it wrong, or does half of it and leaves town. And it's hard waiting on money from government. And not having done this stuff before, now having to do all of them, it's just all trial and error.

April and Richard had problems with contractors but were eventually able to find a reliable worker through word of mouth and realized that cutting corners was not the way to go.

April: Trying to find reliable people has been the most difficult thing. Right now we've come to the conclusion, if we can find someone who knows what they're doing and is going to be reliable, we're willing to pay for it. Because we've lost so much money trying to save money, it's just better to find someone you know is going to be able to do it. [We are relying on] word of mouth, mostly. We are getting multiple estimates. But this guy that's been in and out of here, Antonio, he's really been helping us out the most. And he was referred to us by friends.

Antonio put an addition on a friend's mom's house, and he said, "Come check it out. This guy does good work." So we hooked up with him, and he does really good work. Something that was frustrating a lot of people in the city [is that it] seems like when they [contractors] work on houses, they just patch up and cover up stuff instead of really repairing it, and so that's something we really appreciate about [Antonio] because he'll point stuff out to us like, "This wood is rotten." He's really like a friend now. We hang out with him and stuff. He's always over here, just drops by and watches TV and stuff.

So that is something. We were so relieved to find someone who's really wanting to do work that way. It's a little more expensive, but in the end it's better because you feel good about putting people in that house. And you know you're not going to have to come back in two months because something broke.

He's been kind of our main guy. And he has usually a couple of different people with him. Sometimes he'll go pick people up, like day laborers who wait outside Lowe's or whatever. Sometimes he'll pick some of them up.[50] And he usually always has at least one person living with him that he know that came up from Houston or wherever that's skilled. It's been a help, with him having his own tools and vehicle—it frees us up to go take care of SBA stuff. Go to this meeting and that meeting.

Sometimes we'll work with him. At first we were really gung-ho about doing a lot of our own work, but we realized that [this was not the] time to experiment and learn to do stuff because we're trying to get properties up and running so we can be at a financially stable place. We're putting money into these houses—some of it is insurance money, some of it out of our own pockets.

Because Richard and April were rehabbing rental properties, it was a double strain on their finances. Not only did they have to find the resources necessary to make the repairs, they were simultaneously losing money in lost rent for every month it took to get the properties in order.

April: And we're putting money into houses that aren't producing income as of right now, so we trying to do it as fast as possible so we can get renters in there. But we've done all our own painting, so we saved money there. It will take the rest of this year. We've made a lot of progress, but a lot of it's taken a lot more time than we [expected].

Homeowner's supposed to get up to $150,000 to compensate for what they lost, but the program is just taking so long to get money to people who don't have any, it's just ridiculous. It's like they're saying to us, "We're going to give you $120,000." Then you get to closing, "Oh, we brought it down to $60,000." And we're like, "Wait a minute. I'm not signing that." So now, it's the whole process again.

Well, we haven't looked into the landlord program, really, yet. But we qualify for our personal house. We'd love to be able to have money for our personal house and [to] make repairs. Where it's really tying us up right now is his mom's house. It is still sitting there gutted, but no repairs have been done because she's waiting on the money and she's in one of our rental units, which could be renting out, but she's staying because she's Mom. That is [a loss of] $1,500 a month for us.

In the landlord program, they give you up to $65,000 or $75,000 to repair your house. But you've got to keep your rent at a certain level. You got to weigh your options, and that's what people are doing. And on top of that is just additional paperwork because we've got so much stuff going on with insurance, mortgages, this SBA loan, that SBA loan, and bills. And keeping track of it, sending in receipts, doing this, and then you get—what's it called—a supplement check from the insurance. You found something else that was wrong, so you apply for it, so they give it to you—now SBA loan is decreased per month. You have to fill out this paperwork and that paperwork.

When you have an opportunity, then it seems like the way the government is set up is to say, "We don't want you to make too much. We'll give you this, but if you get this, you've got to give this back." That's only part of the mentality. So at the same [time], you've got that other thing going on where people are trying to scam and sneak around, and "I know this person, so I have access to this grant that I'm not supposed to." So that's why all those stipulations are in place.

As far as the government's performance after the disaster, April has a charitable outlook but is still critical. Richard, however, believes that individuals should also be held accountable.

April: I wouldn't want to be the one in charge and making decisions for how it would go down, so I don't want to be quick to judge and say this should've been done like this or that, because I don't really know all the inner workings of it, but I don't see how you could watch what went on and say they did the best possible response they could. It does seem disappointing—I hate to see ranting and raving about this and that organization on TV, but it does seem like FEMA—an organization that, from the beginning, was meant to respond to disaster—shouldn't they have some type of a plan in place?

Richard: People got to learn to take their responsibilities, too. The man say get out, get out. You didn't get out.

April: Some people couldn't get out . . . some people didn't have access to transportation and all that.

Richard: Well, I think it's just like everybody knew how bad the city was and they just wasn't prepared for something that—the city just couldn't take on that response. It wasn't prepared for it. That kind of situation, they should have took the time.

Like others, April and Richard viewed the distribution of government money in the months following Katrina as haphazard and confusing.

Richard: Instead of dishing out money, mailing, faxing them information, showing the deeds with your name on the house. I'm not just sending people money for no reason. You don't just hand out money to people. When we were in Mississippi and they just start putting money straight in your checking account.
[First] they wouldn't give you any letters or anything. A couple of months later, oh, there's some more. And there were some people that could never get a penny of FEMA money.

So we signed up. So then when FEMA sent a letter, "This is for your losses and help." And then here comes $10,000. And then, a couple months later come a letter in the mail, "You can only spend this money on XYZ. You may have to pay it all back." And you're like, "You just put that right in my checking account." So FEMA's been a little confusing. Because it's like, "We give you $10,000."

We were still getting paychecks, which a lot of people weren't. We were saving our money. We were able to save a lot of money during that period. That's what really helped us get jump-started before we got money from SBA. We saved the FEMA money, saved our paychecks, and donations and stuff. That's what really helped us get started. Because right about now, we'd be just getting started, right about now. We really just started getting our SBA money. [We applied for that] over a year ago, right after the storm. It just started coming through the system. There's always paperwork that you sent them, and they say they didn't get. And we've faxed them things five and six times.

Richard and April explain how the way they spend their time now is different from before Katrina.

Richard: [We spend most of our time now] doing paperwork. Basically, it's just work. I'm coaching at the high school, so I've been trying to substitute every now and then and coaching football in the evening, trying to find time to rest. It's just work, work, work. We do a lot of work.

April: That's a new thing for me, being self-employed, because you can work straight through the weekend. So you have to tell yourself, "Take a day off because you can go work on your houses."

We spend time with Richard's family and stuff. We have a couple friends around here.

My circle of friends was really limited pretty much to people I was working with because I had only lived here for a year before the storm. And pretty much everything I did was within that circle. And most of them are—well, it's probably split about half and half—a lot of them are in Baton Rouge with the school right now.

Some of Richard's friends, them are still living down here. He's got some people that he'd been knowing a long time. We see them pretty frequently. He's coaching with a couple of guys that he'd known since high school. So we'll see them and their wives, and of course his family is around. One of his friends got a job driving a truck, so he's out of town all the time. So some people are around, but it's not really like they're just down the street like they used to be.

Like many of the people we interviewed, April has strong views on why some communities rebounded and others did not. She believes that the high percentage of renters is to blame.[51]

April: Well, I think some of it is just [happened] naturally— places like the [French] Quarter that didn't get that much water anyways—some of those places obviously sustained less damage so it's easier for them to get back up and running. But there are sections of the city—I mean, tourism is the main industry, so I think those parts were focused on more quickly because if those parts die out, the city dies out, basically. But as far as pockets of housing, the city has such a high percentage of renters that, until those landlords come back and fix up the houses, the renters can't return. I think it would be different if you had a city full of homeowners where everyone wanted to come back and set up camp in a trailer in front of their house and make their repairs. I think that would have been a lot faster. But some people own 20 or 30 houses and weren't that great of landlords to begin with and probably might not even have had insurance on those properties. So then you've got those big gaps where everything is kind of sitting at a standstill. Plus the city had a lot of blighted housing to begin with.

Nobody really knows who owns them—so there's a lot of that stuff going on there too. I think mostly the biggest thing is the renters and the people who didn't have insurance and are waiting on programs like Road Home and trying to figure out how they're going to move forward with restoring their properties.

April believes that if appropriate housing were available, people would come back because of how attached they are to the city.[52]

April: There's no place like New Orleans, good and bad. So if people had the money to buy a house and renovate a house, they'd be back. But by the city being mostly populated by renters, that's the problem. Basically, it's a waiting game for those people that come back in the city. Some of it might be age, but then you have some older people that have only known New Orleans, too, and they're dying to get back. I think some of it is just people's personality and where they ended up evacuating. Because some people ended up evacuating to a city that they loved, and their kids are thriving in school, and they have a supportive community, and they just realized, "I have it a lot better off here than I did in New Orleans." I think there's a number of people that are just happy where they ended up.

Katrina has given April a new way of looking at life. Like so many of the people we interviewed, she reports being more grateful for the smaller things in life than she was before Katrina.

April: For me it's gotten a lot better. I was really surprised when we came back at all the small everyday things I was taking for granted—not having those things really made me stressed out. Like, even when we were married and moved in here and had to take those cabinets out, and we didn't have countertops and a kitchen sink, that drove me crazy. It's like, you didn't want to cook anything, and then if you did, you had to wash your dishes in the bathroom sink. And the small things that you think, that shouldn't be a big deal, that just makes a strain. And then you try to fix a plate and you don't have anywhere to set it down. Just little things like that, you want to throw your hands up. And I had it so much better off than so many other people. But it's amazing how much that stuff will really get to you. Yes, it's little things like that. [It's better] since we've got our house straight, where we can feel comfortable when we come home.

We were able to interview some residents twice to track their progress. In May 2008, just over a year after our initial interview with Richard and April, we checked in on how they were doing with their efforts.

> **Richard:** Mom is still in one of our rental properties. Her house has been gutted, and we've been able to get some volunteers to help with her house on a couple different occasions. Just the week before last, we found out that a program through the Red Cross in partnership with another organization is gonna help her actually do her house. They did it as a fast-track project, so it's actually gonna be done, hopefully within a couple months, I think. It's something—it's some program that they said they haven't gone public with yet. Hers is one of the first houses for them in the program.
>
> I don't know [how they chose her]. They just drove around and just kind of selected certain houses that looked like they were still structurally sound enough. Then she filled out some applications for that. I think it's just God providing for her and for us.

Since speaking to Richard previously, he has transitioned from a volunteer football coaching position to a paid coaching job. This paid position is in addition to managing the reconstruction of their properties. April, now expecting a baby, did not return to ministry work. She instead continued to work with their property and took on the task of home schooling their nephew. They have found a church in Metairie. And April and Richard have made real progress on their rental properties and now have tenants. However, their personal residence is still in need of significant repairs.

> **Richard:** We've got two more major renovations. We are dealing with our personal property in the Lower Ninth Ward across the canal. We have another property that we just got from my mom that we're doing a total renovation on. That's the two major ones. We've got a small, minor renovation where my mom is living at. It's minor compared to some of the other ones, but it's still going to be pretty major. It's a house that wasn't flooded, so we didn't make any repairs to it. We haven't made any

repairs to it since the storm. It's just some real minor stuff. It's an older home, and we want to try to restore it. It's in a historic district. We're trying to change some stuff to increase the value of it, also just to make it nicer.

We did have a tenant, right after the storm, in one half of that. Then some guys that were doing some work for us [moved into] that unit when the other people moved out. [My mother's] been in the other half the whole time. When her house is finished, she'll move. We're already starting to work on that half. Structurally, it's, as far as we know, it's pretty good. We did some leveling of it, but it's basically just cosmetic stuff.

This home we are in now, it will become a rental property. Right now this is our personal property house. We had a house across the canal in the Lower Ninth Ward, a rental house. After the storm, we thought about renovating it, but eventually realized it wasn't really worth it. We tore it down, and now it's just an empty lot. With us having the baby and taking in our nephew and talking about possibly taking in some other kids, this house is just too small. We had the idea to build on the empty lot over there. It's right across Claiborne from all those Brad Pitt houses.[53]

Well, we're gonna build a pretty tall house if it works out the way with the plans that we had drawn up. The idea is it's gonna be basically three levels. The bottom level will be just kinda like all concrete. It will be like a garage and then like a rec room so we can have a place where can have the Bible studies for the high school kids and that kinda stuff. So if it does flood, hopefully we will be able to kind of just hose it down and go from there. As long as we have insurance we're fine. And as long as we're not sitting on the roof when the hurricane comes, we can deal with the rest of it. Right, if we get anything higher than a Category 2, we gonna leave.

April and Richard now feel optimistic about the rebuilding process. Although they believe government must play a role in that recovery, they do not underestimate the power of the community.

Richard: A lot of the properties were owned by people who are living their whole lives. We drive through there. People are rebuilding. They are building some pretty decent houses, too.

I just passed it like two days ago and saw a man finishing up on a metal stud house. He framed the whole house.

We feel pretty good about the city as far as rebuilding wise. I think it was slowed down by all that fraud that went down with the contractors. I think people are getting a lot wiser like we did also. I think the city is headed in the right direction, especially from a real estate standpoint.

The citizens [though] are the ones who have to step up and make the final calls. The local government can only do so much, I mean. They can only do so much because a city is bigger than a local government. There's only one mayor, and he got a certain team of people, so there's only so much they can do.

We gotta do for ourselves. Not to diminish the role the government plays, whatever, but I really agree with that. People on the news and stuff, people protesting this and that. They put so much pressure on the city to fix the problems and the crime problems and all this stuff. It's just impossible. You can't have enough police on every street to solve the drug problem. You just can't fix all that stuff from the government standpoint. Some of it, yeah you can make a difference with the policies you put in place and whatnot. A lot of it is just on the people that live here.

April and Richard have learned a few lessons from their experience. Among them is the value of patience and the need to find a way to deal with stress.

April: [We've learned to] take our time, for me, and not just jump into a situation and try to get our house done. Just be patient and trust God. Initially, too, when there's so much stuff to be done, it's easy to get frantic and scramble. We really just sit back and take time with the decisions. It's been turning out a lot better. Just to be prayerful about stuff and not try and do everything on our own and race around just stressed out. It doesn't work like that. Now we take our time. I think a lot of people are very stressed out still. A lot of people are still struggling with stress from the storm.

[Our advice to others is to] be patient. Don't turn down any opportunities for assistance, but don't bank on assistance. Go ahead and start figuring out how to do it yourself. Make sure you stay connected to some people outside of the chaotic situation so you're not constantly dealing with people who are as stressed as yourself.

I think our faith, obviously, has been the main thing. We both feel like this is where God wants us to be right now, and we wouldn't feel comfortable going somewhere else just because it seems easier.

MELVIN

Melvin, an 87-year-old black male, is a 79-year resident of the Ninth Ward.

My first wife died in 1949. My [second] wife died in 2003. We was married 54 years. I've always been close to the Almighty God. I've always been around a church all my life. Right now, I'm an usher at Corpus Christi. This is the Ninth Ward. This is the Upper Nine, not the Lower Nine. And on a Sunday morning, I go [to] Lady Star of the Sea on St. Roche Street, more south of here. Right around there is the Seventh Ward. And I enjoy working for Almighty God. That's all I do now. I look forward to that every week.

My mother played the organ for the same church where I'm now. It brings back a lot of memories. I was the altar boy, but sometimes I couldn't serve at the mass because I had to go up in the balcony up there and pump the organ for my mother.

My mother played the organ, and they had the big pipe organ with beautiful brass pipes. And she would play the keys, and I'd be back just a-pumping and I'd get tired, you know, 'cause I was 10 years old. I was a man at 10 years old because my daddy died when I was 10 years old. My dad was 37 years old when he died. His health went bad. He got lung trouble and there was no cure for it. Now it's all right, but during those days, there was no cure for lung trouble—lung cancer. He was a mail carrier.

There's only two of us left in my family. There's my sister. Marian is her name. She's in Houston, Texas. They're coming back after the school closed. They will come back to New Orleans. [Before Katrina], she lived right around here on the Seventh Ward. The majority of [my extended family is] from

New Orleans. [I am related to] the president that runs the Liberty Banks here in New Orleans, Louisiana. He has I don't know how many banks, Liberty Banks. That's my first cousin.

Melvin, like most of the others we interviewed in the Ninth Ward, had a positive view of his community before Katrina.

This was a nice community, beautiful, beautiful. You know when you tell people that—especially a lotta people say, "Oh, you from the Desire area." I say, "That's right. I raised five boys in the Desire area and never had a ball in my window." And people in Pontchartrain Park, all these big shots and living in Pontchartrain Park, every home had a ball [through their window].[54] This was a beautiful community. Quiet just like it is now. In the '60s. Yeah. In the '60s, yeah, in the '70s, the '80s, it was just like it is now. In the '90s. This was a beautiful community. A guy told me one time, he said, "Man, Melvin, you buying a house 'round the Desire projects?" I said, "That's right." He said, "Man, you're gonna have some trouble with your boys." I said, "Well, I trust in the good Lord." And you know what? Between you and I, five boys, I've never had a police knock at my door. You know what the neighbors used to say? "Mr. Melvin," the neighbors say, "You a good father, but you're kinda hard on your boys." I say, "Well, I mighta been hard on 'em, but I made men out of 'em." They had to do what I said. You see now, the children is raising the parents. The children's telling the parents what to do. They all on drugs, the parents and the children.

It is not uncommon for Ninth Ward residents to blame the federal government for the flooding that followed Katrina.[55] Melvin is no different.

All these buildings around here is just like they was the day after Katrina. It's 18 months and look at 'em. Everybody's living in trailers waiting for the Road Home. You see, that's what keeping a lotta people from coming back to New Orleans, too. They don't have any money. They waiting for the federal government to help 'em. There's over 100,000 people right now in Texas, just Houston alone, and they can't come back. The federal government destroyed all their property, the Corp of Engineers. The levee didn't hold up what they built. In Betsy, in 1965 right in this house here, my wife and I was walking around with water up to our knees, and my house was 5 feet off the ground. But this time, I had about 13 feet of water. And right now, I'm higher than the street. I'm about 3 feet higher than the street.

Before Katrina, Melvin was friendly with his neighbors but describes himself as a very private person.

I been here a long time, but I always mind my own business. We didn't have people running in and out of our house. It's good to have neighbors and be friends with your neighbors. I always was friendly. They all respected me. I respected them. Mostly, we would socialize at the church whenever we'd meet. Now my wife, sometimes some of her auxiliary, Knights of Peter Claver members, would drop by after church and we'd have a little coffee or something. But I was always the type of fellow, I was always to myself mostly. But I respect every nationality, every race. Right now, I'm a member of the Knights of Columbus, which is a Catholic organization. You know the Knights of Columbus is all over the world, all over the United States—and the Knights of Peter Claver. Peter Claver was a priest. He was white priest and he helped to free the slaves, Peter Claver. I'm a Knight of Peter Claver about 15 years, and I was just initiated into the Knights of Columbus up in Houston, Texas. I was their only black American, but they had other blacks, but they was from Nigeria in Africa.

As with many in New Orleans, his church life was very important to him.

My parish right now is Our Lady Star of Sea on St. Roche Street, by the St. Roche Cemetery. But I do help at Corpus Christi every Saturday evening. I go there and help. By the way, there's another organization there that's called the Men in Christ. There's 15 of us. We meet over there by Corpus Christi. And then they depend on the men that belong to the organizations to do the church work, you see? And I been doing it so long, it's part of my life. I wanna be close to Almighty God, continue doing His work if I have my health and strength.

Melvin evacuated with his friend Vita but had to leave his dog, Bandit, behind. He experienced firsthand the misery of the Superdome.

I evacuated the evening before the storm, the day before. The 28th of August. I took my car—a Lumina Chevrolet. Vita and I drove. I said, "Vita, we got to get away from here." I said, "That storm is—the wind's gonna gust up to 225 miles an hour." I said, "We got to go." She said, "Melvin, I'm not leaving." I said, "Well, good-bye then. I'm out." She said, "Wait, wait, Melvin. Don't leave me. Don't leave me." [I went to] the Superdome. And I'm sorry I did. I was in there five days, always just thinking about Bandit, my dog. I left him on the porch right here with a bucket of dry food and a bucket of water. [I was worried about] how Bandit made out. But they found Bandit on Franklin Avenue after the storm. How Bandit got from this porch to Franklin Avenue, I don't know. He was on the porch with the screen door open right there. I put a wedge down there and drove the wedge tight so the wind wouldn't close the door on Bandit and trap him and he would drown.

[The Superdome was] miserable. It was really sad. The muggers tore all that up all the way around. I thought they was gonna tear down the Superdome, it looked so bad after the storm. When we first went in the Superdome, they put us in seats. We had to sleep in the seats on the 20-yard line. It was sad. The ladies couldn't go to the restroom or nothing. The stuff was piled up so high on top of toilets. I would just go ahead and relieve myself against the wall. It was all wet all the time. It was flowing out to the concession. It was miserable. And you had to be sure your feet was wiped good before you go back to where you was sleeping. Yeah. I didn't see too many [people from this neighborhood] in the Superdome. I saw a few, not too many.

The fifth day they would take 1,000 people, and the National Guard would have a barricade all the way across the entrance—Poydras Street entrance, the main entrance, and they would let these 1,000 people come through. They was pushing and pushing, 42,000 people trying to get out. So they let us out and come through and they'd spread out about 15 abreast and go a little bit at a time till you get to the main gate. And Vita and I got in that line, and we got about 50 feet from the gate. I'd say about 100 feet from the gate. I had chest pains. So I told Vita. She said, "You can't hold up. We're almost out the Superdome." That was the fifth day. No, that was the fourth day. I said, "Well, I'm gonna try to hold up," but my pains got worse. They wouldn't let nobody out. You couldn't get out if you wanted to get out. So I asked one of the soldiers. I said, "I have chest pains." He said, "What you do about it?" I said, "I took a nitroglycerin," 'cause I found my nitroglycerin. It was in my little pouch. He said, "Did it do any good?" I said, "No, I still have the pain." He said, "Well, brother, there isn't much we can do for you. That's all we can give you is a nitroglycerin. So you better just try to hold up and try to make the best of it and just take your nitroglycerin. That's all we can do for you. You done took that. Once you've come out this line, you can't get back."

The next day I got back in line and I got out. There was five feet of water all around the Superdome. I seen bodies floating around the Superdome. They would put ya in a bus. There was about three feet a water. So they put us in the school buses. There was 25 school buses. Load 'em down with—there were 25 school buses. They would load 'em down with people. You got quite a few people. I asked the driver, I said, "Where we going?" He said, "I don't know. I think they gonna St. Bernard Parish." You know St. Bernard Parish. There was still water. We were driving in the little water on the street, driving slow. I remember that. When we got close to St. Bernard Parish, they had the State Police and the National Guard with the rifles, machine guns. And the buses stopped. So I was in the third bus, and I got out and the driver said—no, a guy came in there with the bullhorn. "All passengers. Stay on your bus. Do not get off your bus." So I asked the driver, I said, "What's the trouble?"

Across diverse populations, New Orleans residents believed that race played a critical role in how they were treated during and after the storm. Whites often complained that blacks became the face of the disaster to the outside world and so received most of the direct assistance. Blacks complained that their vulnerable situation and the roadblocks that they encountered as they tried to evacuate the city and to return to rebuild were part of an intentional or unintentional pattern that would keep blacks from returning to New Orleans. Melvin is no different. The fact that he was evacuated to a jail cell did not help.

"Man," he said, "them people don't want y'all in St. Bernard." It was mostly blacks [on the bus]. "We have to turn around and go back." So they went to Baton Rouge, Louisiana, see? We was going east to St. Bernard Parish, then we had to turn around and go west towards Baton Rouge. So when we get to Baton Rouge, they put us in four or five Greyhound buses. And guess where they took us. We get to Dallas, Texas—we got about three miles outta Dallas, Texas, and all the buses pull on the side of the road. So we see some big officials talk to the State Police. They came back and they told us that the places they was gonna bring us wasn't ready 'cause we arrived too soon. So they gonna have to put us in another place, but they didn't tell me what the place was.

You know what the place was? It was the old jail. They built a new jail and all the prisoners they put in the new jail, and the old jail was empty, so they put us in the old jail with the iron bars and the bunk beds and all that. There was two right across from me—two bunk beds across from me, and Vita had the bottom bed on the other side. I had the top. The restroom—they had no restroom. They had a curtain right in the cell . . . a curtain with a bucket, and you relieved yourself in that. You pulled your curtain. We was over there a day—two days—one day. [I called my daughter and she] did come—she did—I ain't gonna lie. That's one thing she really did act on that. That's one time she acts. She came from Houston, Texas, to pick Vita and I when she heard that we was in that jail.

Melvin had left New Orleans under the assumption that it was simply a routine storm and that he would be back in a few days.

I didn't take anything, not a thing. I lost everything, everything. I never thought—I didn't worry about taking anything. Had I known the levee was gonna break. But nobody knew the levee was gonna break. [I thought I'd just sit out the hurricane in the Superdome and] then come back and take care of Bandit. That's why I left a bucket of dry food and a bucket of water. I figured that'd last him a couple a days and I'd come back. [I stayed in Houston] for 11 months. We came back here in August. In Houston, I stayed in an apartment, Broadway Square Apartments. I had a nice apartment. It was upstairs, second floor. I didn't have Bandit then. There was always a lady named Miss Sandra. [She] is from Canada.[56] She used to always call or write and tell me about Bandit. She was still trying to get Bandit back, and she'd done a lot for me, too. We still communicate with each other.

Though many people cite the negative aspects of the government's response, Melvin sees the positive of the Social Security system and is grateful for FEMA's assistance.

Financially? Well, like I said, I'm retired with the federal government, and wherever I went, [I had] my annuity, like in Dallas and Houston. I was always with the Chase Bank in Houston. My annuity check and my Social Security check [would go right into my account]. That's how I survived. FEMA did send me a check for $21,000. I didn't expect anything, so [it was] more than I expected.

I had to come back. Not only Bandit, I had to come back to see about my property 'cause I had no one here, no one to see about the property. The property's in my name and my first wife's name. Right now, I can't get anything because I have to get her name off the deed, my first wife. And my son, Phillip, that's the boy that really helped me, and he's still helping. But I didn't raise him. See, my first wife died after childbirth and Phillip was a child. He's my power of attorney. And [my other son], Marcus, he helped me. That's the only two there is now that's really helping me—that's close to me. Marian and Stanley was [Phillip's godparents who raised him]. My wife died two days after childbirth when Phillip was born. Man, I been through the mill. I'm gonna tell ya. I swear I don't see how—I thank God—if I wasn't close to the Almighty God, I'd a been gone long ago. I'd been in a nuthouse somewhere.

The first thing Melvin did when he returned was to check on his dog, Bandit. Next was to assess the damage.

> [My first priority when I came back was,] well, I had to try to get in touch with someone concerning the Road Home and try to sign up to be interviewed and to let 'em know I was here. I had to go get [Bandit]. The lady brought Bandit. Miss Sandra and another lady. She presented Bandit to me after almost a year, close to a year. I had that dog for 12 years [before the storm]. He's a good watchdog. All you want a dog is to let you know somebody's around.
>
> The water did all the damage, everything inside. I lost everything. About six feet of water from the floor. But there's a mark on the sill on the door. The water stayed there so long, it left this mark.

Katrina and the work required to reestablish his life has made Melvin consider changing his lifestyle.

> I waiting on the Road Home. I am thinking about selling the property. I spoke to the lady yesterday, and she's one that I had the interview with concerning the Road Home. She told me that if I get the grant that it would go with the property. Whoever buys the property would get the grant, also.
>
> That would be the easiest way, and at my age, 87, I'll get me an apartment with the senior citizens—a nice apartment where I can go like I want and come when I want and live the rest of my life. I can't take care of property like it should be. Right now, I'm doing it. I got the push lawnmower in the garage back there, and I got a Weed eater. That's all I use.

Melvin attributes the slow pace of recovery to government corruption and incompetency.

> It's slow. They're coming back, but slow. Yeah. I would say mostly around the business area, the area is all right. They're about up to almost 100 percent. But get away from the business area, I don't think they not even 50 percent back. You're not even 25 percent back here.

Everybody's getting their hands on the money. Road Home, it's politicians. They all want a piece of the pie. [The government should] give [the people] the grant. Give 'em the grant so they can repair their property. There's a lot of people want to come back, but they don't have any money to repair their property. The federal government destroyed their property. Right now my house woulda been in tip-top shape if it wasn't for that water. I had $400 of wind damage, I'm telling ya. You can see my house. Do it look damaged?

Melvin gets food from the church pantry to help make ends meet. He appreciates the trailer and the financial help he received from FEMA.

I'm getting right now—I just got commodity stuff, you know, like cheese, cereal, and some beans from Sacred Heart Church and Angels Church. Right now, the only [reason] I go is to pick up the cheese. I went there. You know to pick up cheese [and] beans. But sometimes, if you get too much of that. There's no need taking something you're not gonna use. I got canned goods in there, I never use. I could get food every week, but I don't do it because I don't—it's the same thing. It's all the time the same kinda goods: French-style string beans, or butter beans, tomatoes, tomato sauce, cream, evaporated milk, grits, oatmeal, cereal, a lotta things.

Only thing I got from the government—and I thank God for that—is my FEMA trailer. I thank God for that. I mean, I don't know where I'd be if I had to pay my way right now. But when I was in Texas, I got the FEMA paying my rent. Paid my light bill, too, FEMA, federal government. I got 90 percent of help from the federal government. It was more than I expected. If it wasn't for FEMA—I tell ya, they didn't have to do that.

When asked how he got through the hurricane and all that followed, Melvin tells us the story of when he lost his first wife. He got through these tragedies in similar ways.

It was rough. It was rough. I'm gonna tell you what happened. We built a new church, okay? What happened, we had an empty lot back in 1947. It was a group of men and ladies got together. We bought a lot not too far from here. We decided that we went to Jackson Barracks right here—Jackson Barracks right here on St. Florence Street, north. We went over there to see about getting a building to put on this lot to start us a church 'cause we was holding a service in a placed called the Delta Theater. They used to have a theater over there. It was called the Delta Theater. And we used to have service in the Delta Theater upstairs because you had segregation.

[Eventually, we built a church] and we got all the foundation. We had to put a foundation first before we put the floor section. But anyhow, we built this church. My wife, Elaine, and I, Elaine, she was one of the—she was always close to the church, too. I met Elaine at a church festival. Anyhow, we started building. We got the building almost completed. All I had to do is put the bell tower—I built the bell tower, oh, about 3½ feet square. It was an old bell. And we got the bell up there. Elaine was working in the church with the ladies mopping and everything, getting it ready for the dedication. It was about three weeks after it was dedicated, Elaine had the baby. The surgeon that operated on her said she had a little tumor on her brain, but she didn't know it—probably didn't know it was like smaller than—about like a green pea, smaller than a green [pea]. He said it burst [because] of the strain of labor. I tell ya, I been through a lot. You gotta be close to Almighty God. That's the only thing help me get through this, nothing else. Nothing else helps.

2

CENTRAL CITY

Central City is a subdistrict of the Central City/Garden District Area, located just below Uptown and just above the Central Business District. Adjacent to some of the most prosperous sections of New Orleans, it is bordered by South Claiborne Avenue, Pontchartrain Expressway, St. Charles Avenue, and Louisiana Avenue. Although Central City was never as affluent as the neighboring Garden District, it did have its heyday of middle-class prosperity, a lively business district, racial tolerance, and civil rights activism. Unfortunately, however, Central City's story has also been one of economic decline and racial intolerance.

Irish and German immigrants hired to construct the New Basin Canal in the 1830s settled Central City first. From the mid-19th century, Central City was also home to Italian and Eastern European Jewish working-class immigrants, and African Americans were later attracted to the neighborhood. "By the time jazz great Buddy Bolden lived here at the turn of the century, the neighborhood was a polyglot mix of shopkeepers, draymen, porters and laborers. By 1900 this neighborhood was home to a vibrant mix of African-Americans, Italians, Irish, Germans, and Eastern Europeans employed as laborers."[1] Additionally, this area had "its own kosher markets, Orthodox synagogues, and small shopkeepers."[2]

Although the subdivisions of Central City and the Lower Garden District were planned and developed at the same time,

Central City was settled much more slowly. Central City's wet and muddy terrain was not as inviting as the neighboring locations.[3] Though the first Central City neighborhood was settled in the 1830s, not until a modern drainage system was installed in the early 20th century did people start to settle below Claiborne Avenue in substantial numbers.

Architecturally, Central City was both characteristic of New Orleans and, at the same time, distinct from the structures in the surrounding neighborhoods. Many of the houses in Central City were the shotgun houses that are typical in New Orleans.[4] The tracts that contained these shotgun, double shotgun, and camelback houses (shotgun houses with a second story added toward the back of the house), also popular in Central City, were flat parcels with small yards and few trees.[5] These houses were developed as rental housing for workers employed by nearby industries. Peppered throughout these small wooden homes were a few country villas and antebellum mansions that still stand.[6] Although neighborhoods around Central City have maintained their historic character, with villas and antebellum mansions commonplace, the same cannot be said of Central City. In fact, Central City lost half its historic buildings between 1922 and 1997. Unlike the Garden District and Uptown, Central City was caught in the middle of an urban planning debate. On one side of the debate, developers lobbied for suburban-style development and, on the other side, historic preservationists resisted those developments. The urban planners won, destroying the historic architecture that still marks the neighboring districts.

At its height, this diverse working-class neighborhood was often referred to (at least until the 1960s) as the Dryades Street neighborhood because it was centered on Dryades Street, the original business center for this community. From its grand opening in 1849, the Dryades Street Market was an important social space in the community. The feasting celebration at its grand opening, for instance, was heralded by the *Daily Picayune*:

The new market in the Second Ward, at the corner of Dryades and Melpomene streets . . . has been recently opened by one of our more enterprising citizens . . . Two long tables of the market house strained beneath the weight of roast turkeys, ducks, chickens, beef, etc. [with] champagne, claret, etc. to wash the aforementioned articles down. The attendance was large and . . . ample justice was done to the banquet. . . . The feasting continued for about an hour when the eatables and drinkables began to grow scarce in the market. The erection of the present market in the Second Ward will . . . prove highly advantageous to our uptown population.[7]

On Dryades Street, people were always coming and going. "The street was so busy back on Saturday nights [that] shopkeepers would stay open as long as there were customers, sometimes till nine or ten o'clock at night."[8] The nearest competitor to the Dryades Street businesses corridor was the Canal Street district. For Central City's diverse population, Dryades Street had several advantages over Canal Street besides convenience. It was a more congenial, less prejudiced environment in which to shop. Residents noted that Dryades merchants did not follow the same racial practices as merchants on Canal Street, such as forbidding "blacks from trying on clothes. . . . Additionally, while Canal Street merchants were virtually all-White, Dryades Street merchants were diverse. Jews, Blacks, Italians, and others operated side-by-side."[9]

Unfortunately, Dryades Street (Central City) would not always enjoy such economic prosperity nor long keep the reputation of racial tolerance. Central City was, in fact, a mixed bag. It was not only a staging ground for the civil rights movement in the city, but it was also a battlefield. In his documentary *A House Divided*, Avery Alexander notes that "There were a hundred stores and there were no blacks clerking in any of the stores. No managers, no assistant managers. No white collar workers. We didn't believe it was equitable when 90 percent of the customers were black."[10] After months of negotiating with shop owners, protesters organized boycotts and picketing demonstrations.

Many students from local colleges joined the picket lines in the summer of 1960. Oretha Castle was among them.[11] The protestors stood their ground, as did the merchants. In April 1960, the trajectory had been set, and it was clear that the Dryades Street businesses would not survive if they did not give in. Easter, a usually busy time of the year, was quiet for the store owners. The shoppers never returned in full force, and eventually many of the stores went out of business. Even before Katrina, Dryades Street was nothing more than a ghost town, a shell of its former economic glory.[12]

This racially driven economic difficulty partially explains Central City's decline. Another reason, however, was the growing suburban movement. In the 1960s, protestors in New Orleans, as they did elsewhere in the nation, won important desegregation battles. Peter Burns, a professor of political science at Loyola University New Orleans, claims that in New Orleans "desegregation was followed by white flight to the suburbs in the 1960s."[13] Many of the white residents of Central City moved to other areas looking for the picket fence and garage version of the American dream as well as hoping to move away from the seemingly more and more corrupt city government.[14] Consequently, "in the 1960s, dwindling urban population and burgeoning suburban development raised the specter of economic stagnation and created the context in which city leaders would further the development of tourism in the city."[15] Just prior to Katrina, 87 percent of the residents in Central City were African American; less than 10 percent were Caucasian.

In 1939, the city began construction of the B. W. Cooper housing project (also called the Calliope Projects). The C. J. Peete housing development (popularly called the Magnolia Projects) was built in 1941. Fourteen years later, the housing projects were at full capacity. The Guste Homes development (also known as the Melpomene Projects or Melp Projects), taking up 10 city blocks, was built in Central City in 1964. By the time Katrina hit, the Peete (Magnolia), Cooper (Calliope), and

Guste (Melp) housing developments were considered the most violent housing projects in the city.

Even though there were single- and multiple-family private dwellings and college residents in Central City, the area had its problems before Katrina hit. Central City went from being the hotbed of the civil rights movement to a place that was rife with crime, poverty, and social neglect. Only 45 percent of Central City residents, for instance, said they felt safe in their community "before Katrina." Moreover, "85 percent said that 'people being murdered' was a concern."[16]

Thanks to somewhat higher elevations in the neighborhood, Central City did not suffer as much flood damage as other parts of the city, though it did sustain significant wind damage. Vacant homes that were either abandoned or condemned were common in Central City before Katrina, and the storm did not help matters. As in many of the older neighborhoods, Katrina led to "the chipping or peeling paint in many of these homes directly [exposing] children and adults to lead either through direct contact or through inhaling the dust through their lungs, where it then enters the bloodstream."[17] Recovery in the wake of Katrina was slow. By August 2009, 1,277 property owners had received financial assistance from the Road Home program, but within the Central City planning district, there were still 6,255 unoccupied residences, and the city had issued 417 demolition permits.[18]

Though community and city leaders had focused their attention on Central City before the storm, Katrina heightened this attention and attracted resources from outside the community, including human and financial capital, which began to flow into the community. Leaders within the Central City Renaissance Alliance (CCRA), an organization established in 2002 as part of a community planning effort, reasserted their vision for an economically vibrant neighborhood with a high quality of life. The CCRA was awarded a grant that would help it along the way to reconstructing their community after the storm.[19]

Moreover, even a year before Katrina, the Felicity Street Redevelopment Project was working to revitalize Central City by purchasing and redeveloping homes. But before Katrina, the average household income in Central City was $23,237, which was significantly lower than the citywide average income of $43,176. This meant that many of the homes the Felicity Street Redevelopment Project was buying were out of the financial reach of local residents.

In addition to the CCRA and Felicity Street Redevelopment Project, other groups such as the Central City Partnership and the Central City Economic Opportunity Corporation worked toward restoring the vibrancy for which the neighborhood had once been known. Café Reconcile serves tasty, inexpensive meals while it trains at-risk youth to develop skills they can use in the restaurant industry. Similarly, Rachel Glicksman, a member of the Jewish Service Corps, worked with the Jericho Road Organization to develop a community garden in Central City.[20] Additionally, the Central City Artist Project "believe[s] artists play integral roles in healthy communities," and is working toward developing a residency program in Central City.[21]

Whether it is a residency program for artists, a community garden, or "a mixed-income, mixed use housing development containing 263 apartments, 28 market-rate condos, and 4,000 square feet of ground floor commercial space,"[22] many people are fighting against economic and social odds to see Central City rebound after Katrina. There is, however, much work to be done.

ARTHUR

Arthur, an African American, is a retired budget analyst for the Navy and deacon of New Hope Baptist Church in Central City. We interviewed him in his church in fall 2007.

> I was growing up in a neighborhood that to fit in I had to be a hoodlum so I went that route, but when I started going to church, the young people here, the old and young men here,

they gave me an option versus the option that I had in really growing up.

Arthur grew up in a segregated New Orleans and felt that to fit in, he needed to be a tough guy. He credits his church, however, with showing him another way. Many things attach people to a community. In New Orleans, churches are often the hubs of social networks. They can connect people to the place they were raised decades after they have grown up and moved away. Arthur, for instance, grew up in Central City but moved out shortly after his marriage in 1975. The New Hope Baptist Church on La Salle in the heart of Central City, where Arthur is a deacon, keeps him connected to the community of his childhood.[23] New Hope, which started with nine members back in the mid-1950s, numbered 2,200 by the time Katrina hit.

In previous hurricanes the church served as a place of refuge. Katrina was no different.

Well, when the storm came, in fact, that Friday most of them didn't know the storm was going on because we pay attention but we don't pay attention. That Saturday we realized it was a little bit more imminent. Sunday morning our pastor said, "Everybody that can evacuate, we'll ask that they would evacuate." And then, reluctantly, but being the man that he is, he said, "For those people who can't leave, we'll be here." So he and a few others stayed here at the church and had about 80 members, old folks, some young folks, some sick people. They were at the church and, as always, came here for a couple of days. People bring food, they cook, they eat, they laugh, they talk, kids play games, but after three days you go back home. This time it didn't work out that way. So we stayed through and [it was] pretty rough that Sunday. Monday was a real mess after the hurricane, after Katrina passed. A few cars that were in the parking lot were damaged pretty bad. Some of them were kind of messed up, but those that there were operative, we were able to leave out of the church, the pastor and a few other folks. We went down in towards New Orleans East.

When they saw how bad things were and that they could not get back to their homes, they evacuated as a group.

> We just loaded up the cars. We had about three cars here. We siphoned the gas off of every car that was gonna be left and put it in the cars that we had, and we left here in a little caravan and we went 90 West. And at the 310 split, some of us were separated, so some went the 310 and [others] ended up—kept going straight out, but by the grace of the Good Lord, we hooked up again in Lafayette.

The pastor contacted a church in Lake Charles that prepared for their arrival.

> We left the day after the hurricane. That afternoon we just started driving and, once we got there, they had food prepared and everything. They fed everyone, and then we went over to another church, also in Lake Charles, and they had converted their educational building into a mini hotel. We stayed there for maybe two and half, three weeks.

Once resources were available for the group to leave the church in Lake Charles, the pastor of New Hope oversaw that as well.[24]

> He stayed there for the better part of maybe two, two and a half weeks because he wouldn't leave until he made sure all the members that were there, all 80 of us, was disbursed and was going someplace more stable than where we were, with family or some temporary housing, a job, whatever.

New Hope relied on a number of churches within its network for assistance.

> We was one of the first few churches here in the city. And once we came back, the Lord just blessed churches from around the country. They were sending 18-wheeler tractor-trailer loads of everything—clothing, water, food, and canned goods.

They just were sending stuff, and I mean, some of it was [amazing. One man] out of Mississippi, his church was destroyed. He had a school bus and nothing to do with it, a yellow school bus in the backyard. He gave it to us for getting around the city, just trying to do whatever and see people that need help and see if we can do anything with them.

Another church in North Carolina, they sent down two tractor-trailer loads of clothing and supplies and water. Like I say, once we had this thing pretty much intact, we had a room that was just filled up with our eatery. Just filled it up with water and canned goods, and we just opened the doors and had fliers out going out to all the FEMA sites, East Bank and West Bank and by the library, and letting them know that if you need clothing, if you need food supplies, whatever the case may be, you can stop by and get whatever, so people would just come.

Although New Hope Baptist Church had relationships with some of these churches, it did not know many of the churches at all. Through these generous donations, however, the church was able to help Katrina victims beyond its congregants.

Some of these people, we never even knew them. They said they just heard about it. They may know one church or some-body or whatever. And someone would say, "New Hope is down there trying to do the best they can. If you've got some stuff you want to help, send it to New Hope. They'll get it out." So we had people walking, picking up, calling in, they'd come through, ladies, babies, everybody. They'd just come in. There's no restrictions. Get what you needed, get what you can carry or whatever you can put in your truck. I mean, we received furniture, we received mattresses, received food. We just received a whole bunch. There's a guy here, he's a millionaire, I guess. I hope he is. He gave Lake Charles, Baton Rouge, and New Orleans $1 million, and we set up the F. H. Dunn Recovery Center in the building in the back there. Of course, that was all about helping people, pay their rent, get their utilities on, buy different things. They bought brand-new mattresses, different things that people just probably couldn't get or couldn't ship here, but it'd be distributed, and they gave them a check or whatever.

Although other churches in the area were able to open their doors after the storm, a lot more did not reopen.

> Quite a few other churches, the pastor's not there. The churches where the pastor would be back, there's no members because their members haven't come back because it took so long for the city just to get things together. And they keep saying, "We want you to come back," but what am I coming back to? I don't have a school. I need a place to stay that's affordable, and I need a decent job. Without those things in place, what am I coming back to? Two and a half years later a great portion of our population has not come back.

The city, for a long time, refused to provide certain basic services to various communities with the rationale that not enough of their residents had returned. But displaced residents were holding off their return until these basic services were in place.[25] Those who have come back face serious financial hardships.

> Some of the roach-infested rat holes that some people used to pay $200 and $300 to live in, these things are $1,200 and $1,400. They have to be going crazy, but people are trying to do the best that they can and stay as close as they can because, again, a lot of them still don't have transportation so they still have to stay within Central City where they can get around. We found some affordable apartments in different areas of the city, in Metairie and whatever, but their job is way over here and way over . . . I mean, what do you do when you can't get around?

The deacon had a laundry list of what could be done to help people in their recovery efforts; simplifying the process for government aid was at the top of his list.[26]

> They could've made the process of trying to help people a lot easier than what they did. We're dealing with people and again deadlines and all that stuff is fine, but some people just don't know. Some of these people had no idea some stuff was even available.

Many people who were employed pre-Katrina found that their jobs no longer existed post-Katrina, or that they would have to reapply for the position they once held.

> That was another process that puzzles me. How do you have a job pre-Katrina [and] post-Katrina you don't have a job? Post-Katrina your job is now open, but you have to reapply for the job that you had pre-Katrina. I don't understand that. They were working and lost their job and then had to reapply for the job that they had before.

Arthur describes the challenges associated with post-disaster recovery and concludes that piecemeal assistance will not allow people to return.

> I don't know. I'm just passing my own opinion about a lot of this stuff, but again just two and a half years later people are still struggling and trying to get their lives together. I never imagined it would take that long, never even imagined it. But when you look at it, families need a total package. You can't give a man a job with no place to stay. What good is a place to stay if I can't pay the rent? What good is having a place to stay and a job and no place to put my [children in] school and to get a decent education? And everyone for sure wants to live in a safe neighborhood, in spite of what they may think, so a lot of factors need to be in place. And since they're not in place, a lot of people are not that apt to run back here because they're running back to nothing. And some folks, they moved away.[27]

MELROSE

Melrose is a principal of a charter school in the Central City neighborhood. We interviewed her in spring 2006.

> I have been here in New Orleans for about 24 years, coming from Baton Rouge. I always did have a love for New Orleans. I was born in New Orleans at Charity Hospital where everybody

was born, basically, but I've been here for 24 years. I live in New Orleans East.

While Arthur's connection to Central City was maintained through his continued involvement in the New Hope Baptist Church, Melrose's connection developed as a result of the time she has spent educating children from the Central City neighborhood. Even though she lives in another neighborhood, it is very clear that Melrose has tremendous affection for Central City and especially the children who live there.

[Before becoming the principal of this school], I was principal at another school, a prekindergarten to sixth grade public school also in Central City. Well, [this] is an impoverished community, you know, a lot of projects, low-income families. But the kids have drive, they're smart kids, you know, gifted kids, talented kids, you know? They are kids. They [only need to be] given the right opportunity and directions. That's what we try to do: provide the directions. Because kids are our future, you know, those are the kids that you are going to meet on the street. I would rather meet them as [a] doctor [or] lawyer than meet [them] holding me up with a gun in [their] hand. So, I try my best to steer them in the right direction and provide for them the things that they need. I mean, we try to encourage them and let them know that they are not responsible for the situation they were born into, but they can change that. It is important what you are going to grow up to be, not your situation right now, because we know it is not in your control. But once you walk through these doors into this institution, this educational institution, then you have control of that. You are here to learn, and we as administrators and educational leaders have to make sure that teaching and learning is taking place. And we are providing you with the skills necessary to be successful citizens.

Melrose spent more time at the school in Central City with her charges than at her home in New Orleans East. She sees how much the school means to community.

I lived up at the school. I would get there 7 in the morning, stay till 9, 10 o'clock at night. I am just doing what needs to be done, you know. Holding all kinds of activities for the kids and families, you know, just being supportive. And the neighborhood, kind of, like looked out for us, supported us. I mean no matter what was going on, I felt that they supported the school. [For example], we didn't have a parking lot. We parked around the school, and even though it was within the bad neighborhood, we never, we rarely [had any problems]. Maybe once since I was here the incident of a car being broken into or something, but the community members kind of looked out for us.

When she heard the news coverage of Katrina's progress, she was ready to leave. As we saw with Elizabeth and Ervin, people who have lived through Hurricane Betsy tend to either feel bulletproof, so never evacuate when a storm is approaching, or feel extremely vulnerable, so always leave when there is a storm. Melrose falls into the latter camp and believes that the loss of life during Katrina was higher than it might have been because of people's reticence or inability to evacuate as the storm was approaching. She felt particularly vulnerable because she was also going through a personal loss at the same time.

I was kind of like really caught off guard. I had a brother that passed that weekend, so I had taken off that Friday to go to my brother's funeral, and then when I came back, it was time for the evacuation. So we were told to go, and I went through Hurricane Betsy, so when you say "hurricane" it is like I pack up and leave. But I was really concerned about the people that didn't believe that this is going to be [that bad]. A lot of people ride it out, and it is not [always] because they want to, but they don't have transportation. I had a parent who brought his kids to school on the back of a bicycle, and he couldn't ride that bicycle out of New Orleans. And at that time it seems like the government didn't take the threat of storm seriously because they didn't provide transportation out of the city for those people, they just let them walk to the Dome, that's what they usually do. They just go to the Dome if it got too bad.

That's why I think a loss of life came about, [not] because people didn't want to go, but they had no way of getting out of the city, you know, and they were just accustomed to going to places like the Dome, going over to the convention center, and then once it passed over, going back home.

Although Melrose was safely away from New Orleans when Katrina hit, much of what she valued was left behind in New Orleans and was destroyed by the storm; not just her house, but Melrose's entire life was upended by Katrina.[28]

I have relatives in Baton Rouge so I went to Baton Rouge. [I was] looking [at] all the pictures, right, you know, but watching everything on television was devastating. I mean, I just couldn't believe the things that were happening, you know, it is like a nightmare. In one night, I lost my house, my job, my benefits, and I'm 51 years old [with] 25 years in a system. You know, I'm looking at retirement; in a day's time, I'm looking at trying to find employment. It just tipped over like that. That's what I had to do, try to find employment because that was the biggest thing, trying to find employment.

Like others, Melrose's house was badly damaged. Also like others, she believed that if she was allowed back into the city earlier, she would have been able to salvage some of her possessions.

In my house [in New Orleans East], they had about five feet of water downstairs. Upstairs on one end, the roof blew off. So, . . . I think if I could have gotten back, if they had allowed me to get back quicker, I could have saved some things. But because they wouldn't let us back in and the water sat so long, the mold and mildew got on everything, you know.

It was October when we came back—late September or October that we could come back into the city. [Meanwhile] I was calling around because I don't want to leave the state, you know, like I said, I have 25 years in a system, and so 25 years if you retire, you only get 50 percent of your money. And if you do 30 years, you get 80 percent. So I was staying for a long time. I had an investment. I probably would have stayed after 30 years because I enjoy what I'm doing, like working with the kids.

After Katrina, people received help from quarters where they least expected it but often were disappointed when they did not receive help from sources they were certain would come through. This was the case for Melrose, who expected help from the people who had the power and resources to help her. To her surprise, those expectations were dashed.

So, it was like, I knew a lot of people in Baton Rouge . . . if I tell you every person that I thought would help, that had their resources to help, [but] did not . . . They had the resources to help. . . . They had the resources to help. No thank you. No help at all. They just like turned their backs. It is hard for somebody who has always given, who has always had to give, to ask for help, you know, but I am saying it makes you feel like you are begging.

We had a family come in here from California, that came in to volunteer, to really touch lives. They volunteered in our school. They bought supplies for the school. Those people are the ones that really touch and help—people that I don't even know. The people that I knew, and I thought I could depend on, I found out different that I couldn't, that they were not there; they turned their back. They said one thing on television and then in real life they switch. It was really, really hurtful to realize that, but then you know on these things like this, you really found out who people are truly. You really see the real person. Before that you thought this person was great and everything, but then you see the real person, especially the politicians who you thought you knew. So I applied at Southern University Laboratory School because I worked there before . . . and I know my résumé is excellent, you know, I've always got some great evaluations, there couldn't be a problem getting a job. So I just kept calling and calling until I called here. I didn't know that they had added pre-K through 5th, see they always had 6, 7, 8 in this school, and they only had a lead teacher and a director and assistant director. They didn't have a principal.

> So when I called Mr. Evans and I actually told him I was
> looking for a job, we communicated a lot [in the past] because
> some of my kids from [my old school] transferred to this school
> and some of my teachers they come over to change things up.
> So he was like, well, I'll get back with you, and I was invited for
> an interview, and I came down and interviewed, and I got it. I
> was really excited because a lot of my kids were now here. So
> I mean it is really good to know, they knew about, some of the
> other ones, they could tell me, oh, so and so is here, so and so is
> there. So that really helped a lot to know that my kids, a major-
> ity of them, got help.

After Katrina, charter schools that were already in place before
Katrina were at a significant advantage relative to their traditional counterparts.[29]

> This school has been in existence for seven years. It is one of
> the first charters, and it was [one of the first] to reopen after
> the hurricane. This school opened in November. They saw the
> need; they came back. The building was in good shape, and
> the director decided to open up. Because they are [a] charter,
> they opened up. [As a charter school] we don't have all the red
> tape and the politics. We see what needs to be done and do it. I
> mean, if everything could be that easy.

As Melrose states, her charter school is doing well because it is
free from much of the red tape that hampers traditional public
schools. Similarly, the superintendent for schools in St. Bernard
Parish Unified School District used her contacts outside of the
school system to have the schools in her district reopened the
November following Katrina.[30]

Melrose was also very critical of FEMA, which she saw as
inhibiting the return of the schools.

> For instance, the Martin Luther King School, the parents want
> to go in to clean up there, and they didn't even want them
> to go in. FEMA was trying to block that.[31] They wouldn't let
> them go in the building at first. They said some of the building

wasn't stable, but that wasn't the truth. That building didn't get much water. All the materials and all the money they put in the school is gone to waste. Those are taxpayers' dollars. We cry broke, that we don't have money, and then we waste and let it go away. I don't understand that. Why not have FEMA do a warehouse thing? They may put all [that they have to offer] out and let you come and get what you need, but they let it all go to waste. I don't understand it. Those taxpayers' dollar money, we pay for them.

[The public school where I was before] I mean, we weren't a magnet school, we are in a poor area, poor school. Our building left a lot to be desired. I mean, we tried to keep it as clean as we could, but it wasn't a place that I would want children to see. I mean, you know the school I grew up in Baton Rouge, the floors were immaculate, the bathrooms, you could eat off the floor. These bathrooms, my babies would hold it until they get home, they don't want to go in, and they were so filthy. And I was constantly, [as the] principal trying to go out to get resources to get somebody to come in and remodel the bathroom because it was so horrible, and the kids couldn't use [it]. Now can you imagine them measuring me against the school like Ben Franklin?[32] That was a school that had everything. The schools in the public school system are always the haves and the have-nots.

After the hurricane, there was a move to convert many of the public schools to charter schools.[33]

Well, kids need to go to school; they need schools open. So if that's the way they were going to do it, I was like I'm all for it. But then a lot of people are getting into it just for money. They're not getting into it for the kids. They have given these charter schools to whomever comes in with the right connections, I guess, to open it up, and it's all like a money thing. They opened the charter schools in the affluent areas where the parents are middle [class]. They had people that would come out and, say, in big large numbers, we want this open right now. [Parents with] affluent jobs and connections and those are the ones that got open. Those are the ones that got open. [They] want to select what kids you can come . . . come

on now. That's what some of them are doing; they're being
selective. They're not letting anybody come. We take in everybody that comes here that we can take in; in fact, we have [a]
waiting list because this school was really built for like 16 to
1 teacher-pupil ratio. Right now, we're like 25, 26, you know.
We're full; we're at our capacity.

Melrose defends the New Orleans school system but at the same
time laments that parents don't realize their power.

The school system wasn't as bad as they painted it out to be.
We have some success stories but, of course, they never tell all
those success stories. They'd rather harp on what we don't have
and the bickering between the board and [the teachers]. And
they, you know, they could do away with that. We would probably do so much better. And they never consult the people that
are on the front line. They never consult the front line, never.
   I see some of the parents . . . so we talk and find out how different families are or where they are. Some that I came across
said they're not coming back. They want to stay where they are.
Those that are back, they complain to me about them not opening up schools, but they won't get together and go as a group
and complain about it; they will come and complain to me. They
don't know the power that they have. They don't do it. They just
take whatever is dished out. Somebody ought to tell them they
don't have to take that.

Her school not only benefited from an absence of red tape, but
concerned individuals and charities also helped the school
reopen its doors and stock its classrooms.

We get a lot of people coming in to volunteer. Lot of people
are calling us, want to know [what they can do]. Just [inter-
ested] individual families that are concerned and [that] know
that money doesn't trickle down to where it needs to [go]. So
we just had a family in California come and buy $1,000 worth
supplies from Wal-Mart, and they spent all day sorting books
for our library and they read to some kids, this is a husband
and wife and four kids. And they're all on break, and they came

down to do a bit. And then we have church groups, different church organizations that are coming in to do things. They volunteer, come in to assist with us tutoring the kids or either straightening out those books that we have, those donated books, or we have a lot of clothes that was donated. They go in, straighten up the clothes. So they're doing everything. If the building needs painting, they paint; they're doing whatever needs to be done. They ask us, "What do y'all need?" And we're doing this list, and they go from there.

Although Melrose is quite clear about what needs to be done to the school, she has no clear idea about what to do with her house. It also seems to her as if the city has no clear idea of what it needs to do for people to return. Simple things like making sure trash service and street lights are operational are not being done.[34]

Well, [where] my home is concerned, whether I have to raze it or not. My home is built on a concrete slab. I don't know how I'm supposed to raze it, but I don't know if I'm going to be allowed to rebuild until the adjuster comes. I can't get somebody to do the roof. I don't know if I'm going to [be] allowed to purchase insurance because if I don't meet the guidelines [I can't]. Nothing has been written out clearly.

Seeing signs offering to purchase damaged homes, Melrose considered selling. But such signs gave her pause.[35] If someone is willing to buy it, she muses, it must be worth something.

You know, when driving through my neighborhood I saw those signs that said, we will buy your home, cash money, so I'm thinking they know something I don't know. It is something [that] did not come down the grapevine to me. So I am not selling the house, you know, but they are some people who had a $150,000 home selling for like $60,000 and $80,000 because they just want out. You know, they just get nervous and they just want out. You know? But looking at those signs [makes me] wonder why would someone want to buy my house if it's going to be worthless. If the levees are not going to protect it again and it is gonna flood again, why would you want to buy that?

Nonetheless, Melrose, like many New Orleans residents, is frustrated by the slow pace of recovery.

> I just went back there today [eight months after Katrina]; it's still looks like there's no pickup, you know. The trash, the debris is still everywhere. It's like nobody is doing anything. You see individual people working on their own homes, but . . . the lights are still out, even at the intersections, come on. Shouldn't those lights be working by now?

At the time she was interviewed, much of the city's infrastructure was still not working, and she did not understand why that was the case.

> If I can get electricity in my house, why isn't the street light on or working? You know, and then you will see right here on Jackson, the light is not working. Come on. You know, things like that, I think should see more progress. So I called the mayor's office and then just said, may I speak to Mayor Nagin; I am a citizen of New Orleans. I'd like to speak with the mayor. Well, I need to take a message. I knew I wouldn't be able to speak to him. But, you know, my momma would say [that] you better try. So I tried on several occasions, and I left several messages. I tried several times; I left messages, "This is Miss Melrose, this is the principal of a school, and I am very disappointed in what I am seeing." You know, it will get more votes if he responds to people like me than that commercial that's going around. We have one superintendent that I really, really admire. [He] don't care when you called him. If he didn't answer that phone, he would call you back. To me, that's more of a public servant than these people who I can't touch, making decisions about your life.

Melrose did not grow up in New Orleans and, because she was an only child, her mother was not happy with her choice to live in New Orleans. But, to her, New Orleans is now home.[36]

When I got this job, you know—I am an only child—I had sisters and brothers from my dad, but I'm my mother's only child, and she didn't want me to come to New Orleans, and when I decided to move down here, she cried. She thought I was moving to Sodom and Gomorrah.

I always loved New Orleans. I was the only majorette in high school that couldn't come and march in the Carnival parades. I would cry that grandma would never let me come. She wouldn't let me march. She thought somebody would just snatch me out of the parade. So when I was a majorette in college too, and I found that we were coming; when the bus pulled up my mom was sitting on the bus. She knew the bus driver. So she came with us [laughter]. It's college! My freshman year. I was embarrassed, but she came with us. So I told her that's why I live down here. It's rebellion. If you had let me come all those times, I would have gotten it out of my system and I may not have wanted to live here. I had just talked her into moving down here. She moved down here December before last. All her stuff was in my garage. Now I'll never get her back down. She is by her sister [and] she is not coming back. You know I had just gotten her down here.

Melrose credits the school kids with her being able to overcome such challenging odds. She works with and sees her inspiration daily.

[For me, it's] the kids, just seeing these kids and smiles on their faces and, you know, their successes, that keeps me going. It really does. You know it really keeps me going . . . My family said they want me to come back, and my uncle was a minister in my home church and he would say just pray on it. And I'm hanging on and I'm praying. When I got the job [it was clear that] God wants me back in New Orleans. And I can say I'm just excited here. I am excited about getting up in the morning and coming to work . . . if I wasn't I couldn't do it. I couldn't do it if I wasn't.

JOYCE

Joyce, an African American woman in her 40s, has lived in the Central City neighborhood and worked as a mail carrier for at least 10 years. We spoke with Joyce in the fall of 2007.

> I always thought it was a raggedy city. I mean, people come and liked it, but I didn't see it.

Unlike many others that we interviewed, Joyce was not very fond of the city of New Orleans.[37] She feels the minorities and working-class people are treated poorly. She believes that the government officials as well as the politicians are corrupt. And, unlike many we talked to, she considers the churches as part of the corrupt political machine.

> I never liked New Orleans, but my mom and my husband would die if we had to move. I don't like the fact that the areas that the majority of the minorities live in, they put no money into it. [They] take the money and go somewhere else with it; that's what frustrates me. I've been around here so long, you hear everything. People tell me. It's just like the bar. Bartenders, they tell them everything.
>
> Okay. When the money [from the government] came here, they decided that they were going to use it for economic development, which they already have, economic development programs. They kept it hush-hush, but let's say I found out. What they did is gave it to the faith banks, the churches. After that, I see them [the pastors] riding in Mercedes and buying property.
>
> Where is the money? What are you doing with it? There's so much that goes on, you just get frustrated. They just steal and take money and do not use it for what it's supposed to be used for. I've heard so many stories. Now you see why I don't like New Orleans.
>
> Nobody ever saw that money because people don't know. People in the neighborhood, most of them are elderly people. The other ones might not even worry about what's going on in the neighborhood. So they don't know, and most of these people feel, "Okay, they don't know, so we can do whatever. They will never know what money's coming into their neighborhood

and what it's for." So they just take the money and do whatever they want so that all the neighborhoods stay like they are.

The politicians, they own property. When money comes in to help people renovate their houses, they take it and give it to their family members. All this kind of foolishness, and nothing's ever done about it. So that's why I say you'll never get anywhere in this city unless you're crooked or know somebody that's crooked. Just helping your family members. [This is particular to] New Orleans. They got their own style. They have their own style of stealing.

Joyce is quick to evacuate when a hurricane is on the way.

Yes, I evacuate. If they say it's a strong wind, I'm gone. They did not have to say, "You know, it's going to be a tornado or whatever." I leave if it's a little regular storm. I left. My mom and my husband did not want to leave. I had to convince them at the last minute to leave, so we all finally left. I think we stayed gone three months.

Joyce evacuated to a shelter in Mississippi when Katrina hit. She found the people there very helpful and was still very appreciative two years later.

We left and went to Mississippi. We stayed there in a shelter at a church. They were really nice, and I think about them all the time. I keep sending them a cinema card. I'm like, "Okay, it's two years after." But it was nice. It was a nice shelter. We stayed there for two nights, and then we went to Jacksonville with my son. He was in the Navy, so we moved there.

She returned as soon as she was given the all clear.

When they first said people could come back in, then we started to come back in because we didn't have water in this area. We couldn't come back before then because there was no lights, or I guess the water was contaminated.

I had a lot of wind damage . . . I guess it was like a little tornado that was coming through because when you came up

Baronne Street, one house was rubbish, the next house was nothing done to it, the next two houses were just all torn up. My neighbor, it tore the back out from her house, and when it got to mine, it just tore all the boards off and shifted the house.

Like others, Joyce explains how her insurance payout was not what she expected it to be and that she has had to take the issue to court.[38]

I own my house. I had $220,000 worth of insurance, but I got, what, about $50,000. That wouldn't even hardly cover them to shift the house back. I mean, out of $220,000, I could've just gotten $100,000, that's how it worked. But that's the way New Orleans is. [I filed an appeal]. I'm waiting on it. You have to get a lawyer. You have to go do all this kind of stuff.

Joyce was as disappointed with Road Home as she was with the insurance company and New Orleans' city government.[39] According to her, the way that they distributed funds appears to have been arbitrary.[40]

The Road Home, that's another joke. I applied for Road Home. They deduct your insurance money from, supposedly, the $150,000 that they're supposed to give everybody.[41] They deduct the insurance that you get. They have two formulas that they come up with. So out of that, I got $18,000, out of $150,000. All I got was my insurance. I got no FEMA, no SBA, any of that. They said the average that they're giving people is $70,000. No. My supervisor got $2,000. She lives out in the east. It's all a joke. I'm telling you.

I had strictly wind damage. [My supervisor], they had water. I don't think they had as much water as some parts of the east. I guess maybe it depends on who came out to do your house, to adjust it. That determines how much money you got because my aunt . . . she lives in the east, too. She had a lot of water. [The adjuster] didn't even show up, so she called and told him, "I waited for you, and you didn't show up."

He said, "Oh, I couldn't make it, but I'm going to go out, and I'm going to automatically give you 100 percent." It just depends on who comes.

I asked them, "Are these people that you're sending out, are they contractors, licensed, and know what they're doing, or is this just somebody you hired?" Because I know FEMA was just hiring people to just come out. They had no experience, no nothing. So she said, "Oh, yeah. They're experienced, but we don't hire them. Another company hires them."

Okay, [so I asked], "How are these people gonna know what they're looking for?" Nothing. It's a no-win situation, and the city is not back to nowhere near half to where it was originally.

Joyce is surprised and frustrated by the increased cost of living, including higher costs of food and housing. She believes that if the government really wanted to help the poor, rather than providing Section 8 housing, it would put the money provided to rent a two-bedroom apartment toward homeownership.[42] She believes that the reason the government does not pursue this route is that politicians are the ones who own the rental properties.

Everything went [for] three times what it was before the hurricane, as if we hit a gold mine here. You know, it's getting to the point where . . . you can't even live here because the expenses are too high. They need rent control because $1,200 a month for one bedroom is ridiculous. That is totally ridiculous. Most of these people can't afford that. The people who can afford it, they're buying houses. They're living in their own homes.

That's another reason why people can't come back. They can't afford that. Then, Section 8 pays $1,300 for two bedrooms. Now, most of those people can come back that has a Section 8, but what about the people that don't have Section 8?[43] They can't come back here and afford it.

Most people are putting their houses on Section 8 because they want that $1,300, which is a waste of money for you to pay somebody for somebody's house for $1,300. If you want to pay $1,300 for someone on Section 8, do like the other cities. Pay it toward them buying a house. Here, they just throw money because most of the politicians own the property, which is crazy.[44]

Joyce agrees that New Orleans is unique, but she does not understand the place attachment that is common among New Orleanians.[45]

> I could just sell that house and go, but my husband [won't leave]. [My husband] works across the river, and my mom's just been here forever. [My mother] lives upstairs. We have an apartment upstairs, so she lives up there. She knows a lot of people because, like I say, she's been here all her life. So she knows a lot of people. She just don't want to go. I don't know what it is about New Orleans where people feel like this is the only place they can live. It's different from any other place, I agree, but it's not all good.

Joyce's opinions of civic leaders are not far off from her opinions of the government.

> A lot of them say they are leaders. I will tell them, "I don't see much of what you're doing." I saw [a church leader] on TV saying he's trying to do this. He's trying to do that. [They] have a program. But it's not like you're doing much for the community.
> The previous pastor of that church, you could tell him, "Could I get some of the guys to come help me repair my fence?" He would send them, but he would tell you, "Okay, they don't have a regular job. They are in a rehab. You want to donate a couple of dollars?" Which was no problem. You could just give him $10 or $20. He wasn't asking for a whole lot. Now, they'll say, "Oh, they're busy." They are not trying to work in the community. I don't see much leaders.

As a mail carrier, Joyce has a particular view of the neighborhood she lives in. She sees various parts of the neighborhood that might not be visible to others.

I was delivering mail when only the TV station was on this street. This was an abandoned building. You could see clean through it. There was nothing open on this street. That was it. When I first came on this road 10 years ago, that's all that was on this street. I got to know all these people by them coming while [this was my route]. So I know everybody on this street. Really, everybody was there.

I see everything. Yeah, they don't see the people that are on drugs and how they live. You know what I'm saying? I get depressed because I see it every day. You look at it, and you say, "Oh, that could be me." You never know how your life's going to go. I'm wearing this postal uniform making money. Anything could happen. So I don't judge them, but people don't see the lifestyle people are living. People that are homeless, you know?

Now some of the guys, they're just homeless because they want to be homeless. They can get a job. I know one guy was like, "Oh, I don't want to work. I hustle, stand out there with a sign and make $200 or $300." An alcoholic or a drug addict or something.

But there's some of them that's really legit. They don't have nowhere to go, you know what I'm saying. They might not be able to read. They do pretty good at the shelter down the street. Now, they're pretty good with helping the homeless people. I think they do pretty good.

Joyce reiterates that homeowners are not the only ones suffering. She recognizes that those who are renting are having a hard time after Katrina. It is difficult to find a place to live and then to afford one that is in decent shape.

Most of the people in the area don't own their homes. They just rent, and the landlords are not going to fix [the problem]. If they do ask them to fix it, they're going to up the rents, so most of them don't ask. You know what I'm saying. So a lot of them are not fixed. A lot of them was raggedy before the storm. Now they're even raggedier. So, if the landlord decides to fix them, he's going up on the rent.

I know when I first came back, we were delivering mail. This house on Baronne Street, the guy told him, "Oh, we're renovating the house." I think they were paying $300 or something. So he wanted to go up to $800 or $900 because he said he was renovating. The windows are still busted out. What kind of renovation is that? You're going to go up to $800 or $900 from $300 in a raggedy house. But people don't have no choice. They need somewhere to stay for their children. They're struggling to pay the rent. They can't do anything else. It's too bad.

Joyce tells us about the community project she's been involved in. Like other citizens, she tells a tale of seeing something that needed to be done and simply doing it.

Down the street, where they have the statue, the little Martin Luther King, we used to take care of that, me and my husband. But they would never put a water system there where we could water plants and stuff. So me and my husband, we lived two blocks down the street, we used to have to get water, put it in the back of his truck and haul it there. It got ridiculous.

They had benches on this street, and they took them all up because they didn't want the homeless people on this street sitting down and stuff. So they took all of them out. So I had a nonprofit organization, and I applied for a grant and bought some benches to put over there so they could sit over there. They don't bother anybody over there.

[It's the green space] at the corner. They're still out there. But I haven't done anything. I tore my knee up on the road, working. I have to have surgery, so I really can't do too much anymore.

Many people on Joyce's mail route no longer live at the address they did before Katrina. Still, she knows for certain of only one person who will not be returning to New Orleans after evacuating the city.

Yeah, there was one lady on my route, but she didn't come back. She was in Atlanta. She had three kids, four kids, I think. They lived in a one-bedroom house, and they were paying $300 or $400. It was a shack. She really didn't have an income. I guess she was on welfare or whatever. She was nice enough. I'd always talk to her, every day, and she was young.

She left, but you know, by being a mail person, and the mail has to come through me, I see their name, and I see where they went. They changed their addresses, so I wrote her, and she was telling me she was doing okay. She was in Atlanta, then she moved to Texas, and she was saying how she was still struggling and blah, blah, blah. Christmas time was coming up, so I sent her a gift card for her children.

She always writes, but I haven't had time to write her back lately. She was the only one that I knew didn't come back for sure. The others, they're all back that way (north). I don't go that way anymore. I'm all over this way (south), so I don't get to see them.

And some of them died. Crazy stuff. This one lady, she came back, and they didn't have any lights. But she was trying to burn a generator and the fumes from the generator. The same day she came back, she died from the fumes. It was crazy. I know a lot of people died.

The challenges of recovery have had their effect on Joyce's emotional well-being. Yet she stays in New Orleans because of family.

Oh, I've been depressed all the time, but I know being depressed is not going to help, so I try to tell myself to just not worry about it, just let it go and just keep going, you know? It gets hard sometimes. I'm just ready to get away from it.

I just keep it in. I don't really have many friends. My friend just moved. Well, she was in the Navy. She just got out. She lives out of town. Or my mom, she knows how I feel. She's like, "Okay, if you leave, I'll leave. I won't have any choice." But she don't want to leave. My husband, too. They both would leave if I just packed up and left, but they would be miserable.

Joyce recognizes the sense of place that New Orleanians have and has her own theories about why people would come back to New Orleans under these difficult circumstances.

They feel like they've been here so long and can just do whatever. People can stand outside on the sidewalk or sit their chairs out. You can't go nowhere else and do that. I'm serious. That's the kind of stuff that they feel like, "Oh, I miss this. I miss that." Or they miss the food or miss where everything used to be open 24/7. But, I mean, that part, they're going to come back and face reality. Nothing's open no more like that. But most of it is the lifestyle that they lived. They cannot live it somewhere else. By lifestyle I mean: walking down the street, drinking a beer. Sitting outside, they sit out on the stoop in Chicago or whatever. They just put their chair out there and sit anywhere. That kind of stuff. They're used to that. They came up with that kind of stuff.

So they can't get away from it. Most of them have never been anywhere else as far as trying to live somewhere else. So they don't know nothing else. That's what everybody I hear. [They say], "I don't know anywhere else. I grew up in New Orleans, so that's my home. I won't go nowhere else."

They're scared of change. I think that's what my husband's problem is. He's scared of change. He doesn't want to. He feels comfortable and secure in New Orleans because that's where he grew up. So that's why he don't want to leave. That's what I think [explains] most of them. They feel comfortable in New Orleans. This is what they know, and they can't adjust to anywhere else.

SAUNDRA

Saundra is an African American woman who has lived in Central City all her life. Before Katrina, six generations of her family lived in Central City. She is chair of the Central City Renaissance Alliance, a nonprofit organization dedicated to community planning and neighborhood revitalization. We interviewed Saundra in the spring of 2007.

The majority of my family were either raised or lived [in Central City] pre-Katrina. In fact, I have a very New Orleans dynamic to my family in that my sister and I live next door to each other.

And at a point, my sister and I owned property next to her, and my mom lived in the attic apartment in my sister's house, and her adult son . . . lived—she has a, we call it a triplex, but it's a big grand old house that has been cut up into a couple of different sections, and at one point, her son and his wife and children lived in one side of the house; she lived on the other. My mom lived upstairs. I lived in the house next door, and my son, one of my adult sons, lived in a studio apartment near, so we kind of at one point pre-Katrina all kind of conglobed on the corner on this particular street. We all lived in different parts of the city, as well, in the transient way that life takes you around sometimes. But some years ago, my mother moved in with my grandmother and my great-grandmother.

I say all of this so that I can explain to you that there are six generations of us on my maternal side that have lived in this city.

Saundra's grandmothers were a central focus of the extended family, not only because they needed care, but also because they contributed to the family's sense of joy and family cohesion. Katrina exacted a particular kind of toll in this regard.

A few years prior to Katrina, we lost my great-grandmother, the matriarch, at 103. But grandmother, my mother even moved in with the two of them because one had Alzheimer's, and the other was just old, senile [with] dementia. And so my mom, woman that she is, stopped working as a nurse, and she went to take care of them, the two adults.

Institutionalizing them [in a care facility] was really not an option for us because we just, there were just so many of us, and we just figured that keeping our family together, keeping them home was the better quality for their lives, and it really proved to be that. That background is important because my grandmother, who evacuated with us before Katrina even, was in her 90s, and she's not officially listed as a Katrina victim, but she is.

On August 27, which is a Saturday, when we evacuated, [my grandmother] was an Alzheimer's victim, but she was still functioning at a very high level and had a reasonably sweet quality of life. She lost all of our names, but she knew and could recognize people that were related to us, so we all became "Darling" and "Sugar," "My Baby," and all those kinds of sweet things. And she would make her bed 3, 4, 5, or 12 times a day, and rearrange her drawers, her lingerie, and her different kinds of things in her dresser drawer. She lived in her own home and could decide when it was time for her to go to the bathroom, and she was in familiar space. She enjoyed going to church and seeing people that she was used to seeing. Everything was about her. She dipped in everybody's conversation. It was all about her.

I said that so you could hear the high quality of function in her life that she lived, and we loved seeing her. We told her she looked pretty. Oh, it was just the best thing in the world. She had been a beautician for over 50 years.

Well, Katrina sucked all that out. The distance and the difference and the constant change. She was dead by May [of 2006]. The life had been sucked right out of her. She became introverted, then combative, then stopped eating and trauma-like, to the point where by the time she was gone from us, she was frail and as if, she looked like someone who had been in Auschwitz. That's the truth.

We had to put her in a skilled facility in a nursing home the last six or eight weeks of her life because it had gotten to be physically too much for my mom, who had also been affected by the storm, as we all had been, and this is the physical toll. There was an emotional, physical, psychological toll that [Katrina] took on every single person. It changed the dynamics of family; it changed how we related, interrelated.

Because we are and were a very closely connected and closely bonded family; we were the family that little children would ride on the wheelchairs of our elders. And those elders, who didn't even have their names anymore, understood and recognized [the children] and would hug them and keep them together.

We'd have dinner, not a formal dinner. We'd get to the place where [we'd say], "We haven't seen Gram this week," and we'd just all show up and it would be potluck or the boys, I call them boys, but they're men, loved to fish, and if somebody went fishing and there was fresh fish, somebody was boiling potatoes, we'd make potato salad, and it was kind of like that, or, "Let's play charades." It was in a very black kind of way, Ozzie and Harriet.

It was that kind of a familial familiar-ness that bonded us and made us really, really comfortable about being together. The storm took effect. It cast us out like stray pennies in your purse that you just throw up on a bed or throw on a dresser. When we evacuated from the storm, before the storm, we were all together. But the dynamics of what happened as Katrina passed and the levees broke, our home was stolen from us, we had to plight our troth in different directions because there were different families.

Saundra evacuated with her entire family and three dogs, staying at a friend's house in Poplarville, Mississippi. Along the way, the unexpected delay and roads blocked with storm debris culminated in a medical emergency for Saundra's daughter, who required dialysis treatment. Eventually they ended up safely in Baton Rouge, staying with her college roommate. Once it was clear that they would be away from New Orleans for an extended period, practical considerations forced her and her sister's families to separate. Saundra's sister, her children, and grandchildren were able to stay in Houston in a property owned by her late husband's family. Saundra and her immediate family remained in Baton Rouge.

Practicality is what it is, and somebody's gotta be earning a living, and somebody else has gotta be able to get your kids in school, and you have to decide what's going to be from here. Are you gonna stay in Baton Rouge? Are you gonna go anyplace else?

Then there was me and my children. Well I am, at this point, a 30-year state employee. I work for the food stamp and welfare office, and if ever there was need of food stamps and welfare, so it was a natural fit for me to stay in Louisiana, stay in that region, particularly because that region had become North New Orleans because it was so many people that went automatically there.

Though Saundra was appreciative of those who gave her support in Baton Rouge, the time and cultural distance away from New Orleans heightened her desire to return.

Well, the city that I love and the reason that I don't want to live nowhere else, is not a perfect place. And it's extremely unique in that its history and its culture kind of keep me saying these two descriptors "familial" and "familiar." There is so much oldness that informs today, like the music and like the food and like the traditions that every New Orleans commercial or public view puts forward in a very one-dimensional kind of way.

When we were away from the city for a long, long time and were able to come back just for an evening, something that was going on at the Ashé Cultural Arts Center. My church is untraditional in that we have lots of bands and music. It has a very Afro ethnic kind of look and feel to it. Well, we went to this event, and I didn't recognize until it affected everybody because you see how much [different it was from the church in Baton Rouge]. The drums were there, and it was like the heartbeat had got started again, and I didn't realize how much of that I missed or that it was missing in my life. I guess what I didn't realize was how important it was for me to hear that—to kind of enliven my spirit, to quicken my heart.

And that's how it is for a lot of people. The folks in Baton Rouge had to change their culture once we got to Baton Rouge in a commercial kind of way. For example, they had to buy different things to put in the store to satisfy the New Orleans palate. You would think that 80 miles didn't make that much of a difference, but it did.

Hot sausage and red beans had to [be brought] to Baton Rouge. They were there, but not in the volume that we were used to having. We like to put pickled pork in cabbage and greens and red beans. But it was like there's a whole different palate for hot sausage. What they called hot sausage was different. Something as simple as bread. I want some French bread. What they meant by that was a big hot dog bun, and it's very, very simple, very subtle, but it's very complex—the sense of place, the sense of belonging.

Saundra's and her sister's houses both suffered wind damage, but the higher elevation spared them from significant flood damage. Saundra's nephew's home and her mother and grandmother's home were both destroyed by flood. As with many in New Orleans, Saundra experienced the grief associated with the loss of memories and keepsakes that represented her home and family.

My house and my sister's house is on a ridge where we were not affected by the flooding. We were affected by the wind and the damage. My mom's house was in Gentilly, and they got 11 feet of water. So her house was completely destroyed. My mom is back here. We got her an apartment up in Central City, meaning my sister and I, so she's within two minutes of our house.

My nephew lived—his house was facing the St. Claude overpass, the bridge that goes over the Industrial Canal. When he looked out of his front door, he saw the side of the bridge. When he looked at the corner, there was the levee, so his house was completely under. So he lost everything. Mom and my grandma lost everything. My sister and I both have our houses. So in terms of property loss, it was 50/50.

But it was deeper than that—another fine line. All of our memorabilia was at my grandma's house. So we lost all of that: all of our great pictures, all of the baby clothes. I happen to like old furniture; nobody else [does], but [I do]. So I had my great-grandma's bed and her little vanity from when she was a younger woman, but some of that other older furniture and stuff, that I made them not get rid of and my nephew and I would always joke about where in the will I want that vanity with the cheval mirror on it and I'm getting the dishes and that kind of stuff. All that was gone.

My great-grandma had a picture of herself when she was in her 20s and looking ever so pretty—a little sepia-colored picture that someone had dusted her cheeks pink and she had little curls that someone had done with a hot comb and a lovely little lacy blouse, and it was in one of those round mirrors with a dome-kind of glass to it, and when we went into the house and that was on the wall where the color had drained down to a little pocket of water at the bottom, and the image was gone and this little brown water was sitting up there.

My mother is the keeper. She was the person that kept everything, pictures of my dad and me and my sister when we were little. All that's gone. My grandmother in her best days was a craftsperson where she quilted and did latch hook and did embroidery, crocheted, beautiful, lovely things—all gone.

I have a scar on my head from an accident maybe [from when I was] around three or four where my mom was telling the story, I think it was "Alice in the Looking Glass" or something, for me to have a nap or whatever, and she left out of the room and I jumped and jumped in the bed thinking if Alice could do it, me too.

And I jumped into this mirror on the chifferobe, and I don't know if you know what a chifferobe is, but it's an old kind of armoire, old kind of closet that sits on legs, and one side you could hang clothes and then there were drawers, and then there was a little cubbyhole thing with a door on it for you to put your hats and a little compartment there. And I jumped into that chifferobe, and it was a little old antique piece that some-one had given my grandmother. They were all domestics, but it was a piece that had been given to her, and we had that still. We don't have that anymore.

As with many New Orleans faith communities, Saundra's church and congregation have faced significant challenges in the aftermath of Katrina. New leadership has begun to emerge, however, in the face of these challenges.

[There are] all kinds of little intricacies—it's woven like a scotch plaid. There are some threads that are very, very fine, but they run throughout the whole fabric, and some that are bolder that you automatically see, but it's those little fine prints that really make the plaid one piece. But we have a very strong faith tradition in our family. So our connection to our church runs throughout our family. And our church is very culturally and civically astute and active. That's another one of those really, really, really, really, really fine threads that happened to this city. When you think about what the event did, when I tell you that it was more than devastation; it was decimation that occurred.

When all of your churches go down to nothing and all of the supports seen, unseen [are] all gone, and there's no attachment, you can't talk to your pastor; you can't talk to sister and those you're used to seeing at church. Those supports, those quality-of-life kinds of issues that you're used to receiving and giving and bringing and using through your faith tradition and your churches, it's gone because everybody's gone.

Everything is gone; even the building, in some cases, is gone, and so we put so much stock in security of place, gone, gone, gone, gone. And you have to reattach yourself to someone else. And even though ideally your faith tradition is connected primarily to God, really it is connected also to those people who you are used to fellowshipping with. And in a place like New Orleans, fellowship is a good percentage of the quality of your life, even if it's not a faith fellowship, the fact that we are familial and familiar.

I like to think there are zero degrees of separation, and I don't know if you're familiar with this, but if you sit with anybody long enough, you know somebody. They know you're related to them. Period. Anybody of any culture, any race, creed, we are like that. That is one of the very connected kinds of tissue that makes New Orleans so unique.

Every church had a different experience. My pastor lives in the Bay area now. He's in town a couple times a month. He has a great background in community-organizing kinds of work. He does a lot of scholarly and theologically connected kinds of work, so it took us—it has taken us a lot of time to come back.

We met many places all throughout the immediate months after the storm. Like he ended up—he'd go to Houston one weekend, and folks who had evacuated to Houston, they would meet and have service and comradeship and support. And he'd go to Atlanta; he'd come to New Orleans; he'd come to Baton Rouge, some of the major hubs where people got dispersed to, we kept a website presence so that folks could kind of—I didn't even know what blog was, well folks could make little entries and say, "Well, this is where so and so lives and this is where so and so lives. And we're here and this is what's happened to us."

He has [done this] at the expense of his own physical ability; he's been everywhere; he goes everywhere, marrying folks and burying folks and seeing to folks because we had such a connected ministry till people keep saying, "Well pastor, you coming back?" His house was completely destroyed. His job was completely gone. The church is not in a situation where we could financially support his four boys, three of whom are in college.

He has to be someplace where he could earn a living, and his wife's business was completely taken down. She's a massage therapist and had a salon that had just recently opened in New Orleans East. Their house was completely deluged. They have a boy at [university in Florida] and another one at [university in Atlanta], another one that just graduated high school and did his first semester, starting September at a school in California, and a 13-year-old at home.

We're satisfied to have him when we can have him. His associate to him was a woman who is my mentor; she's a dynamic woman of God who is 70 years old, but in the last two years before the storm, she ended up having to have a liver transplant, so to live in this city is toxic for her right now because of her compromised immune system. She lived in Gentilly. Her entire house is gone. So she is permanently moved to Houston, so rocks, stabilizers [are gone].

This is just a microcosm of what happened in my church experience so, there were several, there was all kinds of fine threads again where ministers were in different states of shock and being and ability and inability to be. Some ministers lambasted other ministers for not coming back. "We were charged with feeding the sheep; we can't run. We have to be here at all costs, etc., etc.," and when that logic is being told, that makes so much sense, but when you look at the facts that are the lives of real people and how they are affected, other things become real truths as well.

Our ministry is back at about a third of the size that it was. Some very, very key people to the ministry are not here anymore, so then we are emerging some new leadership and some other people are stepping up.

So God gives you what you need even before you know what you need. So we have some ways that have yet to grow. The seeds are there. One of the things that our pastor always, always, always put forward was leadership development, and he would say, "I'm not planning to die, but what we have to do is plan for what this church is going to look like in 50 years and 100 years, and how we do that."

And one of the ways that he practiced that dynamic to end inculcate systems that were, anybody who served as the head of a ministry in leadership, you can do that for two or three years, but after that, you have to cycle out, so that someone else can get an opportunity to learn what that looks like and how to do that. [We did it this way] so little kingdoms were not built.

Even before she returned to New Orleans, Saundra was collaborating with other community leaders to reignite the CCRA planning initiative. She was particularly keen to ensure that members of the community would be represented in the city's redevelopment planning process.

This started very, very early on within the first two, three weeks after the storm. [We met with] state legislators because it was [as] a representation of civic, medical, cultural, nonprofit [organizations] to have a conversation [about] where we stand, who needs to get talked to, what do we need to say, how is it that we bring the energies to bear and keep our folks represented in the face of those people who would make decisions about our return and ultimately rebuild because this is at a time when people were saying that we were not going to be going back to New Orleans, and that was just not going to happen.

We needed to formulate some kind of cohesive strategy to begin to make this real to people who could not see it. I think it was really wise and brave and smart for us to begin the conversation that soon. That way our hand would stay in. Well, to have to convince people that make policy that we have to do something so different, so new, so avant-garde, for lack of a better word, in order to bring people back home . . . It's hard for me to understand why we need to convince people of that.

You do as much as you can even when it seems to be ludicrous. You keep making the point of what you consider [to be] obvious because what I had to understand was that it was not obvious.

For all the challenges the community has faced, both from the storm and from the political process surrounding the recovery effort, Saundra believes that important lessons have emerged that will guide the community and community organizers like herself through the process.

> We have to stay the course. We have to, and this is an analogy that I love because it's so New Orleans. We are like folks at a Mardi Gras parade. We have to stand in line and throw our hands up at every float that passes in hopes that we catch something, because surely if we don't go to the parade, we don't get nothing. What we mostly get is junk. But if we're not at the parade, we miss the party. We miss the party. We've got to go.[46]
>
> Rebuilding is not somebody else's job. We have to own it ourselves. [I get asked], "How do you balance all of that with family and yourself and the need to get this done?" And I've thought about it a couple of times and [I think] we have to fold in this as our real life and not just our work. To do it any other way separates the work that has to be done in our real life, and we can't separate that. We have to own it as almost the same thing and by doing that we have to include our children and our families in the explaining of how important it is and charging them to be responsible.
>
> We have to model it as a way of life. We have to also care for ourselves. Whenever I can, if I'm ever offered an opportunity to kind of step back some, I take it because I realize that when I'm in it, I'm all the way in it. And we have to understand that. One of the major components of leadership is to help develop others to do some of this because we get to the point where we think, "If I don't do it, it won't get done," and that ain't nothing but ego.
>
> [Another] of the things [I have seen come out of this process] is that we have begun to talk to people across racial, cultural, economic lines in a real, real, real clear way that we've never talked before. We got to see that even when we don't agree on everything, not even on what we want to see happen as a result of [our activism], we all had one story that we could tell and that we were sick and tired of being sick and tired.

Saundra observes that Central City has shown some signs of progress since the storm, though the recovery has been uneven. She holds out hope that the neighborhood can regain its former bustling pulse.

[Central City is rebounding] in certain places. Because there were several ridges where there was not as much water, and it's a pretty wide-ranging expanse of land; there were places that did get up to four or five feet of water in Central City. Those areas are not coming back very easily because they were already old homes in there. And understand there were three housing developments there, empty, divested of people [by] Katrina, which turned my stomach. Still does. They were already de-densified. That's a term [they] used for people— de-densified. Anyway, so [parts of] Central City [as I] stated are coming back; Uptown started coming back faster than any place. Magazine Street, for example, is not in Central City, but it is bustling more and economically vibrant than it's been in 50 years. It's just really wonderful, and I'm glad to see that. That's what I'd like to see happen on O. C. Haley.

So one of the reasons our community organizing is important is because we have to stay at those floats holding up our hands so that as they throw me something, like the beads [that] come down, we can be there to catch some of the good stuff, and some of that is [coming down]. Some of it is starting to show fruition, not enough, not fast enough, not nearly fast enough. But we are at the table and speaking aloud, and people are at least looking in our direction when we talk, paying attention.

3

GENTILLY WOODS, GENTILLY TERRACE, AND PONTCHARTRAIN PARK

G entilly has had various boundaries over the years. Older residents often think of Gentilly as including only some parts of what are now New Orleans East and the Upper Ninth Ward. Today, however, Gentilly includes the Pontchartrain Park, Gentilly Terrace, Gentilly Woods, Dillard, St. Anthony, Fillmore, Lake Terrace/Lake Oaks, and Milneburg neighborhoods. The community is bordered by Lake Pontchartrain on the north and the London Avenue Canal on the west.

This particular area was originally a shallow swamp, but it was reclaimed through the use of levees and an advanced drainage system. In 1727, lured by the booster propaganda of John Law, French colonist Mathurin Dreux and his brother Pierre chose the high ground of Bayou Sauvage (a natural levee) on which to build their plantation.[1] They named the plantation Gentilly after a commune in Paris, France, by that same name.[2] The whole area eventually came to be known as Gentilly.

The first major wave of residents, however, settled Gentilly in the mid-1900s when this area experienced a residential construction boom as part of an effort to provide accommodations for returning World War II veterans and their families. The city of New Orleans was growing, and places were needed to house the growing population. As an answer to that need, Gentilly Woods was developed in the early 1950s after the developers made an agreement with the city to extend public transportation and utilities to the community. In addition to building single-family homes, the developers set aside land for schools, playgrounds, and shopping centers. The idea was to create a complete insular neighborhood that would at the same time be integrated into the larger city through public transportation. These were all appreciated amenities, and the new development filled up quickly.

Similarly, Pontchartrain Park, which sits between five and seven feet below sea level and is bordered by Lake Pontchartrain and the Industrial Canal, is a postwar residential neighborhood in Gentilly that has the distinction of being one of the first subdivisions expressly planned and designed with the middle- and upper-class African American family in mind. The residential neighborhood is known for its "extensive open spaces and recreational amenities."[3] Although, as in every other neighborhood on the lake shore, the swamp that once filled Pontchartrain Park was pumped and drained in 1896, Pontchartrain Park's drainage project was not completed until 1940.[4] The new neighborhood, which was developed soon after the project's completion, contained single-family ranch-type homes priced from $8,000 to $16,000 on large lots bordered by curvy, paved sidewalks. At the center of the neighborhood was a beautiful, green 180-acre park that contained an 18-hole golf course, ball fields, playgrounds, and clubhouses.[5] The golf course was designed by Joe Bartholomew, a black professional golfer who was not allowed to play on public courses around the city. As a "municipal golf course," the city saw it as a response to the threat by black New Orleanians to sue the city for denying them access to the golf courses in City Park and Audubon Park. Thus, from the city's perspective, Pontchartrain Park's golf course solved a political problem. The neighborhood would eventually also contain tennis courts and its own elementary school.

An affordable residential development with such beautiful amenities for African Americans was a rarity in what was then a segregated city. At the time, zoning restrictions and standard real estate practices kept blacks out of the freshly drained areas on the lakeside. In 1924, the New Orleans City Council passed an ordinance that essentially segregated residential areas. As Colten explains, "based on a 1912 state act that authorized the city to withhold building permits for blacks in white neighborhoods and a 1924 act that prohibited blacks from establishing residence (rental or purchase) in a white community, the ordinance formalized existing racial settlement patterns and largely determined for developers which racial group they could sell to."[6] When that ordinance was overturned, deed restrictions were then used to keep neighborhoods segregated. For example, in the late 1920s in one of the recently drained lakefront neighborhoods, developer Andrew Stafford restricted resale of individual lots such that "no person not of the Caucasian race shall be permitted to reside or congregate in any structure erected on said property or any part thereof. This restriction shall not apply to domestic servants living on their master's premises."[7]

Understandably, the growing African American middle class quickly found its way to Pontchartrain Park after it opened in 1954. Indeed, Pontchartrain Park, with its internal recreational facilities and 18-hole golf course, claimed preeminence in the United States as a planned community designed for African Americans.

People moved to Pontchartrain Park because of the amenities and its modern features. Philip Baptiste, who lived in Pontchartrain Park since 1958, remarked, "It was the first time Negroes could buy what you'd call modern housing, with air conditioning."[8] Even after legal action and civil protest whittled away at segregation, and blacks had more choices about where they could live, not many moved out of Pontchartrain Park. They had moved to Pontchartrain Park in the first place because they felt it would provide a better environment for raising their families. Thus, desegregation did not significantly change the character of the neighborhood. Lawrence Guimont, a retired postal worker who raised six children in the neighborhood, grew up in New Orleans and was attracted to the development because in it he had "found a place I thought was a wholesome environment for raising a family, where you didn't have a barroom on every corner."[9]

Interestingly, as Reese and Wolf write, Pontchartrain Park made "no reference to historic Creole, to New Orleans architecture or urbanism; it is an unequivocal rejection of what had been a landscape of oppression for the African-American community."[10] Denying this connection with the city's architectural past symbolized that blacks were able to move forward socially. From this neighborhood, the Pontchartrain Park residents enhanced the reputation of their community by taking their place as civic leaders, activists, politicians, and as leaders in arts and culture.[11] Some of its most famous residents included two New Orleans' mayors, Ernest "Dutch" Morial (the first African American mayor of the city) and his son, Marc Morial; district attorney Eddie Jordan; and actor and producer Wendell Pierce as well as Grammy award–winning musician Terrence Blanchard.[12]

The Pontchartrain Park neighborhood provided middle-class blacks with the types of houses and neighborhood layout that whites enjoyed in adjacent developments and elsewhere across the city. They were the lone black settlement in the sea of whites that surrounded them. Eventually, however, Gentilly Woods would switch from being an exclusively white neighborhood to one in which most of its residents were black. In the 1960s when mandatory desegregation of public schools was enacted, "white flight" followed. Later in the 1980s, the community merged with Pontchartrain Park and began to form the collective identity of "Pontilly," sharing the recreational spaces of Pontchartrain Park and establishing the Pontilly Neighborhood Association.[13]

As of 2000, Pontchartrain Park had approximately 2,600 residents of whom 97 percent were African American. Ninety-two percent of residents owned their homes. Only 10 percent of the residents of this neighborhood were below the poverty line (half the rate of other neighborhoods in New Orleans), and the community was home to a disproportionately high number of residents holding degrees from tertiary institutions.[14] This community saw little turnover, with many parents passing along the houses they purchased to their adult children. Just prior to Katrina, the racial makeup in Gentilly Woods was more diverse. Although the majority of the population was black (68 percent), whites made up 25 percent of the population. Only 14 percent of the residents in Gentilly Woods were at or below the federal poverty line, again, a rate considerably lower than the rest of the parish.[15]

Although there is a natural high ground along Gentilly Ridge and an engineered ridge that raised the land to above sea level along the lakefront, Gentilly was badly damaged by Hurricane Katrina when strong surges sent upward of 12 feet of floodwater over the storm walls. The storm resulted in levee breaches in two different locations in the neighborhood. The waves overtopped the Industrial Canal levee (to the east).[16] When the levees of the London Avenue Canal (to the west) broke, Pontchartrain Park was flooded with 5 to 15 feet of water. It would take several weeks before the water was drained out of the neighborhood.[17] It was this water, sitting stagnant for weeks, and the resultant mold that caused the greatest damage to property in the area.

Two years after Katrina, Pontilly (Gentilly Woods and Pontchartrain Park) was showing slower rates of recovery than other neighborhoods in the Gentilly area. As the *Times-Picayune* reported, the "lowest rate of occupied or rebuilt homes, 16 percent, [is] in the Pontchartrain Park and Gentilly Wood section, reflecting, many say, myriad struggles of an older pre-Katrina population."[18]

By August of 2009, 49 percent fewer Pontchartrain Park households were receiving mail than pre-Katrina. In Gentilly Woods, the range was between 60 percent and 69 percent, and in Gentilly Terrace, between 80 percent and 89 percent of the June 2005 addresses actively receiving mail. The rate of return throughout the Pontilly region is inconsistent.[19] Yet neighborhood residents point to particular events, such as the purchase and redevelopment of the Gentilly Woods Shopping Center in 2009[20] and the opening of a brand-new Gentilly High School in January 2010, as sparks of hope.[21]

EDWARD

Edward, an 80-year-old African American man with some Native American ancestry, was born in Slidell, Louisiana, but has lived in Pontchartrain Park, a subdivision in the Gentilly area of New Orleans, for 50 years. Before the storm, he owned and serviced vending machines.

> [This land] used to be a swamp, and some land developer bought the land and developed it into lots, and they built houses here. They built a subdivision. They were building these houses for middle-class people.[22] I tried to buy a house here, and I couldn't buy a house. They said I was too young. I must have been about 19 or 20. I was too young. So I saw a sign on this lot: "For sale, by owner." I called a man. He wanted $5,000. I said, "Man, I got the money right now." I bought the lot. Then we had the house built, my wife and I. We had two children at the time. Then we had a total of four children.
>
> When I moved into here I had a truck and I was a furniture mover. I did that for 23 years before I quit that. [When we moved here] discrimination was so bad. All they wanted back here was doctors, schoolteachers, lawyers, and postal employees. And then here come an old truck driver.

Not only was Edward able to, in the face of class discrimination, buy a house in the neighborhood, but one of his best friends (his brother-in-law) moved in right next to him, and they eventually became an integral part of the neighborhood.

I knew everybody around here. In fact, . . . when those people over there grew old, I took care of them. I'd go to the grocery for them. They was old and senile. I cut their grass, kept their place manicured. I did that for these people next door, [me and] my friend, until he died.

Tightly knit neighborhood blocks within subdivisions were one facet of community. Further, a local church served to connect residents across neighboring subdivisions.

I go to church in walking distance from here, around the corner. It's called Saint Gabriel the Archangel. It was a large church. It was large enough to take care of Pontchartrain Park, Gentilly Woods, and something else. Three subdivisions was all going to church there. There's still a church there. There was always seating in the church. They all go to the same church. It is a mixed [Catholic] church. You name it, they had it: Chinese, Vietnamese, Japanese, Caucasian, Negroes. We had Hispanics and everything in there. I went to a shopping center right down the street here, a Gentilly Woods shopping center. They had a lot of shopping centers around here. Bad places that make you spend your money, if you had it.

As the first subdivision built for middle-class African Americans, the Pontchartrain Park neighborhood was different from other neighborhoods where African Americans in New Orleans typically resided.[23]

When things settled down, they had mostly schoolteachers back here. If they wasn't schoolteachers, they worked in the school system, you know? People follow people in groups. One came back and told all of them how nice it was, and then they all come. They all come, just like that. It was the nicest thing in New Orleans at the time. All they had at New Orleans at that time for blacks was shacks and bungalows, so this was the nicest thing that came about.

My wife was worse than me. She knew everybody. They formed a group back here. She called it a Rosary Guild. She was friends with the woman across the street, at the corner, around

the corner. They used to have their little things to say sometimes. Sometimes, there was 25 or 30 women in here. . . . She
had a lot of friends.

To Edward, the neighborhood started out as idyllic. Unfortunately, it changed over the years and, according to Edward, it
was a completely different neighborhood by the time Hurricane
Katrina arrived.

It was real nice neighborhood, man. It's different from night and
day the way it was before Katrina. Everybody would be passing,
laughing and knocking, "Hi, Edward. How you doing?" All of the
houses were manicured neatly. It looked like they was always
freshly painted, you know? It was nice. You didn't see a lot of
old cars broke down in the street, you know? They had no cars
parked in the street. Everybody had flowers. They had palm
trees and rosebushes.

Oh, man. Yes, indeed, [it was a good place to raise kids]. It
was remarkable. At that time, you didn't need to put any locks
on the doors. Nobody's going to come in. It was remarkable.
And we had volunteer security back here. There was only two
ways to come in here to get out. We had security down there,
two securities on the end down there.

I've been robbed in this house three times. Those little
babies that were little angels when they was smaller, they grew
up to be devils when they got big. I was here sleeping and
whatnot and a guy came in, took a pane out of a window [and
crawled] like a military crawl, coming into the bedroom. Like
a fool, I jumped up, in my pajamas. I ran him out, you know? I
could've been killed. Fortunately, that didn't happen.

[Before Katrina, there were] robberies, drugs, alcohol. You
name it, man. Most of the kids around here was on easy street.
When you find a group that don't work, they have to do something. They're gonna get in trouble, you know? But the working-
class people, you'll have no trouble with them. All they want to
do is work, bring that check home, and go to the bank. But the
ones that don't work, they want to stand around the car, smoke
whatever, and do everything easy, you know?

Edward, his wife, and their pets evacuated in the face of the storm—a fortunate choice given that their house was completely submerged under water.

Let me tell you about the storm: 9:00 Sunday morning the mayor of New Orleans came on and said, "If you haven't left New Orleans yet, please do so now. This is the real thing. Please go. All I have to tell you is, 'Please go.'" I said, "Look. Let's get out of here. Let's go."

I had four dogs. I'm a dog lover. I had three Yorkshire terriers and one Siberian husky. I paid almost $1,000 for that Siberian husky. He was beautiful. He was one of a kind. So [my wife] had made up her mind, started throwing stuff in the car, you know? I put the dogs in the car. I put her cat in the trunk, and I got all of their leashes and their food and everything put in the trunk. I got ready to pack us a basket, stuff like tuna fish, chicken in the can, crackers, and cookies. I was putting it in the car and we left.

First we went to Jackson, Mississippi. We went somewhere in Mississippi. I'm not too familiar. It was in Mississippi, right on the Georgia state line. So when I left, I went to my son-in-law's house. We stayed at his house, living in Atlanta. I left [my wife] and came back to this house that same week.

Man, you couldn't see this house. We was in a boat, you know? Every once in a while, you'd see over a rooftop. There was so much water back here. I mean, all you could see was rooftops. Rooftops and trees. Branches all over the place. This house was completely under the water.

I stayed in Atlanta three weeks. I came back here, and then I went to New Iberia. My son rented a house there, and we all stayed there. When the water went down, I came back. I swept water out of this house. We had to take all our furniture out and throw it away. I would advise anybody not to put a lot of money into furniture in New Orleans, in general, because we saw three floods in this house. Oh, it was rough. I mean, everything you worked for was cleared away. I had to throw away everything, clothes, shoes, furniture. Everything. If it wasn't nailed down, you had to throw it away. It was a mess.

Although some houses in his neighborhood have been rebuilt, and some people are back (not nearly enough in his opinion), Edward notes that things have changed, and the sadness of Katrina is never far away from the memory.

> Let me tell you something about this house over there. A lady and her husband, they died, and their grandson was living in there. He was a lawyer. He just [become] a lawyer. Him, his girlfriend, and another girl drowned in that house. They wouldn't leave, so they drowned. Now his mother's in the house. Just like this house where the truck's parked? That's [where my] friend [lived]. He drowned. He was in the house doing good, but he walked [out and to tell someone that] he needed help and that he was hungry. As he walked, the water would keep getting higher. When he stepped off the curb, [he hit] his head [and] he drowned. He drowned right there.

Edward still feels connected to his neighborhood. Even so, he claims that if he knew the struggle it would take to get on his feet again, he would have made a different choice—the choice not to come back.

> If I would've known then what I know now, I never would've rebuilt this house. I would've kept going. If I have to evacuate again, I'm not coming back. I'm too old for this. I'm 80 years old. I don't know what made me [come back]. This is home, you know? I lived here and I don't care who you are, there's no place like home. You always want to come back home. It's not always a very good thing, but you always want to come back home. I'm sorry I did it.
>
> My wife and I could have bought a house where we're staying at, a larger house than this. It had a swimming pool, three-car garage, nice big yard, fruit trees in the yard, the works. Nice lawn. I could've bought the house for $100,000, and me, like a fool, I came back here. I spent three times that much here.
>
> Everything was expensive [here]. Before I left here, before Katrina, you could buy a loaf of bread for $1.20. Now the bread costs you $2.40. You could buy a gallon of milk for two-something. Now a gallon of milk here costs you almost $5.00. People

are taken advantage of. I went out yesterday to buy two screws for a lawnmower. Two bolts. That man charged me $5 for two bolts. I told him, "Man, you got what I want, but I tell you what, I won't come here looking for nothing else."[24]

He was able to survive off of his savings, his social security, and his military pension. It has, however, been too costly for him to restart his vending machine business. Like so many of the early returnees, he did not wait for government assistance to get started.[25]

> [The insurance company] didn't treat me fair, but I'm satisfied. [The insurance inspector came in afterwards], and they surveyed the damage. I mean, they treated me all right. What I got out of this place, I got about $130,000. It wasn't enough to rebuild, refurnish, and get everything that I need. I bought insurance for all of that. I bought insurance for the contents. [But] I was able to bounce back right quick. I didn't wait for the Road Home. I didn't wait for FEMA or Red Cross or anything. I just came, and I went to work and got this house back together, you know?

When he did finally apply for assistance through the Road Home program, his claim was denied. He believes that the process for administering rebuilding assistance was unfair and arbitrary.

> I've been waiting a year and a half [for Road Home.] They told me I'm disqualified [and I reapplied]. I got [a response]. I didn't expect anything from [the government]. You gotta take care of yourself. That's why I paid off on this house with the insurance money. I ran out so fast. I spent all of my savings and all my insurance money trying to get back to where I'd like to be. But it's okay.
>
> It looked like the people that are getting the money don't need the money. I've got a daughter-in-law, she's not my daughter-in-law, but she lives with my son. She's a doctor. All the money . . . they gave her $100,000 for being a doctor, and they gave her another $100,000 and something to fix their house. They had no water in the house.

Because he had so little funds and because of untrustworthy contractors, Edward, like many other returnees, had to do much of the work himself.

> I had a Latin American [that we] picked up at a truck stop. [He] came here for two days [to help us gut the place]. We was finished in two days, and then we had to wash it out and everything. I've been doing most of [the work on this house] myself. My son and I. The contractor we hired was for air conditioning, the electrical, and the plumbing. But all the woodwork and the Sheetrock and the painting and the trowelling, we did that ourselves. It was too expensive [otherwise].
> When you're poor, you learn a lot of things.

JACKIE

Jackie is an African American woman in her early to mid-60s who has lived with her husband in Gentilly for close to 20 years.[26]

> I've lived right in this same house close to 20 years. Me and my husband. Didn't raise any of our children here. Our youngest son, he's 38, and he's married and gone. When we bought the house, there wasn't that many kids because all the kids were pretty much grown and just about gone. But the neighborhood was always kept, you know? The lawns were always kept nice. It was always a very quiet area. Quiet and clean, and the neighbors . . . we would look out for one another, like watching one another's houses and stuff. A girlfriend of mine, she passed after Katrina, was by herself. So whenever she went anywhere and stayed a little longer than normal, she would always call us, me and my husband, to say, "I'm on my way home. Look out for me." We'd watch her from my bedroom to see that she got in safely. Ms. Sheila's been around here about 35 years. Betty's been around here close to 35 years. They got a couple of them who are still in the area for at least 30-some-odd years. Over 30 years, actually.
> We never really had neighborhood barbecues. I mean, me and my friend, the one I told you who passed, her and I did that. With my family, whenever I had anything with my family

here in the backyard, she was always invited. Whenever she had anything, I was always invited.

Like many residents, Jackie recalls the racial history of the neighborhood. And according to Jackie, the neighborhood was a good place to live before Katrina.

At one time, years ago, we weren't even allowed back here. Blacks bought in Pontchartrain Park, not Gentilly Wood. I mean, I remember when you couldn't come back this way. You pass on Chef [Highway]. But when the blacks start moving in this area, the white people start moving out. It's predominantly a black area now. If you find whites, you're going to find very, very few.

There's only one white woman who lives on the corner house. But she's the only one that didn't leave. They had two that used to [live] further up the street. Their houses are torn down [after Katrina]. One lady, she was real old, she really wanted to come back, but her kids, they said they wouldn't let her come back because they [worried] about her living alone, you know? She wanted to come back to her house, yeah, but they said no, [worried about her] being by herself.

Thank God, in this area, we don't usually have any problems. If we do, it must be swept under the rug. So that we don't know about it, you know? But so far, on a whole, this is a pretty good [neighborhood]. Even my relatives, when they come, nobody wants to leave. They say, "Oh, I like it around here. It's so clean, and it's so quiet. It's so this and that." So I said, "Well, it always was like that, from the time we moved here."

I guess because the people really try to keep their property and stuff like that for one thing. They keep their lawns manicured. At one time, before Katrina, they were saying that they were going to start giving out prizes or what have you for the best-kept [lawn].

We have a neighborhood association. As a matter of fact, my little daughter, the one I call my daughter, she is considered the captain now. She was saying the other day, she's got to start going from house to house and get the neighbors' names and addresses and telephone numbers. They would get everybody's name, address, phone number, and stuff like that. Then they would run them off, and they'd give everybody a copy. So then

I see something or see somebody strange, they tell you. They used to tell you, if you see anybody strange in the neighborhood who don't belong in this area, there's numbers to call. So pretty much on the whole, everybody gets along, and we don't have any problems, thank God.

Unlike the New Orleans East MQVN neighborhood, there was no single neighborhood church that attracted everyone in Gentilly. Rather, Gentilly residents were much more religiously diverse.

Everybody here attends different churches. You have some that's Catholic, and there's some that's different. My neighbor on this side, she's a Jehovah Witness. I think they may have more Baptists than Catholics. My husband and I attend Corpus Christi Catholic Church. We could go right there to St. Gabriel, which would be closer, but I kept my membership at Corpus Christi. I'm born and raised right there. They did everything, my first communion, confirmation, got married there and all. I was christened there, too.

The most devastating hurricane in Jackie's memory was Hurricane Betsy.[27]

During Betsy, I was living in an apartment on Saint Anthony Street, down in the Seventh Ward, not here. I had a girlfriend of mine, Helen. She let us over there. What they did, her husband and my husband, they took a piece of board, and they put it from her window to my kitchen window. We had to go out the window to get in her house. That's what we did to get stuff like out of my house. If you'd have opened the front door, more water would've got in. We already had water. Lord have mercy. We went, the first night, to John School on Long Island. We stayed in there a night. Then the next day, we came and we stayed at her house. Well, . . . I was on the ground, just like this. But her house was leveled up. So we stayed there until the water started getting lower. That was [Betsy], but Betsy wasn't a turn in the pot for this, for Katrina.

Jackie had to be convinced by friends and family members to evacuate. She indicates that she may have thought the hurricane was more serious if the media had given the advice to evacuate earlier than they did. Eventually, however, she was convinced to go to higher ground.

Me and my husband, we kept watching the news. I kept saying, "I don't understand this because if this thing is going to be as bad as the people are saying it's going to be, why haven't they told us to evacuate?" So Marvin said, "I don't know." Several of the people started getting together, and they started leaving, you know? So one of my cousins, she called me and she said, "Are you evacuating?" I said, "I'm not gonna do anything." So she said, "No, this thing is coming, girl, and it's gonna be bad." I said, "Oh, girl, this thing ain't gonna be bad. We'll just sit here. There ain't gonna be nothing." So she said, "No, you got to go."

I said, "Well, if I go anywhere, I'll go to my youngest son's house because he has an upstairs." He called [and said] "Momma, you can't stay there. You're all right on the ground and if that water comes through." I said, "You all ought to cut that performing out. This thing ain't gonna be nothing." He said, "Oh yeah, Ma. This thing is gonna be something." So I said, "I don't know what news we're listening to."

So we ran outside, and my neighbors, you know, people started to get together and they were leaving. I said, "We better leave." So my little daughter, she said, "Well, Ms. Jackie, what are you all gonna do?" So I said, "Well, more than likely, we'll go by my son. What are you all going to do?

She said, "We're not going. We're going to stay." I said, "Well, my husband wants to stay, and I told him if he stayed, I'll stay." He said, "No, you're not staying. I'm bringing you by our son." So I said, "No, you're not bringing me anywhere. If you're gonna stay, I'm gonna stay." So . . . he finally made up his mind. He said, "Jackie, pack us a little bag. Just get my pajamas and get your gown or whatever and a change of clothes because, more than likely, we'll probably be back home tomorrow morning."

So I did what he said. I packed a little bag. We went by my son. Everything was fine. He lives in Gentilly but not this area. So we all were sitting out for as long as we could look at the television. I kept talking to my neighbor across the street, a really good guy, we're very close. Ricky would call me, and I would call Ricky. I said, "How's everything up at your home?" And he said, "Everything is fine."

So the last phone call I got from Rick, he told me, "Ms. Jackie, guess what?" I said, "What?" He said, "You know that tree you always wanted down?" I said, "Not my big tree in front of my door." It was huge. I said, "Ricky, don't tell me that tree came down." He said, "No, not that one. Thank God. The one next door to you." It used to make a lot of mess and stuff. I hated that little tree, God forgive me. He said, "You don't have to worry about it now. It came down."

I said, "Oh, that's good." We started laughing. So he said, "I don't know if it's good or not." I said, "Don't tell me that tree came on my house, Rick." So he said, "No, but it's on your driveway. It's knocked all your wires out and everything." So if I would've been here, I would've been the first without power. So I said, "Oh, my God. Oh well."

So not long after that, after he had called to tell me that, I tried to get him and I couldn't get him. So I don't know what it was with the communication. I guess the phones was out. That was the end of him and I communicating. After the storm really did hit, I don't know where he had went, didn't know where Cynthia and them went, or what they did if they did wind up staying.

We stayed in New Orleans two days after Katrina. So we were really here for about three days. Finally, the best part about it, we were at my son's house, looking at the television. Nobody would budge. Everybody was looking at the television. All of a sudden, . . . I told my daughter-in-law it felt like the house was shaking.

So anyway, we're at my son and my daughter-in-law's. While the hurricane was going on, I said, "Oh, Lord. I see what you mean. This is gonna be a bad one. You all felt that? The house is shaking." I was getting afraid. So they were laughing at me. I said, "Don't laugh, you all, because that's not funny." So after that, all of a sudden, everything got calm and quiet. So I said, "Oh, thank you Lord. We made it through." Well, we did make it through the storm, but then the levees broke.

Honey, my son happened to go downstairs, because you could leave from out of his dining room and go downstairs. When you went out on those steps, that's where my daughter-in-law had a beauty shop. When he put his feet down a couple of steps, he said, "Oh, my God." So he turned around and came back in the living room by us. I said, "Oh, what's the matter?" He said, "Mom, I hate to tell you. We got water here." I said, "You got water in the house?" Well, we hadn't gotten it in the living room. I said, "You got flooding?" He said, "Oh, yeah, and it's steadily coming. Where is all this water coming from?" We couldn't understand it. So when we look out the window, it looked like Lake Pontchartrain. I said, "Oh, my God. What is this?" Well, we didn't know nothing about no levees. "Oh," I said, "Lord, what are we gonna do?"

Well, they all know how I am. I get so nervous, and I panic, and I go to crying and all this kind of stuff. So he said, my son then, he didn't know what to do. He said, "Oh, my God. What should we do?" So everybody was in the same situation. We didn't know what to do. So he said, "Well, I guess we'll go upstairs." There was no water upstairs. It wasn't that high, yet, in the house. So we wind up staying in his house that night. Then the next morning, he said, "Pack your bags because we're leaving." I said, "Where are we going?" A friend of his, Mr. Dan, had told Oliver, my youngest son, whatever you decide to do, let me know. He stayed home, too.

When the levees broke and the water started to rise, it became obvious that Jackie and her family would need to evacuate. They were able to find aid from her family friends as well as from strangers.

So what we did, we all packed up. It was me, my husband, my son, his wife, their two children, the girl across the street and her fiancé, and her two brothers. So that was 10 of us. Then we had another couple, a young lady who lived on the corner. Her and her fiancé and their two big, old dogs. So we all got into the boat.

So we all got on the bridge there. Then we walked. So we got on at the Elysian Fields all the way down to the Super-dome exit. I couldn't go anymore. We weren't exactly to the

Superdome exit. We still would've had to walk further, but we were just about there. I couldn't make it. I started crying, and I was nervous. I said, "You all go ahead because I can't go no more."

Temperatures were over 90 degrees Fahrenheit in the days following Katrina. The heat and the lack of water posed a serious health risk to those stranded in New Orleans following the storm.

You see, I probably would've been able to do it, but it was so hot. We didn't have no water. You're lugging these bags and stuff like that, and I just knew. "You're all going to wind up picking me up off the ground. You all go and leave me. If you all get any kind of assistance, you can come back and see about me."

"No, we ain't leaving you. You must be crazy, mom." So me and my husband stayed, and my son said, "Well, I'm going to go see if I can get some kind of help or find out what's going on." So he brought his wife, his family, and the other girl and her little brother. So they all went . . . to the convention center. See, we didn't know anything about all this stuff that people were saying about the convention center and the Superdome and all this kind of stuff. We didn't know.

So then a guy came, standing on the bridge next to me, a young fellow. He said, "Miss." I said, "What, dear?" He said, "Would you look over the bridge?" I said, "No. I'm afraid to look over the bridge." Well, he said, "If you did look, they got bodies floating. It looks like hundreds of bodies." I said, "Oh, my God." Why would this boy come stand by me and tell me this? So I said, "Oh, Lord have mercy." Well, that did something to me.

We're sitting on the bags, and here comes this truck. It's a brand-new truck, and it was coming fast. So I told my husband, "Well, I wonder what fool this is driving a truck fast like that with all these people up here." We did have two people that were very nice. Two different families gave us one bottle of water. So we had to divide that bottle of water—including me, my husband, the dog, and the girl's brother and everybody else.

So I said, "Honey, I love ice water." That water was so hot but it tasted like ice water to me that day. So here comes this truck. Finally, when they pull up in front of us and I see my son jumped out the back. So I said, "Whose is this?" So I come to find out there was a friend of his who was a cop. He said, "Momma, come on. I met a friend of mine. He's going to bring us to the convention center wherever we need to go." That's what he said. So they packed all the bags, and they put me in the front. Of course, the boy did have his air conditioning on. They had two other cops in the thing, too.

So we get all the way there and my son said, "Okay." So I got out, and I was thanking the guy because on the way going, he kept looking, you know, you can feel a person looking at you. The guy who was driving was a young fellow. He's looking at me, and I'm looking at him. So I said, "I guess you're wondering why the lady's looking at you." He said, "No. I thought maybe, I was looking at you, too, because your face looks so familiar." I said, "Yours does, too."

The generosity of strangers was something that Jackie experienced over and over again.

So we're talking. He said his name, don't even ask me the child's name because I couldn't tell you. Anyway, when he said it, I said, "The name doesn't really ring a bell. Where are you from?" So when he said, "In the Ninth Ward." So I said, "I bet I got to know your people." But he said, "But Miss, you're Oliver's mother, but your face looks so familiar." I said, "Wait a minute. I have a nephew who's a policeman."

He said, "Oh, you do? What's his name?" I said, "Ernest." So he says, "I thought I knew your face. Ernie looks just like you." So he started laughing. I said, "Yeah, everybody said that." I said, "Do you know Ernie's dad?" He said, "Yes, I do." He said, "You know, Ernie looks like his daddy, but you and Ernest's daddy look just alike." I said, "Of course, we're sister and brother." So we laughed about it. After I got out, I was saying, "We certainly appreciate that." So just when I was getting ready to start walking, he called my son. He said, "Oliver, go get Shelley," that's my son's wife. He said, "Go get Shelley and your family. Where are you all going? What are you all going to do?" So we said we didn't know. So he said, "Well, I'm going to bring you all as far as Baton Rouge," because I think he had to go to Baton Rouge. So I said this was an angel God sent us. David had [the front seat] in that four by four. I was in the backseat. There was one guy, myself, and then the girl's brother. The other two sat in the front, my son and myself, plus about 10 or 12 of them in the back.

We had our two dogs. My son's dog and our little dog. They went through all of that. So he brought us to Baton Rouge, and when we got to Baton Rouge, I was able to call my son-in-law in Corpus Christi, Texas. My children were looking all over for us. They didn't know where we were. They couldn't locate us, so we let them know where we were. So [my son-in-law] said, "I'll be there tomorrow morning to pick you all up."

Some man we don't know, but he was very, very nice, he just took us and tried to help us. He said, "I'm going to try and get help for you all, put you all in one of the shelters or what have you." So he tried, and every shelter he called was full. So he [took us to] a restaurant. He said, "You all got to get something to eat." "Do you all have money?" We said, "Yeah, we have money. We can eat."

So me and my husband, we stayed on the outside of the restaurant with the dogs, and we told them, "You all go eat, and we'll get something after." Maybe let them bring a hamburger or something out or whatever. So we're standing out there and here comes the people just walking up to us. "Are you from New Orleans?" I said, "Well, I don't know who we look like," but they sure could tell. So we said, "Yeah."

I went in the restaurant because I had to use the restroom, and [a lady] was in there. She said, "Oh, I know your face." I said, "Oh, you do?" She said, "Aren't you from New Orleans?" I said, "Yes, I am." She said, "You used to work at so-and-so's?" She named a couple. I said, "Not me." So she said, "Oh, baby, I know your face." I said, "Oh, yeah? You must be taking me for somebody else." She said, "I don't know." Well, honey, after I was out, the lady hadn't come out yet. But her son walked up to me, and he said, "I want to give you something. Please don't tell me no thank you or whatever because at a time like this, you could use it."

So the man pulled out two $100 bills and put them in my hand. I didn't know what it was because I didn't even look. So I said, "Oh, thank you so much. We certainly appreciate that." Well, when his momma come out, she told him, "Oh, I know that lady." I said, "Oh, here she goes again." So the man came back and gave me another $100. We had several people just come and help us, giving us money. We didn't ask anybody for anything, but the people did all that. This other guy told us, "I'm not going to leave you all. Let me call such-and-such a church." He called them. They were booked. So he said, "Oh, Lord have mercy. If I have to take you all home with me, you're all not going to stay out here." He was some kind of big-shot man.

So he said, "Let me try this one here." So he calls them, and I don't know who he talked to, but they said they could put us up. Well, when we got there, we had the dogs, of course. They didn't want dogs. So we told them, well, you all go get some rest, and we're sleeping on the floor because they didn't have no cot. They didn't have no bed. They didn't have no pillow. So I knew I wasn't going to sleep no how.

They had a garage. It was a double garage, and it was open. So me and my husband sat right on the end. He was holding my son's dog, and I'm holding our dog. The dogs were sleeping. They were even snoring. We were watching the dogs, and we sat up all night. We didn't sleep, but the next morning, thank God, my son-in-law was there with one of his workers in another truck. It was a big Suburban thing.

So they both came and picked us up. We made it to Corpus Christi. Everybody was happy then because you're around your family. So we stayed by my daughter. Everybody got showers and stuff like that. But, . . . me and my husband and my son and his family [stayed with my daughter] for three and a half months. The kids went to schools out there. Then my son works for the post office, so he had to come back home. They required him to come back to New Orleans.

When they came back, they were happy with the speed at which FEMA supplied them with a trailer. But the condition of their property and their neighborhood left them devastated.

Naturally, we all came back together. We stayed at his house for about two weeks. God blessed me and my husband again. We got our trailer in no time. So I said, "Oh, thank God. But, how are we going to stay in the trailer? It ain't got no electricity?" It was cold. So we stayed in the trailer maybe two nights. The guy across the street was back, and my neighbor down the block and her husband were back. We were back. We were the only three in this area. Nobody else was back. No more trailers. No more nothing. When it got dark, please believe me, it got dark.

This neighborhood looked like a total disaster. I cried. My house, sometimes I can talk about it good, and sometimes I can't. It just hurt me to my heart when I saw my house and saw all my things. I lost all my photo albums. I must have had about 10 of them. Pictures of my mother, pictures of my children, myself when I was a kid. I mean, pictures like that, you can never replace. The neighborhood—oh, my God. I mean, you look at this neighborhood now, and you say, "Doesn't look like they went through Katrina." If you'd have saw it, you knew we went through Katrina. Then the water stayed back here in this area for about three weeks.

We weren't even allowed back here. You couldn't come back here. But my husband and my son made a trip to New Orleans, and my son was able to get in the area. Him being a security officer for the post office, they let him and his daddy through. That was after the water went down. They came and they checked on our house and their house.

My husband, I made him take the camera. I said, "Take pictures. Don't forget to take a picture of this, and don't forget to take a picture of that." Of course he wouldn't take them because they didn't want me to know how bad all of it really was. But I had my mother's bedroom set, which was about 50-some-odd years old. It looked like it was painted brand new because my mother kept her things. My husband wouldn't tell me for a long time. I said, "I can't believe my ma's set just fell apart." He said, "Jackie, you realize that water stayed back there." Finally, he told me. He said, "Baby, your momma's dresser, it just split in half. You wouldn't have wanted to see it." My little kitchen there, they did take pictures. My refrigerator was upside down. My sister and them, they came to New Orleans before I did. By me being a cancer patient, they didn't want me in the area because of the fumes and stuff. I wasn't allowed to inhale all that kind of stuff, you know?

They wouldn't tell me the details that I really wanted to know. Like my husband said, "Jackie, nothing in the house is worth saving. It's all gone." Even after we got this house together, you're going on, I'm sitting on talking to you, and something might run across my mind. Oh, yeah, girl, I have that. Then I have to think about it. Oh, I had that. I had it.

Although the FEMA trailer was in place, the infrastructure necessary to live a normal functioning life was not.

We were lucky. We got that trailer and after we got it, it was cold. I said, "Ninny,[28] you can't stay in the trailer. It's too cold." So he said, "It was cold, but I was all right." So I said, "If he's going to stay in the trailer, I'm going to stay in the trailer with him." Well, honey, the first night, I froze. He said, "Jackie, you can't stay in here. You're going to have to go back and stay by Ness," my son. So I went back to my son's house and stayed that night. The next day, I think it was, we went and bought a generator. Then we were able to stay until we got our electricity. We were in the trailer, I would say, maybe about 10 months. We were blessed. We were truly blessed through it all.

Jackie and her husband, like so many others, were not satisfied with their insurance payout. They were also dissatisfied with the way the Road Home program distributed the funds. Yet they consider themselves blessed—blessed but frustrated.

Well, we had flood insurance, so that helped us, but as far as the homeowner's, that wasn't much of a help. Every penny we got from flood, you can see where we put it. Everything was down to the bare walls. Road Home gave us a little something, but right now, I'm trying to fight them again because I don't think it was fair because from what they're saying, they should not have used your homeowner's and also your FEMA [against you]. I mean, FEMA didn't give me any money. Some people did wind up getting money from FEMA, but we didn't get anything from FEMA [for this house].

Oh, yeah. They gave us rent assistance. So I think they gave us one check but they were supposed to send another check or something. I told the lady, "We really don't need that because we're going to be going." You know? I mean, why take something if you really don't need it? That don't make no sense, you know? So like I said, on the whole, I think we did considerably good with the help of God. Yes, ma'am. But they were saying, lately, that they shouldn't have used your FEMA and your home-owner's [against you]. They should not have deducted that and they did. You see?

Like I said, I didn't have anything from FEMA. [I only got a] little chump change that my homeowner's gave me; they shouldn't have put that against me. My little friend across the street, the one I call my daughter, she said, "Ma, you got to appeal it."

I said, "Girl, their people ain't going to do anything, tell me they ain't got no money one minute. They're telling you to appeal and all this kind of crap." They told people they were going to help them with shutters and all that kind of stuff. They haven't helped nobody with nothing.

We didn't even have any savings. Then we have to find a living because my husband is retired. We're on a fixed income. I'll put it like that. That's not great. My husband, he used to work at the New Orleans Country Club. He was a laborer, cleaning up. Yeah.

Oh, yeah. The only thing I really don't have is [a new roof]. We need a new roof. It's not that the roof is leaking, but the roof is old, and you're looking at it from a distance, if another hurricane came through here, that's it. I don't think that roof could take it. I was blessed, you know?

When we spoke to Jackie in October 2007, her neighborhood had not yet fully recovered. Not everyone has returned. Those who have returned have had difficulty, like so many others in New Orleans, finding a trustworthy and competent contractor.

We were the only three on this block, us, Ricky, and O'Neal. Then, gradually, people started coming back. People were coming every day, trying to check on their property. The older guy, I don't know if he's coming back or not, but I know he's been working on his house. The house next to it, they said the last time I seen them in the area, they said they were waiting on Road Home to get their house together. But I think, pretty much, the rest of the people, you know?

We didn't do the work ourselves. We hired people. My husband can't do it like he used to. You see him out there, but he's not a well person anymore. Like I said, with his age, and plus he's a diabetic. So that's why I got to watch him. Every now and then, I make him stop. Not that he wants to. He can't be out in that sun. He's 66 years old. I said, "You can't do what you did when you were 26." You know what I'm saying?

But the first guy I hired, well, I think he probably got over on me because I would have to check my books to see exactly what stuff it was that I paid. I didn't see where he was doing that much and then, "Oh, well, Miss Jackie, I need blah, blah, blah [and] you know, you were supposed to." I said, "I was? Do I look like Whitney or National? Which one?" That's the banks.

I said, "Honey, I don't have no money to just give you like that. I don't see where you're progressing, you know?" So, I had it out with him, and I just told him to go and don't come back. So I got rid of him. Then I got another fool. I mean, I look at so many flaws where they just sunk us. They just took our money, you know?

I talk about my bathroom wall and my kitchen wall. I could've done a better job with that Sheetrock, but you want to get in your house. But I can't see just giving you my money. You know what I'm saying? Who do you know that just has money to give away?

Then the man did the garage because the garage opened up like an accordion from the water. The man that did it, it was only down, maybe about five to six weeks at the most. It's got a crack. Then they did the patio. They got a crack in that. You know? I got in contact with the man, and I asked him—I said, "Well, what do you intend on doing?" So he said, "Well, there's nothing I can do."

I said, "So you're telling me it's my loss and your gain? You got my money and that's it?" He said, "Well, concrete will crack." So I had what they call an expert or whatever. The man came and he looked at it. He's a tester, in other words. He said, "If I were you, I'd call my contractor back and let him know." He had told me and my husband what to tell him. I did, and the man jumped all over me and told me the man don't have the right to tell me that because he don't know nothing about cement, as far as putting it down. I said, "I don't know what he

know, but it's one of the people you recommended me to call."
The tester did tell me, "If he won't accept it by word of mouth,
I'll put it in writing for him." Of course, for him to put it in writing, it costs me X amount of dollars. So I'm waiting for that. I
guess that won't come before Monday or Tuesday or whatever,
if it don't get lost in the mail. So once I get it, I'll call him again
and see what he says. But, he don't have no intentions of
redoing it. He's lying.

Whoever you're going to hire, make sure they are licensed
contractors.[29] Okay? You can't be away from your house when
they're working on it, like being in another state or even—if
you're here in this city and a contractor's working on your
house, you need to come every day and check on it to see how
you're progressing. Keep up with them.

Jackie continues to insure her home but at a higher rate
because of a misunderstanding and misfiled claims with her
insurance company.

My insurance policy is higher. It's totally ridiculous. Like I told
my husband, . . . nobody knew how long they're going to be
here because we all are starting to get older now, and I don't
know, with the income that we have, how long we're going
to be able to pay these high premiums. It is ridiculous. What
they did, my flood insurance, I was paying $207 for the year,
and after Katrina, they jumped it from $207 to $565 or $567
for the year.

Well, they claimed the reason why they did that, if you have
two or more claims. I told them, "I didn't have no two or more
claims." So when they went back, I had a claim in 2004, but
it wasn't a flood claim. I had some pipes from a freeze that'd
broken in the walls, and that was the first to be on the homeowner's insurance. When the adjuster came, I told him, "This
goes under homeowner's, right?" He said, "Oh, yes, ma'am."

They claimed he put it under flood. Then I had to use it
again, you see, for Katrina. So that's what made it change. I
tried to get help with that because if I don't have the money
to pay it and another hurricane comes through, well, it's just
my loss.

Jackie notes that after the storm, the neighborhood is now made up of younger people, which is a positive change from her perspective. Her neighbors tend to look after one another more.

> But that's what they were talking about since we had Katrina. Everybody, even though we look out for one another [before Katrina], everybody also come closer together and maybe do things like neighborhood get together [after the storm]. They were talking about barbecuing and stuff like that, just having a little gathering with the ones that want to participate. If you don't want to participate, so be it. They can't make you do it, you know? On the whole, everybody pretty much gets along pretty good.
>
> The neighborhood has more children now. I mean, in one house, the son bought his mother's house. She didn't want to come back, so him and his wife and their kids are there. Then across from them, there's another couple. They're renting, but just about everybody around here own their houses.[30] But this couple here, a young couple, they moved away, but he fixed his house up and he's renting it out. That lady has children. There's quite a few kids back in the block, compared to what we had.

All but Jackie's youngest child live out of state. However, she has been able to find companionship within her neighborhood since Katrina.

> My husband and I grew up in New Orleans. I lived on one street. He lived around the corner. We couldn't stand one another. We laugh about that to this day. I said, "Lord, I never thought I'd see the day that we'd be together." He said, "I did." So he knew better than me.
>
> My daughter and her husband, they used to come regularly. But they're in Texas. They used to be in Corpus Christi, but her husband is getting ready to retire from the Coast Guard. So they built a house in Katy, Texas.
>
> My little girlfriend who's a neighbor of mine, she's like a daughter, like a second daughter because she doesn't have her mother and father. She must be about 49. We became very, very close since Katrina. I said, "Well, I'm your momma

now." She said, "That's true. Well, you be my momma, and your husband—well, he will be my daddy." She calls me mom sometimes. She lives right across the street. Yeah, sweet person, you know? She owns the house and all [and lives with] her husband and their son.

The retail stores that served the neighborhood before the storm were slow to return after Katrina.

I wish they would put up another grocery store. The ones we have, the prices are totally ridiculous. I used to go to Economical, which they've torn down. They're not coming back. It's a family business, and one of their stores is located in Metairie. But you want something closer. Then I had another little favorite store of mine, which was Ferrara [Supermarket].[31] They tore that down, too. Those people are not coming back. It wasn't big stores like Winn-Dixie, Saver Center, and stuff like that. That's really what we need. A little, small grocery store where you could buy different things, even your meats and stuff sometimes. Ferrara was one of the best meat markets. It wasn't a very big store, but they sold beautiful meat. We're not meat lovers, but I would buy veal a lot from them. That was privately owned, just like Economical. They weren't great, big stores, but you could find anything you needed in there. But that Winn-Dixie we got now, the prices are just ridiculous.

In spite of all the challenges that she has had to overcome, Jackie never considered not returning to New Orleans. This is the place of her roots, and those roots run deep.

The only thing I could say is the people back here wanted to come home. Everybody, I mean, all these people, they're like us. All we know is New Orleans. Born and raised in New Orleans. My mother died at 75. My grandmother died at 102. My mother's mother, and long before that. That's where they all come from is New Orleans. My husband's family, too. That's why I am back.

EASTON

Easton is not a native of New Orleans but is married to one. He is originally from Lake Charles, Louisiana, and moved to New Orleans around 1999.

Me and my wife live here, and I got two daughters. They both went to Loyola. They're both nurses. My youngest daughter was just graduating when Katrina hit. She had just graduated, and she didn't get her license yet. We ended up in Gonzalez. During the month and a half that we were out in Gonzalez, she studied for her state license. Then she got her license to be a nurse there.

I've been with Budget Rent-a-Car at the airport about 8 years. Altogether, I've been with them 11. I was a manager in California for 3 years for Budget Rent-a-Car. Then when I moved back to New Orleans, first of all, let me say this, I'm not from New Orleans. My wife is from New Orleans. I'm from Lake Charles, Louisiana.

As a matter of fact, I got married eight years ago in 2000. I moved back here to New Orleans eight years ago, and I decided to downsize myself. I went to barber school. I'm also a licensed barber. Budget wanted me to be a manager. I said, "No, I'm going to barber school." So I went to barber school full time. I became a licensed barber after a year and a half.

I just stayed driving the Budget shuttle bus for benefits, for hospitalization, 401(k) stuff. So that's where I'm at with Budget and what I was doing before the storm and after the storm. But I got 20 years' supervising experience. I also graduated from college with business administration and marketing.

My wife is a branch manager for Chase, right here in New Orleans, in New Orleans East. Like I said, we met eight years ago when I moved back here.[32] We moved into this house. We own it now. Yeah. We didn't own it before Katrina.[33] We owed about $30,000, and thank God we had homeowner's and flood insurance. What the insurance gave us, we paid off the final note. Now we're working on trying to redo it. We haven't got anything from Road Home. I don't know what the holdup is with that, but you hear a lot of people are having problems with Road Home because of various reasons.

Like many people in New Orleans, they maintained strong social ties through their church, and many of their social activities revolved around the church and church-affiliated organizations.

> We spent a lot of our time at St. Paul's, our church. I'm a Knight of Peter Claver, and we always had some function to do at church. I also had a part-time job before the storm. I worked two jobs. I also worked for New Orleans Daiquiri. I was a doorman where you check IDs. This was right here on Bienville and Covington, in what they call it the uptown area.
>
> So me and my wife kind of stayed busy. She didn't really like that I got a part-time [job], I come in and I'm gone. Sunday evenings, I worked there. The reason why I had a part-time job is because I got a 1949 Chrysler that I was restoring. I just kind of did it for extra money. So I stayed busy, pretty much so I couldn't tell you about any neighborhood functions. I got a couple friends now down the street, but it's been since Katrina.
>
> A couple families, they're real nice that I spoke to. I walk all the time, every morning. I'll take this little 30-minute walk. I always spoke to a lot of people, but I didn't really know them personally. It's just like [one of my neighbors]. I never went in his yard. I never talked to him. We might've stopped and talked for a few minutes, but nothing like now. So I don't know about any community functions or nothing like that.

Easton had to convince his wife that evacuation was necessary.

> Katrina didn't hit until the Monday or something. I called my wife and spoke to her. I think I was going to be at the Daiquiri shop [where I worked part time] until 2:00 that night. It closed at a 2:00 on Saturday night.[34] I called her. They decided to close the club. I called her prior to coming home. I said, "Look, we're leaving tonight." She didn't want to leave. The funny thing about it, her and my daughter didn't want to leave, but neither one of them could swim. So I'm like, "How are you all going to stay here?" You got to keep in mind, nobody's thinking about no water coming in.
>
> Me and her kind of went back and forth. I told her, "Look, if you all are not ready when I get home, I'm leaving." I had my

mind made up. I was leaving. Now, like I said, I'm from Lake Charles, where Rita hit. So that's where we left for, my mother lives in Lake Charles.

So I got home, and sure enough, they were ready. The bags were packed. I was serious. She heard it in my voice. I wasn't going to wait until the last minute. So anyway, I left from the Daiquiri shop, got home. We packed a few things, and we took off. We headed to Lake Charles.

As a matter of fact, it was ironic because my class reunion was the same weekend, so that kind of threw all that off. We were supposed to be going to Lake Charles anyway that weekend for my class reunion. I didn't even do that. I got to Lake Charles. As a matter of fact, I stopped before, right outside of Lake Charles, a little town called Iowa.

My first cousin had been calling me, "Man, when are you coming home to visit my parents and us? Why don't you all stop here when you come?" So I stopped at my cousin's house, right outside of Lake Charles, about six miles. We stayed there, and I called my mom and told her where we were. We kind of rode it out there. This is Saturday. So Sunday, the next morning, we jumped up real early because we wanted to beat the crowd back.[35] When we left Saturday night, the traffic flowed pretty good. I would say Baton Rouge is normally an hour drive from here. It might've taken about an hour and a half. So it wasn't bad, but they did have a lot of traffic. The next morning, we said, "We're going to jump up real early." We left my cousin about 7:00. We got to Laplace, the state line.

I did talk to my neighbor the Saturday night. He stayed a couple of houses down. I had their home phone number, and I talked to him. As a matter of fact, I talked to him during the morning when Katrina was hitting, and he was telling me, "Man, we're in here, scared. It sounds like a freight train."

He was in the house, him and his mother and his brother. He said, "Man, I could hear a lot of noise." He said, "It's just a lot of noise, but I don't see any water." This is the night or morning Katrina hit or whatever. I mean, nothing but wind and whistling. He said he can hear stuff popping. Well, I lost contact with him later on that night. The phones died.

Anyway, so we're thinking, as far as we know, everything's all right because the next morning we left to come back. We get here Monday morning, right at the state line, early, about 8:30, 9:00, and the guy said, "You're all not going in because the levees broke."[36] Well, we had no idea the levees broke. "What do you mean?"

He said, "Well, the city is flooding." I said, "What?" We didn't even know because the last of the news we had, the storm was going on. We got up early that morning and didn't look at the news. We just shot out, trying to beat traffic. So we had no idea the levees had broken until we got to Laplace, right outside of New Orleans.

They wouldn't let us in. They're turning people around. Then we went back as far as Gonzalez, which is about 30 minutes from Laplace, 12 miles outside of Baton Rouge. My wife's uncle stayed there. We stopped, and we ended up there, staying with him because it was only him and his wife. His wife, she was terminally ill and bed-ridden.

Easton and his family spent their time away with family. There they met with even more personal tragedy. They were able to get assistance from their insurance company as well as the Red Cross.

He was kind of happy to have us. He didn't have any kids or nothing. We stayed there about a month and a half in Gonzalez. Well, the first week after we was there, his wife died. So we had to do a funeral. So now we got Katrina. We can't come back to the house. And we had the wife dying the first week we were there. He went through all the arrangements for his wife.

Then me and my wife, the first thing we did, we got in touch with State Farm out in Gonzalez and made arrangements. That's when we kind of found out what all to do. They gave us a little aid. Because of the insurance, they gave us a little aid money. Then they had stuff set up in the town of Gonzalez, and they had a couple of other little towns where you went and got food stamps. We did the food stamps. We did the American Red Cross, just the things that we deserved. I think the Red Cross gave about $250.

They gave us some food stamps; I think $250 per month. We only got them twice. We only got them two months. They gave you a little the first month and then the second month, and then I think we were cut off after that. We didn't have to worry about jobs because Budget is at the airport. They didn't get nothing but wind damage. They didn't get any water. Water was just in New Orleans East, Ninth Ward, the lower areas; some in Metairie and Kenner got a little water.

For some people, it took a while to find or resume employment after the storm. That was not the case for Easton and his wife.

I contacted Budget a couple days afterward, and they wanted me to go to work, which I did. They summoned me to work to the airport. They wanted me to work the first week, and I told them, "Look, just give me a little time to think this thing out." I was trying to get the other aids and insurance together.

So I worked in Baton Rouge the second week after Katrina. I started at the Baton Rouge airport. I worked around there, helped them out, moved some cars, this and that. My wife is a branch manager. Chase is everywhere, so she started working in Baton Rouge one week after, too. Neither one of us had problems with different jobs. We didn't have to worry about being out of money because . . . Budget gave us some aid. Bank One gave her some aid. They gave us money. My car and truck was left here, so I didn't have any transportation. So [Budget] gave me a rental car for a month and a half. The company paid for it and everything.

So our companies really did a lot for us. We could've come back into New Orleans about two weeks later, but we didn't want to do it. Bank One wanted us to stay in a trailer on some bank property, with a lot of other bank employees. I wasn't really for that. My wife wasn't either. So we didn't take that offer.

We kept dealing with FEMA and looking for places. Finally, my daughter, through the Internet, she'd pulled up some places on the Internet. So after a month and a half in Gonzalez, we finally found an apartment in Kenner and we moved to Kenner.

My wife was still going to Baton Rouge. I think she was working in Baton Rouge for about a month. Then they started opening a couple branches. She ended up on Britannia back out here. Both of us were really back in New Orleans about three weeks after Katrina. They only had one flight, if I can recall. Southwest was the only airline here for about the first month and a half. Then Delta came next. But for the first three, four months, you only had two to three flights in New Orleans. I was at the airport.

We had passes to get in. You had to have a certain pass to get through the National Guard because they weren't letting anybody back into the city. They gave it to certain companies that they knew was at the airport. So the corporate office, they got that together. I had a pass for Budget. Two months later is when they started letting everybody else in. Three weeks after Katrina, I was at the airport.

I was not able to visit my house at first. They had road-blocks. You couldn't even get this far. There was only so far you could get. I got here and got the house gutted. I was earlier than a lot of people but still probably some three months after Katrina.

Yeah, it was the first time I had seen the house, three months after. I went in. It was stinky. Man, this whole area was horrible. I mean stuff everywhere. It was pretty bad, coming in here off the freeway. You had no lights, so they wouldn't let nobody in. Even when they started letting people come in the day, you could only come in at a certain times.

They did that for a long time, and I don't get it. We stayed in an apartment in Metairie for six months. So you got a month and a half in Gonzalez, six months in an apartment, and so we really didn't get back here, we didn't get this FEMA trailer until about eight months later. Not quite a year. About nine months when they finally brought the FEMA trailer over here.

The first priority when I came back [was to] hire some guys. They came to gut the house and stuff before the FEMA trailer came. All that stuff was out here in the front yard. So that was the first thing, get all that nasty stuff out of the house. We only got about four feet of water, so we gutted maybe six feet, all the way around the whole house. I mean, we just stopped the mold from moving the rest of the way, but it didn't do no good because when we started rebuilding, he still had to tear everything all down again. Even the ceilings, everything had to come out because there was mold behind the drywall.

The city often gets a bad name for the poor way in which it handled evacuation and the rebuilding effort. Easton, however, recognizes what the city did well.

> The city trucks came around and picked up all the stuff that was around. I think they did a pretty good job. They had trucks coming around the neighborhood all day long. I think they did pretty good for the people that could get in and was able to get their stuff out there.

Like others, though, Easton's experience with the Road Home program has been anything but expedient. And like many of his fellow returnees, Easton viewed federal rebuilding assistance to be just compensation for the government's failure to protect the city, not as a handout of any sort. Easton wants only what he believes he deserves, no more but no less.[37]

> I don't know if they're out of money, but they haven't given us anything yet. Before, they said $150,000. They claim if you got $110,000, they was going to deduct that. We're due $40,000, but we haven't seen a penny of it yet. I've been hearing on TV that they're in trouble with money. The mayor and the governor were just in Washington last week to ask for some more Road Home money.
>
> The system is just broken, from what I understand, the little bit I've been hearing. But we weren't unfortunate. We weren't the ones that hadn't got anything. Like I said, we don't want no more than what we deserve. Their formula they told at the beginning was $150,000. They deducted whatever insurance money you got. We got about $100,000 from State Farm, and then we got $8,000 from homeowner's. So we should've deserved at least $40,000.
>
> But I don't know. I've got some neighbors around me that didn't have any insurance. I know of three cases. I'm not going to give any names, but they got $90,000 or more with no insurance. I think it's unfair because I feel like we all lost everything. I lost everything just like my neighbors. I feel it's unfair. I'm not asking for no more than what we deserve. I'm

not trying to beat the system out or nothing. I'm just going by the formula they put together.

Well, these people got paid. They didn't have any insurance, so I don't feel that we should suffer. I think they're looking at me and my wife both work. When you put our salary and that together, that's still irrelevant. We still lost everything just like the neighbor that didn't have insurance. But like I said, some of them got paid.

I think my problem is really [the] people that was running Road Home from out of town, these executives, they reward themselves hundreds of thousands of dollars bonus. Why would they get $100,000 for some work that's not finished? There's still people that still need money.

So I feel that $100,000, two or three people could've got paid out of that. I sure could've got my $40,000. They're going to just give themselves a bonus for the year for doing good? Well, they didn't do good because the program is broken right now.

Easton has also suffered at the hands of inexperienced, incompetent, or untrustworthy contractors. Easton and his wife took steps to make sure they were not mistreated.

Then the next problem you had [was] contractor problems. You see we're here over two years later, and we're still not done. After you get the house gutted and everything, when you start looking for a contractor, you probably got more people needed contractors than you have contractors. So you got the contractors jacking their prices up sky-high. This guy hadn't been no ice cream and cake that's dealing with the house now.

Let me back up. First it took us almost three months to get a contractor that we could afford. They had these contractors coming and giving ridiculous estimates. One wanted $250,000. Well, I can go buy me a brand-new house right outside of town for $185,000.

You'll still use the frame of this house but still charge me ridiculous prices? I'm like, "Man." Then we had one who wanted $185,000. This guy here, we thought was reasonable, so we went with what he did. We also had to borrow money from the

SBA because after we paid the house off, the $30,000, we fell short on the other end. So we still borrowed a little money.

We borrowed a little money from the SBA, about $25,000, to try and help us because of these high prices of these contractors. The SBA gave us a reasonable rate, time to pay them back. We thought it was a reasonable rate for us to pay monthly. So we're still in debt to the SBA, so we still got a lien on the house, $25,000. I paid it off in one sense and kind of still owe some money in another sense.

We're hoping that Road Home would give us the $40,000, and we could pay the SBA and then we'll own the home and might get a little bit for some furniture and stuff. See, because what they still got to realize, we still have to furnish the house and everything.

But Road Home put us in this situation we're in now. We still owe the SBA right now. We're eligible for $40,000, but [Road Home] just give us $25,000. If they'd just give us the $25,000 to pay the SBA off, we'll be all right.

At least we'll have some kind of peace of mind, but we got that little note. Hopefully, I don't know if it'll come through, I don't know if they'll get some more money from the president. I don't know. It's been a long hike.

Now going back to this contractor, we finally dealt with him. Fifty percent along the way, he started shutting down, couldn't get him to come. These contractors are getting too many jobs. They start here, start there, take your money . . . [But] we had a contract with him. We knew where he was. We checked on him before he started.

So we knew, he's from St. Rose. I know where he works at. He also had a regular job. He's a supervisor. So we checked into him. We didn't just . . . like a lot of our neighbors are going by things, trying to get things done. They got in Spanish guys. Cheap labor came in, and they rushed and did stuff. Now they're finding leaks in their houses and stuff like that.

They didn't get people that was licensed. So they got a lot of, I just hear stories all around us. They ran and did stuff too quick. As a matter of fact, there's somebody I went to church with. Her electric is all messed up. One light come on, the fan come on, when she hit a light for bathroom or something.

Now, to get back to him, then what he did, 50 percent along the way, for a whole month, he'd call and say, "I'm coming. I'm coming." But he'd never show up. Then all of a sudden, one day, my wife called me at work and said, "Look, [our contractor] wants us to sit down and talk to him." I'm saying to myself, he charged us, I'm not ashamed of the price, either, $94,500, to redo our house.

So first thing ticking in my mind, this guy he didn't sit down and talk with us when he came up with the price. He walked the house, did what he had to do, went to his house, wrote up a contract, and came and said $94,500. He didn't sit down and negotiate no price with us or nothing. So we thought about it, and we said, "This is the best one." Everybody over him was in the hundreds and almost in the two hundreds. So we said, "Let's go with this." Now, all of a sudden, he wanted to talk again. The situation was he wanted more money.

I told my wife, "What does he got to talk to us about?" I mean, he got two payments then squeezed us out a little bit of the third. He's always ahead on the money, saying he needs this, needs this. But then they stopped working.

He started telling my wife he'd underbid the job. All of a sudden, he wanted $15,000 more. He said he should've bid $100,000. My thing is, look, you wrote a contract. You did all this. Fifty percent along the way, now you done and feel you underbid. That's not our fault.

I got a lawyer, and she did what they call a demand letter. Somebody told me about a lawyer. She did a demand letter for me. We send the letter to his job, his house, and his P.O. box. Well, P.O. box came back.

If somebody sent some mail to me at Budget, Budget got the right to open it because they put it in Budget and my name. So we did it that way. So once the letter got to the job, I think it scared [him]. His bosses must have gave it to him and said, "Hey, look, you need to take care of this business. This came here." Then we had a lot of other, we had all the information.

I had pictures. The lawyer told me like this, "Sometimes this demand letter works."

Anyway, she said, "This letter can work two ways. Most people bite on it, get scared," which he did because I guess he felt—we could've took him to court—if we'd have went to court, we would've had to pay way more money than it took to finish it. "The best thing for you all to do is really try to work it out, and you better hope he bites on this letter." Well, it did scare him, so he came back, running real fast. Now he's about 80 percent done. We've just about closed up all the plumbing. They're getting ready to start painting, and then all we got left is the floors and the cabinets. The lawyer, she told me herself, she had at least 40 cases she was working on with some kind of contractor problems, fraud or different stuff.

The bottom line, the demand letter scared him. So he came back about a month ago. We gave him 45 days. He's getting close to the 45 days. We're a whole lot stuff. If you'd have seen this house, it was just a mess, the walls were open. I have pictures and everything. We still got, like I said, we got floors, they're pretty much closing in and about to paint.

But it's been a long hike, and this bed in [the FEMA trailer] is not nice. It's killing my back, so it's been a long road to recovery, I'll be honest with you. I think FEMA did good. A lot of people complaining. Then the thing they got with fumes. We did have a lot of fumes. I hope they didn't do nothing. I can't tell right now. I've been happy. I've been satisfied with this. It's better than us paying because we couldn't get any money from FEMA when we're paying. We paid the apartment bill ourself. So the trailer's been a help, but it's time now. Our back's killing us, and it's time to get out. It's close to a year and a half now. It's been tough.

The only reason we didn't get nobody else to come in is because I wanted to hold him to the contract. So if I'd have rushed somebody else in to do something, that would've voided my contract with him. But this guy here, I wouldn't refer to anybody. Personality-wise, he seemed like a nice guy; he's Christian and this and that. But I wouldn't refer him. I wouldn't even go through building a house like this. I wanted to buy a house.

A lot of people noticed that the storm made a difference in neighborhood dynamics: some positive, some negative. In Easton's view, the difference in his Gentilly neighborhood was a positive one.

I know the neighbors pretty good. Across the street, me and Marty are always talking. I've gotten to know a lot more a little further down, but I'm gonna be honest with you. I'm not going to lie; everybody pretty much stayed to themselves. The storm brought about a change where people kind of got friendlier, more friendlier with each other and just came together a little better as far as helping each other and talking about ideas, who did this, who did that as far as construction's concerned. Who they got to cut their trees.

So it's brought about a little unity. My wife is something like a loner, and . . . [so] we didn't really associate with a lot of people in the neighborhood.

Well, now, they do have a couple of community meetings. They're getting together about rebuilding the community. I've been to two, and my wife's been to a little bit more than me because she gets off [earlier]. I work 12:30 to 9:00, Monday through Friday. I'm the late shift guy over there, off on the weekends. My wife gets off about 5:00. She's been to a little bit more meetings than me about the rebuilding of the community: what stores they're trying to get open, what things they're trying to close. Now this here was a big mall, strip center right here. It was very busy. They had a grocery store in it and everything. That all got wiped out with Katrina.

Not all the houses in his community were being rebuilt. Some were slated for demolition. The city was responsible for the demolition work but was not moving as fast as many residents would have liked. Easton explains the danger of having an abandoned house next door.

Just before Katrina, . . . the guy to the right of me went to a nursing home, a white guy. I heard, since I've been back, because I talked to his son. His son is a lieutenant for New Orleans police, and he told me that [his father] died. So they're going to demolish his house. It's been on the demolishing list almost a year and a half now.

The city of New Orleans, they put houses of people who's not coming back on a list. And I went and checked downtown for him. He's on the demolishing list. And they told me three months ago that it should be done any day. The thing that's bad about his house, the problem we got with that, is that it had never been cleaned out since Katrina. We're scared rats and everything are going to start running this way the minute they start tearing all this down. Ain't no telling what's over there.

Like I said, I checked on it three months ago. They said it should be demolished any day. It's on the list to be demolished by the city. Nobody's done anything. In his defense, his son got hit, too. He had a home on top of Metairie, but they got hit with water. We only got four feet over here. The water got all the way to the top of their houses. Two blocks from me down here, heading toward the Lakefront Airport, the water got all the way up. More the water set in, the mold took over the whole house, you know? Had to gut it. All the furniture, everything was demolished. I lost a car and truck, also. Me and my wife left in her car.

Easton was one of the few interviewed who did not feel a burning desire to return to New Orleans. His wife, however, did. It was her love for the city and his love for her that brought them back to New Orleans.

I don't know if you know, I can't say all bankers are like this, but everything is saved. She's so tight; she squeaks when she walks. Just like her and my daughter. I summed up the whole thing [like this], she's more of a saver. I spend. Why not spend and be happy?

Prior to it, I can remember, just before Katrina, the week before Katrina, we had a little argument, me and my wife. She said to me, "You could have a whole lot of money saved for what you put into these old cars." I said, "Look, when judgment day comes and we both go to heaven, the Lord looks back and says, 'He was happy on earth. He spent his money on a lot of old cars, but you were miserable and saved everything.'" See, everything is saved to her. She never buys anything.

I'm just giving you an overview of the family of why she stayed here. Why she saved everything. Like I said, she and my daughter don't like to spend it all, so my thing is enjoy some of it. My dad always told me, "If you work, son, enjoy some of life." Some saving is all right. Don't get me wrong. Prior to meeting my wife, when I was single, I didn't know how to ever save anything. I stayed broke, had about five or six credit cards.

Since I met her, I only have one credit card, so that's the positive side of her, what I got out of the saving issue. She's got me down to one credit card now, and that's a good thing. I do save now more than I had prior to being married, but I was still happy, one way or another.

Personally, I wanted to move to Atlanta or maybe outside of Baton Rouge [after Katrina], but my wife is from New Orleans. She's a die-hard Saints fan. No matter what, you can't get them out of here. She's never been nowhere. She's never lived out of New Orleans, other than going out of town.

She just wanted to come back to this but, as far as I was concerned, I'd rather buy. I would've bought a house that was already built. I'd have taken the insurance money, kept the property, and made a rental house out of it. But stay here for what? We've both got careers. We could get jobs anywhere in the United States. She got 25 years in the banking industry. I got two degrees and a barber license. I didn't need to stay here, but I did it to make her happy. But I wouldn't ever go through building a house from the bottom up again. Even if I had the money, I'd rather buy an already built.

I think it's mostly because she's . . . she's scared to make a change. She's never been exposed to nothing else, always been here all her life. I guess you would call her an introvert. She don't really like to deal with a lot of people. She's very quiet.

MICHAEL

Michael is a 50-year-old African American male who has resided in the Gentilly neighborhood of Pontchartrain Park on and off for the past 28 years. We interviewed him on the steps of his friend Marshall's FEMA trailer. With a couple of other childhood friends, they were repairing the roof of Marshall's house.

I've lived in this community for 28 years, about two miles from here. We all grew up, [and] we all went to high school here. That was a mall, and we ate over there in the Gentilly Woods area. That's where most of [us] work when we was in high school and in college. There's a whole bunch of us, you know. Most of them went to private schools, and I went to public schools, and we always see each other. We always kept in touch with each other. I mean, it's no rivalry, you know.

It was a pleasant neighborhood. Everybody knew everybody. I mean, from here all the way back. You take a Friday night, you know, everybody go to the high school football game. You get up Saturday morning, we hook up, you talk about this and that. But everybody was close knit. But when we first moved back here, it was mostly whites back here.

You see, this is considered Gentilly Woods. You go down about two miles, it's a little canal, that's Pontchartrain Park.[38] That's where I came up, there. That was the first historical black district where 90 percent of the people that lived back here were either working for the post office or they were educators. These was brand-new houses, and the average mortgage was less than $215 month; this [was] 57 years ago. And that's why a lot of people are not leaving here; they're coming back because this is a historical district. They're not going to do anything. Just like downtown Bourbon Street. Because it was build up and it was structured around the black community, whites started leaving Gentilly Woods when I was in college. I would say, '84, '85. You know, they got the message and they figure, "Hey, it's best that we get away from you people." And they moved off to the east, and then when we started going to the east, they all moved to Slidell.

There was a lot of tension back here once the park got to a limit, then everybody started coming eastward, you know. When the whites went, the department store, everything went with them. And that's when the brothers came and, you know, anybody that was [an] entrepreneur here had a lot of grease, they went to college, they had meals stores, and they little shoe stores and little pocketbooks and dress stores. Since about '85, that's been predominantly black.

I went to college at Dillard. My sister went to [Southern University at New Orleans] with my little brother. My little sisters went to SUNO. I majored in biology. I work for NASA. I build tanks for the external fuel tank. Coming up, [I was] in a marching band in high school. My teacher always say, "Whatever you do in life, is make sure you have something to fall

back on because you never know what is going to hold you."
It's all nice to set your hopes and dreams, but just don't put it
all in one basket.

Michael, though he was young when Hurricane Betsy hit, remembers that experience quite well.

What I learned when I was a kid is why you have to prepare for
crises. We just saw things different, you know. We went through
Betsy [and when] we went through Camille, and neither one of
those were to the magnitude of this. I was six years old when
Betsy hit. We went to school. And the principal got on the PA
system, "Pack up your belongings, take all your books, take
everything in your desk, and your mom or your dad's going to
be waiting outside to get you."

And we got home, and I think it was a Tuesday. When we
got home, momma was cooking and all the food and stuff that
was in the freezer. She says, "The hurricane's comin'. Go put
your stuff up, pack a bag, go take your bath and put on some
clean clothes, some clean underwear." And then really, the thing
hit, like, about 9:30 that night, the Tuesday night, and we didn't
have to leave. We had about, maybe less than six inches [of]
water on the ground. We didn't have shingles then. Took all the
tarpaper, wherever there was a crack within the beams, just like
we do in here. And, you know, we went and got pots and pans
to collect all the water. That was about it compared to some
other areas down here. I mean, there were 3,000, 4,000 people
drowned during Betsy.

Michael is among those who believe that the Ninth Ward levees were intentionally breached during Betsy to protect the other areas of the city.

When I was a kid, I remember people talking about how
people['s] bodies [were] hanging off the roof because of the
fact that allegedly the levee broke. That's the best way to
phrase it, right? As not to have litigation come up. That's a
whole different story. Yeah, I mean, who am I to accuse? It was
targeted through the black community because that took a lot

of pressure off the people way down there in St. Bernard's. It took a lot of pressure off them people way up there on Lakefront. It took a whole lot of pressure from the people back here. It took a lot of pressure off their part.

Like many, Michael chose initially not to evacuate from the city as Katrina was approaching but, instead, chose to go to higher ground.

When I heard the news that Katrina was coming, me and my ma were back in Pontchartrain Park. We all agreed that we would go out by my sister. Just me, my mom, and the dog, Chip.[39] We were going to go by my sister, off of IHN and Cotter. She lived in the second- and third-floor townhouse.

So, Saturday night about 1:30, you choose which weatherman you want to listen to. Okay, so my mom say, "I need some orange juice and take my medicine." [So I] go get some sandwich meat, you know, filling the cooler with ice and stuff. So about 3:30 the man kept saying, "Hey, if you couldn't get out, stay right there."

So [I] grabbed my little bag at the time [and] put all the medicines in here. I said, "Ma, please put your clothes on." I grabbed Chip['s] bowl and his leash. I said we gotta go call my sisters. Then I came back and took my reciprocating saw, my drill, collect all the wood, board up all the windows and stuff. And about 9:30 Sunday night, we started feeling the effects. By 9:00 Sunday morning, it was on us. It was a lot of wind and very little rain.

So, you know, we all have Walkmans, so we had our Walkmans on and cell phones there. So once the power went out and I, we say, "Okay, have to scrap it now." My sister says, "Okay, well you the boss. You're the eagle scout. How we gonna cook?" So my sister, she works at NASA too, in another unit.

The water was clear. I'd say about 45 minutes later, we kept hearing, "Dm, dm, dm, dm." And after that, the water came black. It came in at rapid rate. Snakes came out; the alligators came out. We saw alligator with a human leg in his mouth. You couldn't see the first floor. The first floor was gone. We jumped in the water; we took the refrigerator and brought it up to the second floor.

And if you didn't have a Walkman, you don't understand what was going on. That's what they say was a break in the levees. We had 28 feet of water less than two miles from here. There was only one radio station in the city that still works and [was] getting people updated as to what was going on. All our cars [were lost]. We lost a total of 13 cars and two houses in a matter of two days.

The water was coming up the stairs. It had 20 steps to get to the second floor. The first floor was gone so [if] the kids had to go to the bathroom, you know, just went down there, grabbed up some of that water, and poured it down the toilet.

She says, "I got about 300 candles." I say, "You got an aluminum pan?" She say, "Yeah, I do. We gonna eat." We ate for four days off those candles and that aluminum pan. Just as long as there was something in there to make some grease, that's how we ate. It was 12 of us. We had six kids with us. We had enough drinking water until that Coast Guard helicopter came pulled us out of that house that Wednesday night. We were there for four days. We had something to eat and something to drink, but the water kept coming.

I had my flashlight. My niece was at Outward Bound, and she had some little emergency road kits that she was selling, to raise money for Outward Bound. That gave all them the flashlight. We had them two aluminum pans. I took one; my sister's old man took one. We went on opposite sides the house on the third level. I went on the other side. So we seen the helicopter, just start flashing lights. And we did that, like, for two nights and then that last night, the guy came down out the helicopter, my sister had made a sign that said, "There's 13 of us in the house." He said, "I can only take nine."

So there was only two men, me and my sister's old man, and he said, "Well, I'll stay here." . . . I have another sister that works . . . at the Department of Agriculture. We took her children and my mom and they flew us out. So my mom started getting sick—she suffered with high blood pressure and diabetes—after that, so we decided, "Hey, let's go." Hopefully, by the time we get where we're going, we can call and figure out just where everybody is. Our major concern was my niece. She was six months pregnant with twins.

When Michael and his family evacuated, it was with the help of the Coast Guard. They made their way to Houston where personal tragedy struck, and strangers would have to help them out in their time of need.

Everybody saying we was going to the Superdome [or] we was going to the convention center, and with the Walkman we heard all the atrocities that was going on, so we decided, no, we weren't going there. We got on that bus, and I asked the bus driver if we'll be going to Houston. We got to Houston [in] about eight and a half, nine hours, and there was so many buses. There was at least four or five hundred buses.

It's, like, about 4:30 in the morning. My mom had already died. My mom had a massive heart attack about two minutes after we got to Houston. We wasn't even there for two minutes. You had to wait in line, so I called one of the security guards, and I told him, I said, "Look, my mom's not feeling good." I said, "I know there's at least 50 to 60 thousand people out here [but] my mom need medical attention." So we took her off the bus, put her on a little golf cart, and took her up there, took her into medical. They took her vitals and said, "I'm sorry. Your mom needs to go to a hospital." Before they took my momma outta that office, I knew my mom was dead. They revived her. They revived her for about six minutes and then called code blue. And then it was just me. I was sitting there. I'm dressed just like I am now, but I didn't have no shoes on. Lady gave me a pair of her slippers, and I heard them people call a code blue, and I saw them people running through. I knew my mom was dead. So they say, "You have any way to get back to the bus?" I said, "No." They said, "Here, take this, and give it to the cab driver to call me a cab." My sister, she's 53, asked me about her. And she freaked, and I just had to keep her calm because I also had them six kids.

At that point, you know, it was nothing we could do. We couldn't bring her body back down here because all this was still under water. We met some black people in Houston that really, really looked out for us. There was this guy, his name is Michael. He heard our story, he came down to the Reliant Center and, you know, I mean, they were very genuine people, they say, "We're in a mortuary business." And he helped us out.

He really did. And he had helped us [when] my brother-in-law died about two months ago. He brought my brother-in-law's body home from Houston. I mean, they're really kind and gentle people. And he's a very genuine person, and he needs to be recognized for his effort. He is one of God's children, and he can help anyone that needs some help. Him and his wife came down and brought my brother's body from Houston, and we had a little repast for him. We gave him a collection and gave him some red beans, and some pickle tips and, you know, they were really impressed. They was just people that saw us on CNN, explaining what had happened to us, and then they were there. I mean, they were genuine.

We stayed in Houston for about 28 days before Rita came. We stayed in a little shabby hotel off of I-10. We moved downtown at the medical district. Yeah, we had to leave Houston. My sister that work for USDA, she went to Grand Prairie [Texas], which is on the opposite side of the interstate. We all packed up, and we all left together because Rita was coming.

We buried mom, and we all went to Grand Prairie. I mean, we even love Grand Prairie, too. So we had two more kids, and then my grandmother came and my nieces; it's always, like, about 30 of us. I told them I felt like a convict. We running from the hurricanes. But we had no choice.

We went to Arlington. We stayed in Arlington, Texas, [until] the first week in October. And they said the water had went down, and they were letting people come back from 7:00 in the morning. At 12:00 noon, we left there and my sister that works for Stennis, for NASA, they gave her a trailer in a trailer park.[40]

Oh, we missed a whole month of September. Like I said, we came back here first week in October. Some of us stayed in Arlington and Grand Prairie. We were like the floating crew. We have to come back down here and assess just what was up.

When Michael and his family drove into New Orleans, they were awestruck by the devastation they saw as well as the amount of crime that was taking place.

Well, it wasn't so bad. I mean, we got to Picayune, and it's like an hour, we saw how the big pines tree just snapped like toothpicks. Then [we] got to Slidell. We couldn't take the Twin Span, had to take the Highway 11 Bridge. That's when we saw the devastation and, the closer we got off that Highway 11 Bridge, the I-10, it was unbelievable.

My sister that lived in a townhouse [and] we were just trying to get all her stuff out. She was on the second and third floor, so all that was dry. So we packed all of her stuff up, and the people she worked with at Stennis, they had some property, so she was able to rent her a three-bedroom house, $500 a month, and took all her stuff over there.

You had people busting into apartments, taking people's living room sets, their bedroom sets, their washers, their dryers, their TVs, you know, their VCR. All kind of nonsense crap, you know. And 90 percent of the police had cleared because they had their families to take care of, which that was understandable, you know. They have families too.[41]

Michael and his family gutted their homes themselves and became a little gutting brigade. One lesson he learned through all of it, besides how hard his sisters could work, was the importance of patience.

And my cousin got his trailer up there around Xavier. We stayed in there for, like, three months with no electricity. We couldn't get electricity. For three months. And it was cold. Everybody was there at one time, so you had to be patient. You know what I'm saying. You have to understand the situation, the predicament we were in. So what we were doing, we just gutted everything out. All the appliances, all the furniture, we got all that out, we went to tearing up the walls.

It was like four of us, two men and two women. I never knew my sisters could work that hard. We gutted one, two, three, four, five, seven houses. And then we have our people up in Gert Town and Hollygrove[42] at Xavier, so we did a nursery, and we did my sister's house off of Read, and we hit my sister's house over off of Hayne and made our way around. We gut my mom's house and then my niece's over there off of Chef Highway, and we took care of her house, and then we headed uptown. It didn't take much resources. It really was a matter of having something to eat, something to drink, a respirator, some gloves. I mean, at that point, we just had to get everything out. You know, it wasn't rebuilding then. You had to get it out because if you let it set in there, that odor would have killed you.

Michael made the decision not to rebuild the house that he owned with his mother. For him, the returns were not worth the effort.

I didn't rebuild the house my mom and I lived in. I sold it. I sold it to Road Home about nine months ago. I just put $15,000 in my mom's house over the past six years. It wasn't worth rebuilding. Water was over the roof. It sat there for three months.

Right now, I live in a motel. I'm still waiting for the money to come. And they better not put it on the market or it's going to be another lawsuit against them. My friend Marshall got his money. He chose not to come back. I only been back in New Orleans now for seven years, from California.

I live in a motel, paying $250 a week until there's money coming in, because all the apartments are inflated. Before Katrina, you could go and get your apartment, get a one-bedroom apartment for about $450 a month, put down half a deposit for the energy, get your electricity turned on.

And now, to go find a one-bedroom apartment it could be anywhere from $1,300 to $1,800. That's first, last month rent and deposit, a copy of your credit report, and a copy of your police history, if you have a history with the police. Yeah, you need all that at time of filing your application. It's unbelievable.

Just a few miles away, another resident, Easton, described his post-Katrina neighborhood as closer and friendlier. Michael, in contrast, says his neighborhood has changed as well, but for the worse.

There's a lot more activity going on in this neighborhood. Negative activity. I mean, people coming back. Well, see, a lot of the parents and the grandparents didn't come back. They sent the kids back on their own, because kids say, "I wanna go home. I don't want to be out here in Dallas. I don't want to be here in no

Iowa. Are you crazy? I want to go back home." By kids I mean anywhere from 21 to maybe 30. It's just their mentality. I mean, you look at them now, you hear all this loud music, everybody got rims, everybody got 22-, 24-inch tires. And that's it, and everybody got them big, stinky, dirty, nasty, baggy pants; they running around all hold[ing] their pants up. The penitentiary style. And it's sad. That generation is lost. It's lost.

For us, I don't know. It all depends on what they want to do because the people gave us options. People gave us choices. What are you going to do with your life? What do you want to do? Them, they run round, and they stealing everybody's central air conditioning units and taking the copper out. [Some] people just building houses. They're stealing anything that got copper in it. They sell it. Copper . . . the price of copper gone up at least 60 percent since the storm.[43]

We asked him why he came back. Michael told us that he came back to help his brother and sisters get their houses together, because he felt a duty toward his nieces and nephews.

After the storm, I had to come back. I had my nieces and my nephew here. This is their future. I mean, my sister's been working since I was in third grade to be able to buy a house here, and you leave that for somebody.

I left it for 15 years, and I came back. I mean, I went on the West Coast and did what I had to do. I figure, hey, I was gonna come back, take care of my momma's house. That's the only reason I left San Diego, California. I worked at an electronics company as an import/export coordinator. It was a good job.

Katrina was so hard on Michael that he has chosen not to live in New Orleans any longer. Instead, he and his best friends plan to move out of the city.

When I get the money, I'm going to go out towards Greensburg with my buddy Marshall.[44] We have a good elderly friend out that way. I just need a little time because, I took it hard, I really did. You see, a year later, I found out my ex-wife, we had just get divorced before Katrina, I found out she drowned during the storm because she was on dialysis, and she got trapped in the nursing home and that was just, like, the icing on the cake. And then my mom [and] brother died. So, I mean, it's just been one tragedy after another. I just asked and prayed that the Lord give me strength and patience, you know, because it's His will. There's nothing we can do about it. I was just, like, Lord, don't let nothing else happen, come on, not right now.

LYDIA

Lydia is a 52-year-old African American woman. Before retiring in late 2005, she was a cook for the New Orleans public school system. She was born and raised in the Uptown neighborhood and spent her adult life in Gentilly Woods where she and her husband raised their three children.

The further you go back into Pontchartrain Park, my fourth-grade English teacher lived down there in Pontchartrain Park. A lot of blacks moved back here. Gentilly Woods was first. But Pontchartrain Park was still predominantly where black people, professionals started to migrate and build houses, so it's a historic [neighborhood]—that's why people don't understand about the Ninth Ward, but the Ninth Ward was one of the few places black people owned down here in New Orleans at one time.

When I grew up, most everybody who owned a home lived down in the Ninth Ward where it opened on the canal. It just wasn't that feasible for black people to own property all over, but the Ninth Ward was all property owned by black people, and that's historical. That's why you see generations of people down there, and it's their people, it's black people.

Lydia sees New Orleans history as her history. In the 1920s, her parents migrated to New Orleans from towns along the Mississippi River in search of work. At 15, her mother started out as a dancer in a dance hall. After her mother and father were married, her mother secured her first job at the City Cleaners, and her father began a 45-year career in the construction industry.

We don't have enough knowledge about our roots. I am tied to New Orleans. I grew up with the culture. I grew up living across the street from the graveyard. I saw the second lines. I knew what that was about. We do funerals here like nobody else, here in New Orleans. We can start a parade for anything. But back when I was a child, it was a sad occasion to see the horn players going to the graveyard. Over when they came out, they would be playing—going in they'd be playing "Just a Closer Walk with Thee," moving real slow and sad, and they'd come out playing "Oh When the Saints Go Marching In."

I grew up on Washington Avenue when the Jewish people had all these little dry goods stores, and our predominant shopping area was Treme Street, not Canal. The blacks went to Tribe. And that's when New Orleans was a real small community, and I think that can happen again. The beauty of the city, the houses and the porches and the neutral grounds [street medians]. You don't go anywhere else and see that, and I think it would be a shame for us to lose that, all those beautiful old houses up and down Esplanade Avenue. I love that. I still like to go and walk down Esplanade just to look at the beauty in the city.

My mom worked in the French Quarter so I would go to the French Quarter often to pick up my mom and just to [sit with the people]. They were some of the most wonderful people. I mean, they became like part of the family. We knew this when my mom retired; she would still go sit with others and visit with her. She'd still go down there to the store. Sometimes Mr. Joe would still stop by and bring my mom a Christmas—even though they were Jewish—they would still bring her a dinner, fix her an already prepared dinner for Christmas. That's what New Orleans is. It's a very small—it's a little big city.

People try to say it's a big city. It's not. We are all so close to being rural in our ways. We can walk everywhere here. Like in most places you've got to have a vehicle, like in Atlanta. I could never live there, never. Couldn't even drive—I was scared to drive on the interstate. But here in New Orleans, if you go to a major supermarket, you're gonna see somebody you know. Even going from school, church, work, hospital, somewhere you know them. It doesn't matter if you're black or white. I see people all the time who say, "I know you from somewhere," and it might be just that we went to the same drugstore, but it's a small town, and I think we kind of got separated along the way with government programs and just problems, just problems.

Before Katrina, Lydia lived with her husband and two of their adult children. Her husband and their daughter were both undergoing dialysis treatment for diabetes.

> My husband, sick as he was, I kid you not, he had no legs and one hand, and that hand had some fingers missing, but he was not a complainer. He was very independent. We had a life, even though he was sick. I had a full-time job. He went to all his appointments. He caught the lift bus. He had two wheelchairs, one to operate manually so he could get around in the house, and the electronic chair so he could go out into the public and use the lift bus and go to his dialysis and his dialysis treatments.

Though Lydia had lived in New Orleans her entire life, she had never heeded calls to evacuate. But given her family's medical conditions, staying was no longer an option once it was clear that Katrina was on its way.

> When we evacuated out that Saturday, my daughter had dialysis, and I called [my friend] and we was talking on the phone that morning like we normally do and she said, "Oh, girl, I'm sitting here looking at this weather." She said, "I need to get up and go to the store. I haven't fixed [my husband] anything to eat." I said, "Well, I'm fixing breakfast now. When I get through with getting everybody situated, I'll bring [your husband] some breakfast." So she was the one who brought the storm to my attention when I was down at her house, and her godson's girlfriend called and said, "You and [your friend], you all need to come down here in Atlanta." She said, "You all need to come up here because you ought to go away for the storm."
>
> Not me. I had never left here for a storm in my entire life, and I was born right in this city. Never left for a hurricane, but I didn't have the sick people leaving before, so the dialysis unit says, "Oh, you all gotta make sure you come and get [your daughter's] route sheet because we won't be open on

Tuesday. We are closing." So that automatically let me know I had to get out.

My husband didn't want to leave. My husband was here. I started packing stuff and boarding up the windows. They were being very lackadaisical. I said, "What are you all gonna do?" My husband said, "Well, I'm gonna wait and see what the children are gonna do." My son said, "I've got a test so I'm going to study." And my [other] daughter who lives on the West Bank said, "I'm not doing anything. I'm just gonna go on and board up the windows and pray."

I said, "Well, me and [my daughter], we're getting out of here. We're going to Atlanta. We're driving up with [my best friend]." And I just—every day I thank God because if I would not have gotten out, they would not have gotten out. And it worked out excellent because my son-in-law, when they started saying mandatory, my son-in-law came and he drove a 15-passenger van, so he took my husband and my son, and they all went up to Alexandria to my husband's family.

And of course we were planning—on that Monday I was getting ready to come back. We were gonna drive back by that Wednesday, and then we're looking at CNN and our levees breached and it's showing water all over, and we knew the areas. Of course, we knew once they said Pontchartrain Lake, that's right over there in Gentilly. And I said, "Oh, girl, what do we do now?"

With her husband in the care of his extended family in Alexandria, Lydia wasted no time in returning to her home in Gentilly Woods. Since her parents had passed away several years earlier, she was free to sell their Uptown property and use the proceeds to begin repairs on her own home.

I came back here because I had a responsibility to the property. My parents' home was [in] Uptown. It flooded also. That was the piece of property that I was responsible for. I couldn't just say, "Well, I'm getting me another job. I'm not going back." So in this house I wanted to—initially I thought, "We'll tear this one down. I'll rebuild the one Uptown because it was on piers."

But when we started tearing down and gutting it, it was so much termite damage until I said, "Oh, Lord, I can't afford to do this." I didn't have the financial backing. I did not have the energy. When I started getting estimates just to see what I could do, I didn't have the energy to deal with two pieces of property, so the best thing I saw to do was to sell [my parents' property].

That's why I was able to do something to my house here because I had some extra resources, and I said to my husband, when he was here in July [2006], I said, "Honey, they're extra resources, but I'll try to save some." And he said, "Well, we're just gonna have to manage on my little income, and we're gonna be all right." I said, "Yeah, because I'll go back to work once I get into the house."

Relative to other people who had returned, Lydia felt fortunate in that she was coming back to a job and that FEMA had been swift in providing a trailer in which she could live temporarily.

They provided me with a three-bedroom, two-bath trailer. All of us [who had returned early on] were in the same condition. When you come in the community right now, there's kids, but when we first came back, there were no children because people didn't return because there were no schools. So when you looked at our community and there were no kids, it was like such a hole. It really was; it was a missing thing. It felt so good to see little children [again]. Children add so much. When I came back here, I mean, I didn't know what to do. Nobody was saying how to gut a house.

I didn't know how to gut a house, but I knew I had a lot of anger and frustration so that awl and that wheelbarrow really was therapeutic for me. A lot of things, when you get into some situations, you feel better when you can do something. That's the therapy, when you're sitting down just looking at it. And some people are still in shock. Some people are still going through a lot because they've lost friends and jobs, and you just can't [get] them back.

The community was one in which people had planned to stay and pass along their property to their children. Although this pattern created a sense of stability pre-Katrina, it was the source of problems post-Katrina.

> We [have] lots of people [in] this community [who are] elderly people, people retired or very near retiring, people who, if they had any kids at home, they were probably in college. But most of the people around here were probably near paying for their homes or had paid for their homes. So we weren't planning on buying another house. Well, I wasn't. This community, most people lived in this neighborhood at least 15 years at least.
>
> The family who lived next door here, when I moved in it was an elderly Caucasian couple. Since I've been here they've both passed away, so I kinda knew them really well. And then their granddaughter moved in their home and her family. She has since passed away since I've been here, and her husband and one of her children are still living in the house. They evacuated to Florida because the property is tied up with community property, and they need to do succession. There's a lot of heirs. That property is probably—the refrigerator is still in it. Nobody took responsibility for it. The elderly people in the neighborhood, they can't take responsibility for the property if they're depending upon their children or government entities, and I call City Hall every day about this house there. I can't even get somebody to just come out and get it gutted. I would gut it. I gutted this house. But I can't do it because it's private property.

Shortly after Katrina hit, Lydia's daughter took a turn for the worse.

> [My daughter] lost her eyesight two years ago to diabetic neuropathy back in October of '05. December of '04 she was having surgery trying to stop the separation of her cornea. She's had seven eye surgeries, and that happened so quick.
>
> By January [2005] she was on dialysis, so all this stuff is going on and then the storm comes. You just have to—and that's been [true for] so many people's story. They were having difficult situations already, then the storm came and it's just

been—I think it's so important that we talk. It's therapeutic for me. That's why I talk about it. To just some days put it out—it was like releasing it, getting it off of my mind, telling somebody who wants to listen. Because a lot of times people get tired of hearing the Katrina pity parties. It sounds like you're just sitting around whining, waiting on the government, and that's not the truth. That's not—like I said, I gutted my house myself. I came here with an awl and went and bought me a wheelbarrow, and I busted up Sheetrock and took it down myself. That was in '05. When I first came back, the house was gutted by Christmas. And I was going to work, and on my days off I would come out here, and it was really isolated. Nobody was here.

In May 2007, Lydia received the tragic news that her best friend had passed away.

I'll tell you, I think out of all the things that has happened through this storm, that has been the worst, her death. It was like we talked on the phone. Like we had a church member die that Thursday, and she called me, "Girl, guess who died." And then every night we would talk. Sometimes I would just be trying to wait until 6:00. I didn't want to call her before 6:00, and sometimes I'd be waiting and she'd call me.

I got a phone call from her like at 4:00, and I was on the interstate. So I looked at the caller ID, and I said, "I'm gonna call you right back. I'm almost home." And I didn't even hear her voice. I just remember I said—I didn't hear her. I just answered the phone and said, "I'm gonna call you right back." And we did that all the time. So I get another phone call and it's her nephew saying—right after that she calls me right back. I'm thinking it's her, and I said, "What?" And he said, "Ms. Lydia, I just wanted to tell you my aunt, she passed away."

It was like so unbelievable. It was my husband's birthday. And my son used to work, and he was very close to her. She was such a confidante. She was that type of person. She just— I used to call her my 911 person. If you had an emergency, no matter what time it was, no matter how extreme it was, you could call her.

She was gonna Johnny up and whatever was needed she was gonna come and do whatever was needed. She was just like that, and I learned so much from her. That's why whenever there was a crisis, I never cried. She taught me that, how to be an emergency person, how to be the one who can rationalize the situation and do first things first. And I was so glad we just had that kind of relationship.

When she died, I just thought, "I can't go on any more."

I miss [the fun we had together]. I miss that a whole lot, but you hold on to the memories. You cling to that. I still bust out laughing at stuff she would say. I still bust—I still talk to her some days. It's therapeutic, but those are the hard things.

Within the same year, tragedy would strike again with the death of Lydia's husband. The emotional and financial strain was taking a toll, but she was nonetheless proud of what she had accomplished.

My husband and I were married 32 years, and that'll be—just to call him in the morning and just—I was going down like every other weekend, and when I'd go to the farmers market Uptown I'd get some ribs and say, "I'm gonna cook this old rib [for him]." Container it all up so, and it goes—that's gotta be the difficult part, [not being able to do that anymore], but I'm sure he's in a better place and he wouldn't want to come back here.

He kinda was telling me all along, he kept saying, "I'm not coming back." He said just—the first time he stayed a week here, he was so depressed. I went and stayed a week out [in Alexandria] with him. He was just—and it was not just his health. Now, when he came the last time, he came—I fried some fish and invited a few members from the church. He never came in the house. He never did. And we had Sheetrock up. The floors weren't done, but the Sheetrock was up. You could see the individual rooms. He never came in. He stayed in the driveway.

Our daughter said, "My daddy knew he wasn't coming back." She said, "Because he had told me a lot of things about how it is for him to be down here." But you've gotta just do what you gotta do. You've gotta go, keep marching on.

Even though my husband was old, I never thought about him going. So now I'm looking, and I spent my savings. I spent my 401(k), I spent the future, money of the future. I spent money that I found in the car seat of the car. I spent it all, but I see light at the end of the tunnel. Take a look at my house. It's restored basically, other than a few rooms.

When you just—you do the best you can in every circumstance. There is no guidelines when you lose your family. There's no book that says, "This is how you move forward." There's no book that says, "This is what you do after a major disaster," so you're just trying to pray about it and get advice from people who are knowledgeable about building.

If I'm gonna tear the house out, even the doors, so I looked for people and got the advice, and I think I made the best decision when I look at the overall picture and how the resources were used. When I needed to resign from my job, I didn't have to really panic because I had some money. Some people said, "Well, you're living in a FEMA trailer. Isn't that rent-free?" "Yeah, that's rent-free, but utilities aren't rent-free and medicine isn't free and food isn't free and gas for the new car I had to buy isn't free."

So all those things you take into consideration, but we were managing. We are managing, and it takes a lot of sacrifice, but then it gets changed. [Before Katrina] my husband had, like, a 60-inch football TV screen. Because [of his disabilities] he was home all day, and he loves sports so that was his entertainment. But [after Katrina] when I'm pushing and rolling that thing to the street, I'm like, "I will never have this again." I didn't want it from the beginning, but I'm thinking, "You downsize your life."

Whereas I would've pulled out a credit card and go and buy something to wear, now I go to the consignment shops and the thrift stores and stuff. I'm really buying a lot of stuff that's better than what I could've afforded instead of buying it with a credit card. You learn to make groceries last a week. You learn to save. We'll have half of this chicken tonight and then tomorrow we'll have this chicken and then something else. When you've got limited resources, limited space, you kind of bear things with a different attitude, and that's helped for me to really deal with my finances.

A volunteer group arranged through Catholic Charities provided a critical source of support in the rebuilding process. But legal complications arose after her husband died that held up her Road Home rebuilding assistance application.

I've always been civic minded. I don't know why. I guess I just like my city, so then there were all these outreach programs, so every time I heard about something I just signed up. And one night I was at work, Friday, and I had gutted—I signed up to get the house gutted, and of course I was working on it already, but I still had the ceilings, and I had the cabinets that were not mounted on the wall. They were made into the wall, and I couldn't get them out.

And that Friday night I got a call from Catholic Charities saying that they were sending out some volunteers to gut my house, so I was off that Saturday. I was so excited, and I got my ice chest, I got water and Gatorade and everything and came out here. I got out here at 9:00. When I turned the corner, I could see the cabinets on the curb.

It was eight, four women and four men, and they were now taking up the tiles. They had these little tools that take up the tile, and they said, "Was somebody working on your house?" I said, "Me." They said, "You?" I said, "Yeah, me." And I helped them, and by 1:30 we were having sandwiches and talking.

So I got connected. Then they called me for a meeting, and I went over to St. Raymond's, and I saw that there were five contractors there, and they told me that they were going to try to help me to restore my home. And they asked me had I went through the Road Home, and I said, "Yes, I had did that, but I wasn't getting that much." I was getting $31,285, and I said, "And I still have a mortgage because I was underinsured. [And now] the [payment has] doubled. My insurance company wouldn't accept my insurance again so the mortgage company put insurance in place, and they just paid for it and then they added it to my mortgage." [The pastor] said, "Well, we're gonna let you talk to a contractor." So they contracted my house for $31,000. They were willing. Now, you don't think that's God?

I was going to closing for the Road Home on August 17. My husband died August 16. So of course I had to open up the succession, and I haven't gotten a dime from the Road Home yet. I haven't been able. The succession cost a little bit more than I had, so I'm still waiting on money from the funeral insurance to finish paying the attorney to do the succession. And then I'll go back to Road Home. This is a community property state. So he had a will. He willed 25 percent of his half to me, which gave me

75 percent. But of course, my kids are on the other half of his half, and of course they are willing to sign over, but you can't just—they were all there saying, "We'll sign. We are giving it to her." They said, "No. We have to do the succession," so [that] costs $2,350 [in attorney and court fees]. And my lawyer is very good, but I haven't even gotten a death certificate yet. That's how slow the system is. See, these are the things you wouldn't know [from the outside]. And he started the succession without the death certificate, but I was short of some of the money, so I'm just waiting because when people die some things you have to pay for, even if you have insurance. It's a delay. It's not a denial. I'll get it. I think that I will get the money.

Lydia continues to worry about her family but is nonetheless optimistic about the future.

My son is [also] a diabetic, and he was going through such a difficult time. And then we moved out here to these trailers, and he has the little trailer over there, and he's a severe diabetic and was standing in the shower and he stepped into the water and the water was so hot it scalded his feet. And that was in April, and he's still trying to recoup, and he was so depressed from that, and then his dad died. But yesterday he started working with AmeriCorps. He's teaching adult literacy down in St. Bernard Parish, and then he works with a little evening program at Coghill Elementary School, and he has this little boy that has some kind of disability, some kind of tremor thing where he shakes a lot or something. And he said those people just inspire him so much.

And he was so happy Friday. He called me Friday. He didn't have health care, see. So the other day he calls me up, and he says, "Guess what?" He says, "I've got $3,600 in doctor visits from my job." He said, "So I called Kenner Regional," and they were able to see him, and they'll see him with his wound care. He got compression stockings so his legs are [getting better], and Friday he called me and he said, "Mom," he said, "I can see light at the end of the tunnel."

I have been very fortunate. I talk to people who wish they could've come back every day, and I feel very fortunate, and I have nothing to complain about. I've got a brand-new house here, and it wasn't this nice I can tell you, and I didn't have these nice hardwood floors and all that. I'm making memories now. I won't have a lot of stuff anymore, but I'm gonna have me some really nice memories. When the smoke clears, I'll be able to talk about all of the wonderful people that I met and the times that I shared in the restoration of my house, and it'll be good stuff. And God has done allowed me to cook up a whole bunch of good memories with friends, and I'm not worried anymore. At first I was worried, but God builds my confidence up with every time something looks like it's not happening, God says, "Oh, yeah, I got that." Or send somebody along to say, "I'm gonna take care of that for you."

It's been amazing. I almost could say Katrina was a good thing. For some of us, it really was.

4

THE MARY QUEEN OF VIETNAM COMMUNITY IN VILLAGE DE L'EST

Village de l'Est is on the eastern side of the New Orleans East community. Built on what was once marshland, it has experienced sinking and other subsidence issues. The Michoud Bayou was built through the neighborhood to aid with drainage.[1] The community is bordered by the Bayou Sauvage National Wildlife Refuge at its southeastern corner, Parish Road at the west, Chef Menteur Highway at the south, and Lake Pontchartrain on the northwest borders. The levees along the lake were known to be unstable. To add to the vulnerability of the region, this area is some eight feet below sea level.[2] The Louisiana State University Hurricane Center predicted that a hurricane the size of Katrina could result in mass flooding along Lake Pontchartrain's shores, indicating that the swells along the canal near the New Orleans East part of the city could reach up to 16 feet and overwhelm the levees.[3]

The Village de l'Est neighborhood was among the hardest-hit communities in New Orleans post-Katrina. According to the Urban Land Institute, the principal consulting group advising the Bring New Orleans Back Commission, the area around Village de l'Est "experienced some of the city's most severe flooding, with flood depths ranging from 5 to more than 12."[4]

Early recommendations in the redevelopment planning process suggested the area's proximity to the Bayou Sauvage National Wildlife Refuge made this neighborhood a good candidate for conversion to open space. This neighborhood, however, recovered more quickly than others in New Orleans that had similar damage.

Village de l'Est has a distinctive ethnic and racial makeup. The 2000 US Census reports a population of 12,912. Fifty-five percent of this neighborhood is African American. Those of Asian descent are the second-largest group in the area, at 37 percent. In other areas of New Orleans such as New Orleans East, directly adjacent to Village de l'Est, the percentage of Asian residents hovers around 6.5 percent. Village de l'Est has the largest concentration of Vietnamese in the city. Before Katrina, they had created an insular enclave tucked within a larger, predominantly African American community. Mary Queen of Vietnam Catholic Church, located on Willowbrook Drive, is at the center of this Vietnamese community, with the homes of most of its congregants as well as Vietnamese restaurants, grocery stores, and the like reaching out from this core like spokes on a wheel.[5]

When Katrina made her appearance, the church was firmly in place as the heart of the Vietnamese community. MQVN was the home of cultural events, including carnivals, fairs, a weekly farmers' market, and youth events. These events were not simply church programs. Along with the church leadership, MQVN's lay leadership imagined and brought to life many community projects. These projects, such as an extensive urban gardening project and a housing project for seniors, were both outcomes and drivers of cohesiveness within the community. The community's two Vietnamese-owned, -operated, and -focused shopping centers contributed to the community's self-sufficiency and its closeness.

The overwhelming majority of MQVN's congregants live within a one-mile radius of the building.[6] However, the church was not just a building in the geographic center of the community. Nor was it simply a bastion of spiritual safety. MQVN undergirded the characteristics that made this community unique. As Chamlee-Wright and Storr explain, MQVN provided its members an ethnic-specific, Vietnamese-language community.[7] MQVN, for instance, offers Vietnamese language classes and conducts its services in Vietnamese (even a version of its website is in Vietnamese). Additionally, MQVN (along with the Van Hanh Buddhist Center) helps organize and sponsor Tet Nguyên Đán, the Vietnamese New Year, a three-day cultural celebration held on the first day of the lunar year. As with any major holiday, the preparation and celebration far outlast the actual holiday, and this almost month-long celebration draws the community together.[8]

This community was established in the mid-1970s as Vietnamese citizens fled their war-torn country and refugee camps outside of Vietnam to find refuge in the United States. With the assistance of Catholic Charities, many of them made their way to New Orleans. This group of émigrés settled in the West Bank, Algiers, and Avondale. Village de l'Est, however, became home to the highest concentration of Vietnamese immigrants. The group that settled in Village de l'Est comprised refugees from three distinct northern Vietnamese villages that shared a common religion, the desire to be free of communist Vietnamese rule, and the courage to brave a journey to a new land to start a new life. When the partition of Vietnam precipitated an exodus of people from the north to the south of the country, residents from the mostly Catholic villages of Bui Chi province found their way to the coastal town of Vung Tau.[9] After the fall of Saigon, with the help of Roman Catholic charities, refugees from these villages settled in Village de l'Est.

As with other immigrant communities, the first wave of settlers blazed a trail for their countrymen to follow. By the mid-1970s more than 2,000 Vietnamese had settled in Village de l'Est. First living in an apartment complex and eventually moving into single-family dwellings, they established a closely knit community with a distinctly Vietnamese character. Elders from the three separate northern villages developed stronger social ties. As adult children began to intermarry, the community was drawn even closer through familial ties.

As the community grew, the MQVN congregation grew; so much so that they also outgrew the little chapel where they initially worshipped. Consequently, they petitioned the diocese for a larger place to worship and, by 1985, the Mary Queen of Vietnam church with a 6,000-person capacity was built.[10] This became the first Roman Catholic Church in the United States to offer mass in the Vietnamese language.[11]

Another milestone was reached in 2003, when Father Vien Nguyen (known to his parishioners as Father Vien) became priest of the Mary Queen of Vietnam church. He, along with his pastoral team of two priests and five support staff, took on the dual role that previous MQVN priests have performed. Father Vien was not only the religious leader of his flock but also a community leader.[12]

Before Katrina, this community was fairly insular. As MQVN's Father Luke described, "Our ministry is typically about the Vietnamese." Before Katrina, there was a grassroots system consisting of block captains who organized the community to facilitate mostly ministry-related events.[13] As Father Luke described, "We divided [our members] into how you call divisions or zones. I don't know the term but . . . we have eight total, and each leader among the zones [is] in charge of the members of that zone. So any news spreading from the church is spreading through those eight . . . leaders and those leaders go to spread out the news."[14]

Many of the members of MQVN explained that the neighborhood was uniquely suited to their needs. After Katrina, when opportunities presented themselves in other cities, they did not even consider not returning to Village de l'Est. One of the most important elements that drew them back to their New Orleans neighborhood was the Vietnamese-language community it supported. Although the younger generation is comfortably bilingual, some of the older residents could not speak English, and many more had only a transactional knowledge of the English language. In the Village de l'Est neighborhood, Vietnamese is spoken in the majority of commercial and social spaces, leaving native speakers feeling at ease.

Another aspect of the community that drew residents back to Village de l'Est after Katrina was the informal system of communication. It takes almost no time at all to spread the word of an upcoming gathering, a community problem, or a social happening such as a birth or an engagement. As Mary tells us, "Everyone is related to someone in any other way. I'll be related to this person [who] will be related to this person, so the whole community relay[s] messages really quick."[15] As descendants from the original three villages intermarried, a web of family relationships and close social ties evolved. As Quang explains, "Around here everybody knows each other."[16]

Additionally, this community has preserved the customs and cuisines of their homeland, with key ingredients found within blocks of their homes in the Village de l'Est neighborhood. The fact that almost anything residents might need can be found within walking distance of the church and their homes was an attribute residents displaced by Katrina longed for as they endured their time away from New Orleans. The Vietnamese-owned businesses in the Village de l'Est neighborhood include apothecaries selling traditional medicine, pharmacies, and the professional services of Vietnamese-speaking accountants, lawyers, and doctors. And the knowledge of how to find these things and how to navigate the city in general is something that the residents value and were loath to give up.[17] Bill, a Village de l'Est entrepreneur and resident, explained, "Yeah, I love New Orleans. I've been here since 1975. I like New Orleans. I don't like other [places]. In Houston [where he was evacuated], everything is divided. If you're in Houston, [it takes] an hour or forty five minutes; . . . here . . . three minutes, four minutes . . . boom-boom-boom. Everything is close by."[18]

Speaking through an interpreter, Lai explains that she is dependent on neighborhood businesses. She walks to grocery stores, her doctor, and her local pharmacy.[19]

Given the critical role that MQVN played within this community before Katrina, it should come as no surprise that MQVN was active in looking after its congregants from the moment it was clear that Katrina was a serious threat, through the evacuation and exile of many of its members from New Orleans in the hours, weeks, and months following Katrina, to when its members began to return and rebuild.

MQVN was a shelter for those who, for whatever reason, chose not to evacuate the city. Father Vien stayed behind with them, going from house to house in some instances to make sure that everyone was safely evacuated or on church grounds. As the waters rose from the levee breech, Father Vien led a group that went by boat to gather those who had returned home thinking the storm had ended and the danger had passed.

Even those parishioners who did evacuate did not leave the care of MQVN. Once the immediate crisis was over, Father Vien traveled from evacuation site to evacuation site checking on his parishioners, helping them locate missing family members, passing news of friends and family between one city and another, describing to them what was going on in each site, and working with his staff and the lay leadership to set the stage for a return.

Father Vien convinced FEMA to put trailers on the church property so the elderly could all be together and thus feel safe. He negotiated with the utility company to ensure that electricity was being provided. He and the lay leadership organized volunteers into working groups that systematically gutted houses. Very soon after Katrina, MQVN's leadership realized that they needed an organization to facilitate the return of displaced residents and started a community development center that performed many of the functions necessary for return, including helping residents fill out Road Home and other aid applications.

As a result of MQVN's efforts, by April 2006, 1,200 of the 4,000 residents who lived within a one-mile radius of the church had returned. Within a year of the storm, more than 3,000 residents had returned. By the summer of 2007, approximately 90 percent of the MQVN residents were back; at this time the rate of return in New Orleans overall remained at only 45 percent.[20] Within a year of the storm, 70 of the 75 Vietnamese-owned businesses in the MQVN neighborhood were also up and running.

Their tenacity to rebuild their community was bolstered by their support for one another. For instance, Lynn, a 30-year resident and business owner in Village de l'Est, was able to focus on getting her business (a hair salon) up and running because of her sister's help. When asked what her first priority was upon returning, she explained that "the first time coming back, I just turn back to look at the shop."[21] Lynn even slept in her shop before repairing her house. She was able to do this because her sister aided her by shopping and cooking for her, thereby freeing her to work on the salon.[22] Samantha reiterated how important it is to have that family support. "That was also one of the motivating factors to stay here, because you have your family, the support system, especially at this time. We were able to help each other get back on our feet."[23]

By 2009, both the Vietnamese residential and business communities were back and in most cases recovered from Katrina. This return began almost immediately. Not only did business owners hope to restore businesses to the pre-Katrina state, but many business owners also hoped that the "clean slate" that Katrina provided might allow them a platform to expand.[24] For instance, a businessman opened and expanded his flea market right after Katrina. He credits the fact that the MQVN church network was fully functional for the swift return of a customer base. "Before, nobody would stay here," he said "[but] the people come back here now [that] Father open the church back up."[25] When he came up with his idea to build the flea market, he received a pledge of support from Father Vien. "I asked Father Vien, he said, 'Everybody will help you open a flea market.'"[26]

Within five years of Katrina, though the residents recognized that there was still work to be done, the MQVN neighborhood was a bustling, thriving community.

KIM

Kim, a 23-year-old Vietnamese American woman, was born and raised in the MQVN community.

> I stay with my parents. My family includes six siblings, and all of my siblings live in Texas, and I'm the only here with my parents. Basically, I help them physically and to get them to the doctors because they don't speak the language. My parents are late 50s. My father came in 1977–78. My mother came in 1980 in America. I was the first one to be born in America. I'm 23.
>
> I had a bachelor in business administration. . . . After graduation, I worked six months for [state] Senator Jon Johnson. He's a senator of Louisiana. I was his executive secretary doing his paperwork [and screening his phone calls]. He also owned some businesses, so I managed the payroll for the people who work in the businesses for him. And he has some clinics, some free clinics out there, and I also keep in touch with the doctor. He had a lot of businesses so I've been assisting him to manage all that when he's out of the office.

Kim's Katrina evacuation experience began as it had with many other storms.

> When Katrina came, my family evacuated two days prior to the storm, and we went to Texas. And we just stayed there thinking that it would be three days like. Every other year [it] would be three days, so basically [we] didn't bring anything besides three pairs of clothes. I just thought it was a vacation. And as the storm came in, then we realized that we were not allowed to come back. On [the] news, we saw flooding, levee

breaching, and a lot of chaos going on in New Orleans where helicopters [were] coming in picking up people.

Like others, her evacuation destination was dictated by family connections. She went to Houston because her siblings lived there. Although she was safely out of harm's way, her boyfriend remained in New Orleans to care for his ailing mother.

I left, but my boyfriend's family didn't leave because of his situation. His mother was bed-ridden, and she needs feeding tubes and assistance where they need electricity. So it wasn't a time for him to evacuate because he couldn't [leave his parents]; so he stayed back. And, apparently, their house is the only house that has those old phones where it's [a] wired phone so I still kept in touch with him when he was still at the house, which is across the street from the church. When the storm [didn't come in] yet and [before the water rose].

I [had] been calling, and we [had] been talking and asking the situation. And as soon as the phone service got turned off, there's no other contact besides watching the news. I just had a feeling when you see the news, everything was flooded. So we knew that we were below sea level, so we're all like, "There's no way. How we can overcome this?" [But] I didn't give up my hope. I constantly called the house line and hoping that somebody picks up. So I called, and his niece picked up. She said, "The water is rising, and it's above my waistline now." She's only 14 years old, and she says to my waistline now, and it's getting higher and higher. And I said, "So where are you going now? What are you doing? Where is your uncle, [my boyfriend]?"

I just told her, "Tell him to call me." But he never called, and like a whole day goes by and I was freaking out. At night I called again, and his brother picked up. I asked if everybody was okay. Did everybody evacuate to school because it was [a] given that when hurricane seasons come, the school was always open, the church was always open. So people who couldn't have evacuated, they would have to come here for high ground. And he said, "Everybody, about 300 people are [t]here. Food is running low." "I'm home to get some food that's on the shelf up high and hadn't got water yet, and I'm going to bring it back." And I said, "Okay well, get him [my boyfriend] to call me as soon as possible."

And they put numbers on the [television] screens. People who need assistance and some of that [call here]. I called that number and I told them that, you know, "There is a community of 300 to 400." And the response I got from the Coast Guard and the 911 service agency is that, "The wind is still too rough, and the water is rising and we can't make it out that way." And I think I asked, "Are you just going to leave those people there? There [are] 300." And they just said that, "The whole city is flooded so we have to work basically from the most devastated area all the way out." I heard that [and] I just didn't know what to do. Bishop [Luong was] our pastor here before he got ordained to become bishop in California. I called my best friend in California, and I told her, "I don't care what you do, find me the number to the bishop." And she found the number and I called the bishop. And he asked me how I know, and I just told him that I called home to the house and got hold of one of the landline and they told me of the situation. And I cried out for help, and then I told him that, "You have to do something. You have to call on all services or all agencies that can come and assist us." And so he told me to keep in touch and just pray. I don't know if he made any contact with any of the Coast Guard rescue teams. I also made phone calls. I'm very close linked to all the priests [in the Vietnamese area]. I have many priests that are close to my family, so I made phone calls to all the priests throughout the United States.

There was one in Houston, one in Louisiana, and one in New York. We made phone calls everywhere, and I was crying out and I was telling them, "You know if you can gather some of your community members, your parishioners that are willing to come down and save these people. If you can have any transportation to come down and assist these people, please do." And so I was calling on the church itself, the power of God, and the power of all the priests and all the nuns in the church to connect and to actually come down here and see if they can evacuate the people.

And one of the priests that I contacted in Houston called me back, and he's like, "I heard Father Vien's voice on the radio." And he's telling about the situation, and he is saying that you know 300 parishioners that came here had been evacuated to a higher ground to [Chef Menteur] Highway with one of his assistant priests. He left with the 300, and Father Vien stayed there because of my boyfriend's mother. She couldn't leave so he had to wait for a helicopter to come. And at that time, the generator was here so if she leaves, she won't be able to live. So they stayed there. And so he was telling everybody the whole situation over the radio, a [Vietnamese] radio network in Houston.

Kim reaffirms what we've heard about the Vietnamese American community in New Orleans: they are a very close group, with their own particular lines of communication.

The best thing about our community is we're really closely knitted so everybody is always in everybody's business. Everybody knows where everybody is at. So at that time, we knew exactly where to contact, where to make the phone calls. And so people have been calling back and forth, my family getting in touch with our family members, and all that, and filling each other in with the situation here. And of course, through that line of passing on the information, of course a little bit taken off here and a little bit added on [can] make things worse. A lot of the stuff, we really didn't actually know because a lot of [people] were saying that it was [chaotic], a lot of looting going on. And then there was a time where they say that a lot our community were at gunpoint from other people trying to rob what we have, the food and all that. And there were just a lot of rumors, and we didn't know what to believe. But at that time, we just all prayed. My family and everybody, we just prayed.

Her time in Houston was an arduous one for Kim and her family. Although Houston had accommodated many evacuees, like many, Kim and her family found it difficult to navigate.

I came back in October. I could have stayed [in Houston], but knowing that my parents' heart is here, I decided to come back. And my father, the reason for him to come back is that he doesn't know English, and he felt that it would be so difficult for him to find employment in a new state. He can drive; my parents can drive, but being in a new state and new area you know they wouldn't drive. My father is a mechanic. He works for Alpine Plastic, a company that makes [plastic] to distribute to Wal-Mart and . . . all of [the] superstores. And so he fixes the machinery there. And he's been working there for over 16 years. And here, he knows everywhere, any street, any road. He might not know the name, but he knows exactly where it's at. In Texas, he felt like he was a handicap person, that he was disabled. He couldn't drive anywhere. He didn't know where to go. And so it was very difficult for me because I was trying to find a job to keep stable. My siblings, they have restaurants and business and jobs as well, but they don't have the time [to look after my parents] because we have the file for FEMA, SBA loans, Red Cross assistance, and all that. So they couldn't take off their time to take my parents, so I had to manage that.

I had to learn the streets and roads. And I have to take my parents for two months straight to get everything in order. And it's very difficult because it's stressful. You try to use the time, you try to beat everybody to the lines, and you're gone all day, and, you know, coming there and not have enough information. We have to drive back to get all your paperwork and all that.

As with others, Kim's evacuation to Houston extended for several months.

[Well,] eventually three days became two months. So we stayed in Texas for two months.

I came back with my parents [in October], we came back and the road was blocked up. There were National Guards, and they didn't let anyone go in this area. We sneaked in the back way. The first priority was going back to the house and salvage all the papers we didn't bring, take all the paper we didn't bring. And so our first priority is to come home, take all of the documents that we have. So we snuck in and the door was jammed, we couldn't get [in because] all the stuff that was blocking the door. So we used some force, we really pushed in and pushed in. And as the door opened, we're just, we stood there. We just didn't know what to do. I was pretty calm; I didn't cry. My parents cried. My parents think I didn't cry; I didn't want to break down. So they just froze for a bit, [but] I knew where all the documents were. I knew what I needed to take so I just went and salvaged whatever it is [possible to take]. And after a while, my parents saw me doing it, so they started going, they started moving, trying to find where they put . . . our birth certificates . . . where's all this and that? So we took all of that, and we just left. And the next morning, we came back in three in the morning, drive from and took some clothes, we took out clothes and whatever is there.

[It is exactly one year later] and my home is repaired. We went back to Texas for a week, and then we came back. My parents decided to come back so I came back with them. And that was actually the 13th. We came back and we gutted the house. [While we gutted the house], we stayed in my aunt's house [in West Bank]. We were at my aunt's house for up until December, roughly three months.

The biggest challenge was getting [the insurance company to send an adjuster up]. It was very hectic to get him [to come out] because we couldn't do anything until they come out to estimate. The reason we were so late gutting out our house and [fixing it] because the insurance company said that if we gut out, it's our loss. They won't be able to see what's the damages we had. I just want to [gut] it and start coming back. And they said, "No, I can't let you do that. I just have to come back and see it firsthand." So months after months, we couldn't [gut]. The only thing we took out was the refrigerator. We couldn't touch the rest until [the adjuster come].

While they were waiting for the insurance adjuster (a common pastime among Katrina returnees), Kim received help from family but chose not to accept help from the community and had received none from the government.

Yes, my aunt was there for us to help us. When it comes to gutting, it's just my parents and my [niece]. And siblings from Texas, they took turns to come down and started helping . . . to [gut] out the house and fix up the house. So we didn't have any government [help]. At that time, the community has organized people to go around and [gut] houses and assisted. But it was just too many houses and too little volunteers. We couldn't wait for that to come. So we just went ahead to [gut] it ourselves.

Luckily for Kim, she was able to continue working at her pre-Katrina job.

> As I came back in October, I went back to my previous job.
> My job . . . is to screen all applicants through [the offender] registry, fingerprints and all that, to ensure that they have no criminal background before hiring because they're going to work for security and they're going to be armed. I've been working there for eight months before Katrina.
> [When I returned after Katrina] they still had the company, and they still need the assistance because 50 percent of them didn't come back. And everything was so backed up, every company, every contract that we had, they are still needing the security so we were in [the process] of hiring more security, new security. So [in the days] after Katrina, I would interview and process at least 45 applicants. And so it would be very, very hectic, and there are days when things backed up. But everything went well.

Although she was not able to move in right away, like many New Orleanians, she commuted from outside New Orleans.

> So [I was] working and then coming down on weekends. We didn't stay here because my family and my parents' house flooded two feet. And so when we had the permission to come back, our house was already [moldy], you know, eight feet, so we had to gut the house. It wasn't livable at that time so we were traveling back and forth from the [West Bank]. So I worked, and I go Wednesday and on a weekend, we come back here to celebrate mass with the community. And you know during this, after mass, the church and people from the community, they organized hot meals right at the mass. Our families at the mass have something to eat as they gut the house. They had tetanus shot, hepatitis A and B. I coordinated that.

Kim had always been community oriented. When she saw an opportunity to benefit the community, she sprang into action.

I went and got my shot. And then I asked if it's possible if
[Heart to Heart], which is the organization who was giving out
free shots, were able to come down to the community and give
a shot to them because [language was a barrier and] transportation was as well. And so they volunteered to come down
one day, and so I coordinated that. I told the community that
there will be tetanus shot, hepatitis A and B, flu shot, so that it
would be beneficial to the community, especially the elderly. So
they came on and gave out up to 300 shots. And we also were
[distributing] food, something like dry food, canned food, [non]
perishable food, anything like toiletries, cleaning supplies. And
at that time, I wasn't [on] staff with the church or the community, just a parishioner of the community. I didn't come aboard
until December. I knew of the project in November, but I didn't
come aboard until Father Vien, our pastor, asked me to come
aboard. Maybe the beginning of November, he asked me to
come and start kind of assisting around here.

And I hesitated because I didn't want to leave my company.
I had a paying job, and I didn't think it was fair for my company
because they were also in need of assistance. And I told Father
that I need some time to think about it. He's very, very per-
suasive, so I told him, "Give me a month so at least I can tie up
what I started on the project on the company so that I can train
the new employee that's coming in."

Another recruit of Father Vien, Kim helped coordinate the
Katrina cleanup effort in the MQVN community. With no prior
training, Kim nonetheless made a significant contribution to her
community's rebound and recovery by organizing the influx of
volunteer groups.

When I came aboard to Father Vien to assist the community, my
first project here was to be a volunteer coordinator. We had volunteers from all over the United States. Some weeks 20, some
weeks 50, there's weeks where it's 150. And we house them at
the school. And my job was to go out, evaluate the houses that
[signed up for it] . . . well basically it's not even my background
so I don't even know what I'm supposed to look for. But then
I did research to [gut] out my own house; I knew exactly what

is it best that needs to be done. So before the volunteers come in, I had to go in and make sure it was safe, you know nothing was falling off the roof. And that I had to keep in touch with the homeowner and make sure that they took all of the items that they need. I don't want the volunteers to throw out anything that they'd say that they need to keep. So I made sure that the owner came to the house when I arrived there, walked through with them, tell me what exactly what [they] want, need to do. And I make a checklist, and when the volunteers come, I split the teams and I distribute them to the houses. We helped gut the house, and when the gutting was finished, we helped to [protect] the house. We assist[ed] about 300 families.

There was a group out there. One of the biggest groups that came down was Workgroup Camp. They came down with 100, then in the summer, they came down for seven weeks, each week with 100 volunteers. They first came down in November. And that's when I came to work here. The first group was, I'd say, 50 people. They came down. They just came down and start assisting us. The Workgroup Camp was just a base, a headquarters. They volunteered themselves from all over the United States. You know, they are just all faiths, religions coming together.

And when I came aboard to be a volunteer coordinator, every time I send one out, my heart just melts. I had other houses to do. And my house was on the way, but I couldn't cut [in front of] other people. It was hard for me because my parents were frankly frustrated. They were angry. "You have a house, too; your house is also devastated. Why you're not doing your house? You're going out to do somebody else's house." And they just didn't understand my job.

Kim and her family depended on different funding sources to get their house back together again. Government rebuilding assistance was less than what they expected, given some of the higher payouts others had received.

Well, when we came back with the FEMA assistance and all the SBA loans and all that, we thought we didn't have to prove anything of our house. We [thought that it was a] given that, everybody's house [was] damaged. There was a long

waiting [list for] assistance, you know, it was just to the point
that, we have to call everyday to see if assistance is coming
in. And the only assistance we had [was] $2,000, the first
assistance. Other than that, we didn't get anything. And I was
really upset 'cause everybody calling, "We got $26,000. Oh, I
got $10,000. Oh I got rental assistance." I was like, "Well what
happened to my family?"

[Thankfully], my parents and I have savings. Also, my
brother, sister, you know, kind of assist us, chipping in, and we
just put out pocket money. [Also,] we were in the process of
SBA loans. But it was slow. So we took it easy. One bit at a time.
[We did] whatever [was] necessary first. We just kind of worked
at it. And so we gut out the house first and left the house
standing for a whole month. And finally, we had an adjustment
amount of the only $3,000. I wondered, "What is it that you
want me to do with this?" They told me that I can go buy paint
for 25 cents a gallon. And I said, "Why don't you go buy it for
me? Bring it here. I can't I find paint for 25 cents a gallon." And
then I got really mad, and I called insurance again and I blew
up. I yelled at them, and they had another adjuster come out
and they said, "Yeah, this is wrong." They apologized, and he
said, "Just keep this $3,000. And do whatever you got to do."
With that first $3,000, we brought some insulation. We started
putting it together.

Kim acknowledged that although she had problems with her
insurance company and what she considered underpayment
from FEMA, things were even tougher for those who had to tra-
verse a language barrier and who were not college educated.

In cases that some of the families that don't have anyone to do
the translation, they would come to church and do the translation for them. That's when we came aboard as staff, and we
do the translation. We read FEMA [papers]. Keep in mind that
none of us are trained for any of this. So we learned as we go. I
guess it's just survival skills, you know. You have to do what has
to be done. As I did it, I learned the way to do it, and then that's
when I helped the other families.

I felt like it was time. That was my time to give back to the
community. The community has given me so much. I was born

and raised here. I didn't know anything other than this community, other than this city. I went to Southern University at New Orleans, about 10 minutes away.

So as I came on board, Father has given me the opportunity to travel, to visit other communities to see their development. I had to go visit volunteer groups, and well, ask them to come down. And I had to go to Berkeley University to be on a panel and to represent the community.

Kim credits the closeness of the MQVN community for its swift return but acknowledges that the community's isolation pre-Katrina might have played a part in the way their recovery efforts were hampered.

I would say that the best part of our community is that because we're close knitted, so our recovery and returning is much quicker than other communities. But the failure that we have is [little] knowledge of government assistance or not knowing that there's assistance out there. Because I guess we exclude ourselves for so long prior to Katrina. We excluded ourselves as a minority, as a community. Most of the government assistance weren't knowledgeable to our community. Other community, as they come back, they had all other assistance, government assistance. And that's what their advantage and that was our disadvantage.

They look at us as one community that came back, the first community came back, and we were the role model of developing and rebuilding without government to assist us. But we look towards [other communities] because they were the one who had the support, had the government knowledge, and had knew [ways to get] assistance.

[We'll be better prepared next time.] See the history of our community is that our elderly traveled from Vietnam to America, and so they stay close together. They had gone through years of being refugees and evacuating and leaving and all that. So they have survival skills. So if it will happen again, we're prepared. We are always ready. It's just that this time, it came so sudden, we just didn't expect it. And, so yes, when the next time comes around, everybody will be more prepared.

FATHER VIEN

When Katrina hit, Father Vien was the rector of the Mary Queen of Vietnam Roman Catholic Church. We interviewed Father Vien in spring 2006.

I'm the pastor here at Mary Queen of Vietnam Church. This Vietnamese community was established in 1975. With the original exodus in 1975, we were in the refugee camps throughout this country. The Archbishop of New Orleans went to the camps. He invited the people to come to New Orleans and live there. Not only did he invite us, he also invited the priest there to come to New Orleans and establish a community. As people began their life here, they would congregate along [with] their priest.

At age 13 or 14, we moved here to New Orleans. I spent my teen years in New Orleans. I attended public schools: junior high [and] high school. I entered the seminary. We had four major Vietnamese communities and one minor one. This is the largest concentrated Vietnamese community outside of Vietnam. And then there's three communities on the West Bank: Algiers, Avondale, and Aurora. And then there's a minor community comprised of all the people outside of this area, from Greater New Orleans. My predecessor was chosen to be auxiliary bishop for Orange County, [California], and . . . that's how I came to be the pastor here.

Pre-Katrina, we were a pretty insular community. We kept to ourselves. We kept a fairly low profile. We were a very tightly knit community. In order to understand us, you have to understand that this community is comprised of three different communities from North Vietnam. In 1964, those three communities migrated to South Vietnam into three different areas, and they lived together, [though] each village stays in its own . . . and then came the 1975 event. And then all three communities came here. [For example,] two elderly ladies [from] that generation know each other—not only each other, but each other's ancestors, families for 70, 80 years, 100 years. They were from the same village. Once they got here, they began to intermarry and made the other connection. So one is the village connection, the other one is now the connection from intermarrying. So [after] two and a half years, I'm not even sure who's related to

whom or who knows whom. We were fairly content with what
we had here because we've had it going for about 30 years.

Many in New Orleans drew upon Hurricane Betsy as their
benchmark for whether they would or would not evacuate.
Arriving in the 1970s, however, the Vietnamese community had
to draw upon more recent memories, such as Hurricane Ivan,
which hit the Gulf of Mexico in 2004. Given the strength of the
hurricane, many evacuated in anticipation of Ivan, though the
damage it caused in New Orleans was relatively minor. Thus,
when officials warned residents to leave in anticipation of Hurricane Katrina, many were reluctant to leave.

> When Katrina came, [it] was just another storm, because we
> had evacuated before, for Ivan, which came to nothing. And the
> evacuation was successful.
>
> Some of our people did not evacuate because that Friday
> morning, Katrina was aiming for the Florida panhandle. We
> weren't even in the pathway. Friday evening a wake took place
> in this church with more than a thousand people. And then the
> next day, approximately a thousand people were at the funeral.
> And so when we gathered at the time it was done, about 1 p.m.,
> I was on my way to answer to a conference call. Waiting for the
> ferry, I heard St. Bernard and Jackson Parish were under man-
> datory evacuation. Katrina was aiming towards here. Then when
> I came home from the meeting, I was monitoring it on the TV.
> When we had mass that evening, I told the people to get out.
> But knowing that some of them could not [leave], I would keep
> the school open so they could take refuge. It has two stories in
> case of flooding. And then the next morning, we kept shorten-
> ing the masses, and we told people to get out. Around noon, we
> opened up the school building, and people trickled in.
>
> Basically, that's what transpired. A number of our people
> were caught surprised. A number of our elderly people had no
> transportation, and a number of people who were sick, they
> could not be moved. And they just didn't want to after the Ivan
> evacuation. They just couldn't imagine going through the same
> thing again. So that's how, at the end, we had 500 people who
> remained. And we had a lot of wind damage.

There was a small window between when the winds of the storm died down and when the water from the levee breach came rolling in. During that window, some who had found refuge in the church went back home. It wasn't long before they realized that they would have to return to the church for safety. With the help of other parishioners, Father Vien was able to bring most of the residents back to the church's school building where they could be evacuated.

The center of the eye hit St. Bernard Parish. And so we caught the much lesser part, so it was primarily wind rather than water. And so when the storm ended at 2:30 we cleared out of here. The storm, the wind kicked in really hard at approximately 10:00 p.m. on Sunday. And, then at 2:00 a.m., it [was] much stronger. Five minutes after 4:00 a.m. is when the power went out, and so it went on till 2:30 p.m. the next day. And so we were, because the wind was coming in this way, the southeast direction, and then when it whipped around, it came from the northwestern direction. So from this side [. . .] we had the church to protect us. And when it came from this way, we had the school building to protect us. I just thanked God that no one was injured. At 2:30, the storm died down, I drove around to survey the damage. But it was okay. We were on the street, you know, we found they had about 3 inches of water. And so I went out again at 5:30, and I thought, "It seems like the water is higher." And so I came back, and several of my people here said that the level of water was rising. So I walked around, and sure enough 15 minutes later I can see it moved up strongly. And then I listened to the radio, and I was told that in St. Bernard, parts of the levee breached. And so I drove around, I tried to get all of my people who went back to their homes. And so I tried to remember as many people as possible, where they lived, to pick them up. I was driving a 15-passenger van.

Because it was dark, I had people shining flashlights when I drove. When I drove, the water rolls up and blocked the headlight. And so we had to use the flashlight to drive. By 8:30, the water was too deep to drive by then. So we started to use boats to get my people. And I remember going to this one place, about a mile from here, to try to bring a family back.

And along the way, we heard of one lady who had just given birth and she didn't evacuate. So we went over to the house to try to bring her in. And there was a man that was with her who used to be a fisherman. So he rowed the boat. We went to the house. I went in. And he put the boat up on the ground. We stayed for about a minute trying to knock on the door to get her out. No one responded. So we turned around, the boat was gone. The water rose so fast, it whipped the boat away. We finally found it caught in a fence. So we started rowing. And he says, "Father, the current is too strong. We have to find a motor boat." And we turned around and looked for motorboats, but the water wasn't high enough at that location to get it off of its truck. But the rescue work continued. We brought the people back here. And so we monitored the news by listening to the radio. And so on Wednesday, the rescue was coming to help us, I think. They got in boats. They had people out there. At the end, there was some 350 people over here in the school building. And so the evacuation completed at approximately 5:30. I sent my assistant with the rest of the people. I had to stay behind with a family, a lady who was on a [breathing machine]. They could not evacuate her; she was sick. And so I decided to stay behind with her, her husband, and two children. And the daughter is also invalid. So we remained behind. And so people evacuated. It was a real eerie feeling that happened. We had 350 people out here, and then suddenly there was no one else here. And so everything was quiet. It was totally dark. I've never seen it so dark. I mean there was no power anywhere.

As it turned out, those who evacuated were placed in even greater danger, because they were left on Chef Menteur Highway overnight with no provisions.

Okay. And so the next morning, I heard voices calling. And I said, why are these people still here? I thought they were just stubborn. I heard and I knew whose voice it was. He didn't want to go. He wanted to stay here. That's how I found out all my people who had gotten out to Chef Menteur Highway had been left there overnight.

So they were out there all night, and by that time it was 400 people. No tents, just open air. And they were told not to bring anything because they were going to be brought over the Superdome, convention center, they have food and water there and all of that. The boats were only able to bring only the sick, elderly, and children. The strong people were to walk from here to Chef Menteur Highway, walk in about three and a half feet of water, which is about an hour [walk].

That was on Wednesday. They only carried what they could carry. We left all the water and food behind. But they stayed overnight out there, all of them, [including] elderly people. And I told the people that came back, to get all the cooking materials out of here: the propane tank and to get a drum, a big five-gallon drum out there, and build a temporary toilet facility. That was close to the morning. And so the rescuers continued to pick up the rest of the people who were stranded and brought them out. So by the end, there were about 450 people. My feeling was that it is not good. Then I heard about the convention center and the Superdome. I had heard that the Superdome was overwhelmed. Periodically, we plugged the TV into the generator. So we saw some images, so I knew what was down there. When I heard that my people were fighting, I got on a boat and went out there to talk to them. But by the time I arrived, there were about four or five military vehicles. And all my people were on them. So I told them just take care of each other.

Father Vien used his connections to ensure that his congregants who had evacuated to other states received help.

Our telephone lines were doing okay. So I spoke with my connections on the outside and asked them to get ready to receive my people, because I knew they were going to Texas. They left. I get a call from my assistant on his cell phone and [found out] that they arrived at about 5:30. I had heard that the National Guard had arrived, but that they just stayed outside the convention center and that there have been no food, no water given to them at all. He said that for the last two hours [that] there's been riots. I told them to protect each other and so they did. There was no med-evac; they put [the sick lady I waited behind with] on the back of a pickup truck and took off to meet an ambulance that was picking up someone else. And I caught a

ride on the truck. I heard that they would go to San Antonio. I
was on my way to San Antonio when I found out that [some]
were on their way to Arkansas. It was midnight when I arrived
at San Antonio. So we decided to leave the next day. I get a
call from my assistant at about 2:00 a.m. He had just arrived in
Austin. And I [went to Austin the next day].

The residents of Village de l'Est were not permitted to return
to their homes until the first week of October, over a month
after Katrina.

> We were allowed to return the fifth of October, a little over
> a month after the storm. During that time, I was traveling in
> between all locations and trying to bring them into one area. I
> brought all of the people who were in Arkansas back to Austin.
> Some stayed there. Some left to Houston to join their people. I
> found out a week later that one lady was missing. I went back
> again to every place to look for that lady. At the same time, I
> kept each community appraised. I had a digital camera. So I
> took pictures. I took my computer, too, so that each commu-
> nity can get in touch with the other. I organized each location,
> you know, with leaders. Some of the people who were more
> able-bodied would be the first in turn to prepare the way. By
> that time, we were actually all ready for a return in an organized
> manner back to our community.

Although the Village de l'Est residents were exiled from their
homes, they were not without community. The Vietnamese
community in Houston opened their homes and offered support
to members of the MQVN community.

> Austin was the only place that people stayed in [shelters of
> any sort]; the rest of the locations, the people were out of
> [the shelters] as soon as possible because the Vietnamese
> communities there would take them in, especially in Houston.
> I don't think any of the Vietnamese from here stayed [in a
> shelter] in Houston.
>   The [Vietnamese community elders] in Houston called
> on the Vietnamese community there to take in our people.

And our people congregated around a Vietnamese shopping center, and Vietnamese were driving up and holding up fingers to tell how many people they can take in their home. So if your family is that number, you just jump in their car, and they'll take you home. So there was really no interaction with the formal governmental relief. They lined up to register for whatever is given. But that's it, then they go back to the homes. That's how it worked. The different churches, religious communities, took people in. I know one religious community had some 200 evacuees. Another church had [another] 200.

Though they were prepared to return in early October, not all the utilities were functioning, making the logistics of return extremely difficult. For instance, the water had to be trucked in.

I mean we all were just holding our breath to return. The question that was asked of me was how and when can we get back? So I met with my leaders, to divide up the responsibilities. I heard that we were allowed to come in on the fifth of October. And I spoke with a pastor from the West Bank and asked him to allow us to use his community center for a month as the staging area. We arrived Tuesday and set up.

The biggest issue when we brought people back was the lack of water. Therefore, we had to use a staging ground that's 23 miles away. I have a small pickup truck, where I would put some trash barrels and fill them with water, and I drove over here and handed out the water. Our people were coming to wash after the day of working in their home. We, as a community, were able to pull together.

The MQVN community had been through much hardship before Katrina and, according to Father Vien, they considered the problems that arose when they returned as "minor inconveniences." Yet for the entire community to return, municipal services such as trash removal and electricity were a must.

Remember now, my people have migrated from North to South Vietnam in 1964 and then here in 1975. And they are from where there are no running water and electricity. For our elderly [and actually] anyone who's over 30 or 35, the evacuation and the cleanup afterwards is a minor inconvenience. [This is] because we've been damaged several times in our lives. And, therefore, we were not concerned that much. Still, we knew that we need to have electricity to bring all our people back. And then that's what we did the negotiating with Entergy.[27]

I did that together with city councilwoman from this district. She was really good. We came here on Wednesday, October 5. And I remember that there was someone who came by who knew about our church and asked if we would have a mass here on the Sunday. My concern was that there wouldn't be that many people. He said there'll be a lot of people. So I said, you contact them and tell them that there'll be a mass here at 10:00 a.m. Three hundred people showed up on that Sunday. I was truly surprised. So Monday, I called this council lady and told her that the community was starting cleaning up already. So she called a cleanup crew. Tuesday someone from the cleanup crew came, and then he saw all the trash, the debris that we were putting up. He said, "I know the community is back. So I'll send someone over on Thursday." He sent someone on that Thursday; they haven't stopped. So I mean cleanup here for us it's not an issue. Because the good thing about it is that they will be paid by the load. So the more we put out, the happier they were.

The congresswoman called Entergy. She also called city water. I had someone to contact Entergy, and he said that he can have electricity in for us that weekend. He was thinking about temporary setup. Just to our facility, because it was the church, people were coming in. And so when I called Cynthia, she was the councilwoman. She was really surprised, because when she talked to them they said it would be another two to six months. So and then when she heard what I said, she called him again. [By this time], rumors were spreading that I've got power by that weekend. And he called me up and he said, "Look, we need to talk." We met in Baton Rouge, and he explained to me the situation, at the time there were up to 24 power stations for New Orleans. There were only 13 functioning. Of that 13 functioning, only 2 of them were at full capacity. And so they have been directed to downtown as well as midtown for reconstruction. Then he tells us that all of the backbone has been set up for our area and shows us the maps of the area our people could return. And we were going along with that.

But we must justify the load in order for them to divert power out here; we must justify that there are people here planning to receive it. So they needed paying customers. We were always the paying customers. So they needed us in order to go back to their parent company and ask them for more money from having to rebuild. They [didn't] mention an exact number, but he would say something like, I guess you could come up with, say, 100 households. And I gave him pictures that we took of our people in mass. First mass was 300, second mass was 800, third mass we invited all the people from New Orleans, and we had more than 2,000. So I had those pictures to show him. He said, "We need a list." And so we went and got what he asked. We called our people to put their names down and their addresses and also to tell us how deep the water was in their home, so that they can know how high. You see all the outlets [were 16 inches high]. So I guess if the water was under that [mark], then it could take [care of it]. So we helped them with that. I called the people. We printed out sign-up sheets and all of that. So within one week, I went back to Lafayette, to his office; I said, "We have 500 petitioners." So, the first week of November, we had power. And we were the only people with power.

Although they had much greater success with the electrical company and with garbage removal than some other communities, they experienced the same frustrations with the insurance companies that other New Orleanians reported.

[When people came back] they were staying in our school building at the time. We've been outside of our home for five weeks, and they were covered with molds. But the other aspect that we struggled with was that a lot of the insurance companies did not allow our people [to begin work]. I bought cameras for them so that they can take pictures and then begin to remove the bad materials they find. They had called their insurance companies, and they refused to allow them to do that. And the problem is when the adjusters came, let's say if there was roof damage or wind damage. Remember Rita brought in six inches of rain to this area. They refused to allow my people to do [what was necessary to] stop it from further deterioration. When they came in, they said, "Well, there's only the roof damage; we pay for that." I'm still looking at a class action suit. You see, they had adjusters that come in, did the adjustment, agree on the number. They better give us in writing on the number.

My people were using their own savings to fix their roofs and fix everything else inside. They came back later, and guess what, [the adjusters] looked and they said, "Well, there's no damage." Can you believe that? I mean I am surprised that to this point none of [the insurance adjusters] have been killed yet. I mean to go through all of this and now they low-ball us this way. I'm trying to calm them down and telling that I'm bringing in lawyers; otherwise, they will kill somebody. Those adjusters don't know what they're getting into.

With a little help from a FEMA executive, a couple of US senators, and the threat of civil protest, this community was able to secure FEMA trailers on a site that allowed them all to be together.

For us, FEMA has been nothing but good. FEMA has come through on delivery with us. The head of FEMA housing at Grover Station in Baton Rouge, I think he's still there. He sought me out in the shelter that we have in Baton Rouge. And I met with him. So as long as I did not get any lease paper from the government then we can do an exclusive group site just for our people. I had my people sign up on October that we stopped at 500. He says that site could only hold so many. I remember at one of the meetings, I brought him the list, so that they can put my people in, and he said, "No, no. You determine who's going to go in there." That was on the 19th of October [that] we did the paperwork and brought it to the mayor's office. We had our people call and email the mayor. We had the Archdiocese in the discussion. The mayor refused to sign it. He refused to sign it . . . so November 21st was a Monday. And if they had to bring it up at the commission's meeting on the Monday. I called the Archbishop, because he was on the commission. I told him that unless the mayor signed it on that day, we will set up a tent city because my people are living in moldy homes waiting for FEMA. That evening, the Archbishop called me and said that [the mayor] signed it. But nothing moved for a whole week. And so I called them again, and I said that Monday, if it doesn't happen, that [tent] city's going up. It was cold, in the lower 40s here. And then we had to go purchase heaters, and we backed out for a moment, and remember, December 6th, 7th, and 8th, the mayor sent his people out to Atlanta, Dallas, Houston, and invited the people to return. And, [why] he sent his people out to invite the evacuees to return? We are here already. And yet he has impeded our return. So, is it racial? That's the question. Is it because we're not of the right color? So few of them caught up on that, and some senators came out here.

Well, Hillary Clinton and Mary Landrieu were coming in at the weekend after. So they came to this place. And my understanding was that they called the head of FEMA, and that person was able to reach the mayor that day. The next day, Senator[s] Clinton and Landrieu were going to see the mayor. Only then were we able to come in to do that. Now we had to negotiate how many trailers, exactly how we set [them] up, and all of that. That piece of property [was owned by the] Archdiocese. The problem is who is going to pay for liability insurance. [I said] I will have all of my people sign a waiver before they came in. The Archdiocese finally said, "Okay, we will take the liability insurance." That's when it was fine. And then it came down to how it was going to be lined up. FEMA had a meeting.

Entergy had called me before about long-term recovery. They knew that we had intended to build a retirement community on that side for a long time. So they were trying to [figure out] how we can prepare now, so that the infrastructure [they set up now] can be used [later in that project]. They came in with the long-term people; all of them came in to meet with us. The approved contractor kept on saying, you can't do this and you can't do that, and we had a conference call with the FEMA housing director. And we discussed the situation. I asked the FEMA person, do I have permission to do everything we need to be done? The FEMA director said, yes, that we have permission to do what has to be done. So we had a meeting. And again, [the contractor] kept on saying, it can't be worked out.

I got so angry, and I said, well if this guy can't do it, tell him to get the hell out. Then we'll have another contractor. He was just being difficult. He didn't want what it was. He had wanted to do the aboveground infrastructure. So we went back and forth on that. Finally, they gave in and said they will do exactly what we asked. The trailers will be able to move in on the 20th of May. I remember the original list was 500. But people are still coming. So how many will we require them? I do not know. It depends upon the condition of their home [on the weekends].

Within a one-mile radius of the church pre-Katrina according to the last census, we had some 4,000 people. We have approximately 1,200 people having returned here already permanently. But a large number of them have not received payment from the insurance company. So they're still waiting for that. We are helping out. We're distributing money to get Sheetrock and things like that. But on weekends, however, we have approximately 2,300 to 2,600 people attending mass every weekend. And they drive in from elsewhere far out, because they work on their homes then.

Father Vien explains how a Katrina fatality has added a sense of urgency to their plans for permanent housing for senior citizens across from the church.

And as our people became more financially stable, they bought houses in different districts, and then they built homes on that street. The people are still living back there as well. So you see more elderly people in that direction [the other direction from the rich folk]. That low-income housing, my elderly people who live there were always terrified. Low-income housing is not safe; they're often assaulted and robbed. Even if I were to go and visit them, I would have to call them beforehand; otherwise they wouldn't have cracked the shutters. And so we had a plan to deal with that pre-Katrina. Post-Katrina, it brought on an additional urgency because the lady that I was looking for, she died in her home. I found her on the 29th of September. She died about three or four days before, I [think] she ran out of water. And after Katrina, I managed to come back, and I didn't know she was there. And I know that she was scared, you know what I mean? You see, the rescue team journeyed to her building and didn't enter because that building did not flood, that whole area did not flood at all. So they didn't enter.

So we lost her. But had it been a place where we have control, I would have gone into, would have opened each and every door in search of them. None of our people died of the flood; she died because she didn't have water.

But basically, FEMA again sat in as we did the planning charrette [for the senior housing facility]. We brought in some experts from all over the country. We paid for that. Yeah, we brought in two architects from Vietnam as well. We showed to all of them. And so that was done and [was] completed almost two months ago. So that's how we did. You see, what else can I ask from FEMA? Nothing.

Father Vien noted that Katrina gave the community an opportunity to act on plans that seemed too expensive before Katrina.

The flood map probably will change, but it won't affect us that much. Whether it changed or not, we are planning on elevating our new buildings to an elevation of six to eight feet anyway. Pre-Katrina, the Vietnamese architecture calls for buildings that would be on stilts, so I was advocating that using a bottom-flooded garage. The people in our development team didn't like that because it would be extremely costly. They were trying to find a way to spare cost, you see. Now after the storm, everyone agrees that it has to be. We don't own [the land yet]. However, just keep in mind that of the 4,000 people within a one-mile radius of the [church], at least 3,800 of them are Catholic. We don't own it, but we can call our people together. I think of all of the businesses, there may be [only] two or three business owners who are not Catholic.

We want to create the first Viet Town in the United States. So I have people think of Little Saigon in California. Little Saigon in California are just strips and strips of mall. Here we redesign it according to Vietnamese architecture. And so that's the difference. I mean there they started out with some businesses, and then it grew according to the consumer base. But here we design it from the beginning.

Not only it will break the insularity, because of what we are aiming for in designing Viet Town is that it would be a tourist attraction for the whole area, you see. Because the [Bring] New Orleans [Back] Commission[28] plans the light rail

would extend to a line that goes from the Central Business
District out. So we would use, utilize that and build around
the traffic-oriented retail.

Father Vien understands that the church and the people can do
a lot. But he also recognizes the need for government that oper-
ates effectively, one that supports the community rebuilding
effort, and he is determined to mobilize politically to support
candidates who support their causes.

Basically I believe that if the city, the leadership, is good enough
to sit down together and put together a plan, the federal
government will fund it. The problem here is we're scattered all
over the place. That's why the next election is so crucial that we
choose the right people to do that. I believe it will happen. If it
does, it could be a tremendous boon for our area, because then
this being the terminus [of the light rail], then we would capture
all of the people from the east, you see. I believe that it will happen in the next 10 years because we are trying to get our plan
to be incorporated into the city's master plan.

And that's what we stipulate for the community to support
a candidate. We have mobilized for the first time in 13 years,
both the East Bank and the West Bank community. The community will vote bloc. If you support these issues, you have a
very good chance of getting our votes. Basically, that's what
we're working on right now.

Katrina transformed the MQVN community from an insular community to one that is politically engaged. Father Vien
believes that this political engagement is necessary because he
sees many signs that the city and state governments are trying to
hamper the return of his community.

Next thing, I'll tell you about the landfill. Well, the mayor made
an executive order to put a temporary landfill that's about less
than a mile from where we are. And it's right next to the largest
national wildlife refuge in the continental US.[29] It's separated
only by a canal, by a 68-foot canal.

Now, that canal is connected to the canal that's along our area. Okay. And so and we're using the water to water the gardens, okay.[30] And so they're talking about the whole cleanup effort will be 12.5 million cubic yards. And they're talking of putting 5 million cubic yards there. They're calling it a temporary landfill. How is it gonna be temporary? I mean this is what we're dealing with. [They] think we're nuts. We aren't nuts. They're nuts.

This is all wetland, the water table is about two to three feet under the ground. Okay. So with all of that passing down, it's gonna leak out into our water. Okay. But on top of that, in New Orleans East, about 1,500 people who have returned, in the whole New Orleans East, other than the 4,000 with FEMA, out of that 1,200 are ours. Out of the 70 businesses that have reopened in New Orleans East, we have reopened 40 of them; that's in a one-mile radius. And now they're dumping the dumpsite right next to our community. So I believe that's a deliberate intention of hampering our return. So let me talk to you more about the state. They're determining that they won't reopen any public schools here till the next school year. And, then [they]'re talking about charter school.

The state cannot assure that it will open a charter school here. And they said they won't make that decision until June or July. June or July? My people make decisions about the children's future now, not June or July [2006]. Also, there's no hospital here, [but] we have the only doctor's office in the whole of New Orleans East, two pharmacies, [and one] dentist's office for the whole of New Orleans East.[31] And this is what they do to us. I believe it is deliberate.

We've been through it before, worse than this. Again, this is a minor inconvenience. We are unified. I mean we have very clear leadership, and we speak with one voice. And when I need to call on my people to the rally, they'll be there.

MARY

Mary, a 26-year-old Vietnamese American woman who has lived in the MQVN community all her life, was a graduate student when Katrina hit. We spoke with Mary in spring 2006.

I live with my dad and my stepmother and another sister. I'm the oldest. I was a member of the Daughters of Mary. It is just [an organization] of younger women. Every first Sunday of the month, we would have, like [a] two-hour prayer service. We would try to raise money for the poor, the hungry. We have a walk for the hungry [once a] month here. And then so we would try to raise money for that.

Before Katrina, we have a lot of challenges. The first challenge I remember was the landfill. I think I was about 10 because it happened around 1990. I remember like everyone had these "No Big Oak Landfill" signs. You know, like we have the bumper stickers. And so that was my first time actually being in a rally. We were just like walking around the church like holding signs, "No Big Oak Landfills." And so we overcome that. We won that.

Like many New Orleanians, Mary originally did not want to evacuate. For her, the decision to stay was complicated by personal dislikes, family peculiarities, past storm experiences, and familial loyalty.

I never evacuate. I don't like sitting in traffic, so [I said], "No, you know, let's not." And then I have a sister that has Down's syndrome. So if we were to go stay with someone else, we think that that would be a burden to them. So we're like we would like, "Let's just stay home." So we are all content on staying home for Katrina, because we're like, you know, it's just going to be another storm, like any other storm. It's going to pass by, we'll be back.

Eventually Mary's father's best friend convinced him to evacuate to DeRidder, Louisiana, where the best friend's brother had a house. DeRidder is about 240 miles west of New Orleans. Mary's fiancé's sister's boyfriend is the one who finally convinced her to evacuate. Though Mary was able to choose her evacuation city, nonetheless, like those who were not able to choose their destination, she spent much of her time in exile separated from some of her closest family members. Her decision to come back was not based on a pull to be back in New Orleans or a desire to leave Houston but rather a sense of duty.

Father Vien actually called me because they needed people to work. He called me, and then I was kind of reluctant because, you know, my family was in Houston and then my stepmom was going to give birth at the beginning of December. So I kind of don't want to, but then, it's really hard to say no to Father Vien [and] in the end I was like, all right. I came back. November, after Thanksgiving, I came back by myself.

I kept [asking] my dad, "Do you want to fix up the house?" Because the house, we gutted everything out, but it was just still sitting there. So I asked my dad, "Do you want to fix up the house, because I'm here." I was [living in] Homa. When I got back in November, that's where I lived because we had a house there. And I was like, "No, I don't want to live with other people." So I was just driving for that hour, back and forth.

The decision to rebuild was a difficult one. Returning to a post-disaster context only makes sense if you believe that most of your neighbors will return. Many residents will wait for signs that the community is rebounding before they commit to a return. But that same logic of return holds for everyone else in the community. In the MQVN community, Father Vien and the MQVN church played a key role in helping this community overcome this "collective action problem."[32]

So then I stayed in Homa for probably about a month, a month and a half. And so my dad was like, "Okay well, let's just start with the roof," because he was kind of [iffy]. He was like, "If these people weren't going to return, you know, because there's nothing, we're going to be wasting our money in fixing up the house." It was like late November, early December. So I was like, "You know, let's just fix up the house because, you know, this community is going to come back, you know." And then he was like, "Okay well, if you say it's going to come back, [then] let's start fixing up the house."

Mary accepted Father Vien's request to coordinate the returnees into FEMA trailers as quickly as possible. This decision set Mary on a path that would eventually find her in the role of executive director of a newly created nonprofit.

[My friend] Kim was getting paid through Catholic Charities when she came. I was being paid through the National Alliance of Vietnamese American Service Agencies (NAVASA).[33] NAVASA funded me. And then, so I was to help with the FEMA trailers; whoever needed one, they would come to me to sign up for one. And so that was what I was mainly doing.

Now I'm the executive director for the CDC [Community Development Corporation]. It was incorporated on May 9 of [2006]. Father Vien was like, we need the Community Development Corporation because we just have the church, and you know, for us to do all these developments, you know, the church shouldn't be involved, so we should have a CDC. So then I did the research. I went to talk to a lawyer, and so she did the papers. And so mainly I was the one that did all the paperwork for the CDC. I asked Father Vien how he's going to find an executive director because the lawyer was like, "I need to know who's the executive director [ED] going to be." So then Father Vien was going to put out a national ad for an executive director. A month later, I talked to Father Vien. I need to know who is going to be the ED, you know; the lawyer needs to know so she can put in the papers. So he said, "You're going to be the ED." I'm like, "No." And then I say, "I don't want to do it." So he left it off like that. [The] next week we had the pastoral council meeting and then he introduced me as the ED.

So it seems like I got stuck in it. I've never been an ED. I have no experience in what ED does. That was my biggest challenge. I don't know how to be an ED. I'm supposed to like run the CDC. I'm supposed to try to find funding for it, try to make it organized, and so, I'm still working on it right now. I've been doing this for five months now.

We work with Providence Community Housing.[34] So they develop affordable housing for like low income. They're based in New Orleans. We're co-developing with them to do the senior housing. Senior housing is one of the biggest priorities for this community right now. We're applying for the tax credit application which is due in eight days. So we're working on that. We're developing 110 independent units. We hope to have it in two years. The next project is going to be the charter school.

Mary's family demonstrates how savings can play a key role in an individual's or family's ability to return. When the insurance company shorted their claim and they had to put $80,000 into rebuilding their house, it came out of her father's personal savings.

I found a couple of contractors that the people here were recommending. I contacted them. You know, my dad gave me $10,000 [from our savings] to like start with whatever I can.

So I fixed up the roof, and [then] they were putting up Sheetrock and stuff. There were like a lot of [volunteers] my age or younger. And they had two like experienced Sheetrockers. I don't know how to put up the Sheetrock, but when they did it, I thought it looked fine. But then my dad came home, and he's like, "Oh my God, you know, they did a horrible job!" And then so, some parts of the house was nice, you know, some parts we have to knock it down to put up new Sheetrock.

Dealing with contractors [was the biggest challenge]. I think I made a lot of mistakes. A lot of times I got ripped off, you know. Paying too much just to install the bathrooms or something and just keeping up with them. Basically it's like I don't know how they're doing it. I just see them working and I'm like "OK." You know, my dad is like, "Make sure they're doing it right." I'm like, "I don't know how it is supposed to look like for me to think that it's right." And trying to see if afterwards if their work was right. You know, like the plumbing guy came and charged me like $500, $550, when the work is supposed to be $200, you know. Some of my uncles were coming. They're like, "You got ripped off." But I had to decide fast because it was flooded, my whole place.

I made a lot of Home Depot runs. I carried a lot of stuff on myself, took care of it by myself. At the same time, I was helping other people with their problems, like FEMA problems, insurance problems. I was helping with them, and then I would come home. On break time, I would run home to check on contractors.

Mary attributes the success of the rebuilding effort in her community to the fact that they are a close community. Additionally, she believes that the members of her community are determined to make it work in New Orleans because it would just be harder to start life over elsewhere.

> You've probably heard it about a million times already, but we're really very close. We're just really close. I mean everyone is related to someone in any other way. I'll be related to this person, which will be related to this person . . . the whole community. We relay messages really quick. And then so we wanted to return because this is the only place we know of. For my dad, who's 56, to move into another state to rebuild his life, buy a house, to get even familiar with the road. I mean in Houston we got lost every day.
>
> [My dad speaks English] but very rarely, not socially. Like, you know, he would speak English at work, but when he comes home, he speaks Vietnamese, so it's very minimal, you know. So that's why it's really hard to adjust. And then even with the seniors, you know, they're so used to this community, you know, you drive two minutes to the Vietnamese market if you need something, you know. So our success, I think it's because we're really determined. We're very determined. We wanted to come back.

Conclusion
STORIES OF RESILIENCE

As we ready this collection of oral histories for press, we are anticipating Katrina's 10th anniversary. For many New Orleanians, this milestone is bittersweet. On the one hand, the population rebound for the city as a whole has been impressive. Between 2007 and 2013, population growth in New Orleans was 28 percent, ranking it first among the 111 US cities with populations greater than 200,000.[1] The city's population of 379,000, however, is still below its pre-Katrina level of 484,000.[2] To date, 38 of New Orleans' 72 neighborhoods have recovered over 90 percent of their pre-Katrina population, including Central City, Pontchartrain Park, Gentilly Terrace, and the Bywater neighborhood in the Upper Ninth Ward.[3] Since 2010, the percentage growth of residences actively receiving mail (a widely cited proxy for community rebound) has grown more than 20 percent in Central City, Pontchartrain Park, the Desire and Florida Avenue neighborhoods in the Upper Ninth Ward, and the Lower Ninth and Holy Cross neighborhoods.[4] But the Lower Ninth Ward still has less than half the population it had before Katrina.[5] Some neighborhoods have experienced a sort of renaissance. The Bywater neighborhood, for example, boasts a trendy new arts district, new cafés, experimental theater, and a $3.7 million project to renovate the St. Roch Market.[6] In response to the Deepwater Horizon BP oil spill, the MQVN community has developed an aquaponics co-op that has allowed community fishers to restore their income and expand vegetable sales to local restaurants and markets.[7] Other communities continue to experience high rates of concentrated poverty, a weakened infrastructure, the loss of key amenities, and persistent blight.[8]

Understanding the reasons behind this variation from one community to another has been the grand question that has guided our research from the start of this project. As the references to our social scientific work suggest, addressing this question is a complex enterprise involving multiple disciplines from political economy to sociology, to cultural and urban studies. But even with the comprehensive approach we have taken, something is missing in our understanding of community recovery if we do not hear the fuller stories of particular people who survived, returned, and rebuilt those communities.

The oral histories highlighted here point to challenges that make any recovery (even if incomplete) remarkable. A history of tragedy and loss might render some incapable of taking on the hardships of post-disaster recovery, but narratives such as Miriam's remind us that resilience is possible even in the wake of the most devastating kind of personal tragedy. These fuller stories help us appreciate the scale of destruction Katrina wrought and the challenge that such destruction presented to the average person, in ways that are not appropriately conveyed by aggregate citywide estimates of property damage. The fuller narratives help us understand that Katrina's destructive force continued well beyond the point when floodwaters had subsided. The loss of elders and loved ones in poor health, though never formally counted among the casualties of the storm, is part of many people's Katrina stories. Such emotional burdens compounded those associated with rebuilding a home, regaining financial security, and maintaining a sense of well-being. These stories also remind us that as difficult as it was to manage the physical and emotional damage Katrina inflicted, the confusion, delay, and bureaucratic runaround so many experienced at the hands of insurance companies, FEMA, the SBA, the Road Home program, repairs in the city's infrastructure, return of critical services, and other forms of "help" was in many ways worse than dealing with the physical damage.

More importantly, fuller narratives like those featured here point to the capacity of individuals and communities to overcome such obstacles. It is in someone's fuller story that we are able to identify the sources of resilience upon which they rely, and how they deploy such resources to fit the turbulent and unfamiliar challenges a post-disaster context presents.

External resources were certainly part of the story of recovery. In addition to the varied sources of government relief and insurance payouts, communities benefited from the philanthropic and charitable acts of others. The stories presented here acknowledge the invaluable forms of support church groups, volunteer organizations, and private citizens offered New Orleanians immediately following the storm and after their return. But such stories also help us identify various sources of resilience found among individuals and within communities directly impacted by the storm.

Some forms of resilience are personal. Miriam's ability to swiftly adapt to radically changed circumstances, for example, was clearly on display in the underground economy she operated in the convention center. This adaptability was also on display as she took on the role of "pioneer" in the potentially dangerous early days following Katrina. As she recalled,

> I got my house together, move in here and chain that generator up through that porch. Got me some cords to watch TV, put my air mattress right there in the middle of that floor. Took one dog, put him outside, took two dogs, put them inside. I can hear him outside but you can [also] hear [people] running from the MP. See, they was up to no good. They were stealing people's things [from] their houses.

For others, their personal source of resilience was spiritual in origin. Kim from the Ninth Ward saw her interactions with people who lived on the neighborhood as her street-corner ministry.

> [T]his is where God wanted me, outside of church. I [used to] go to church on Tuesday night, Wednesday night, Saturday morning, and Sunday. When I opened this grocery store, I wasn't able to do that. But I then kind of felt like I'd given my own little ministry right here on this corner.

She came back not only to restore her livelihood but also to provide support to the people in the neighborhood who needed her. Again, Kim's spiritual resources were the source of her personal resilience that enabled her to withstand the challenges of post-disaster recovery. As she remarked,

> I'm just a person that—I don't let nothing get me down. No matter what, I'm always smiling. I never cried over anything that was lost because it's just material things. And I feel that I have something bigger and better that I'm working towards, you know. I heard people crying over their house or whatever. I just always say, "Don't worry about that. God's got a mansion for us." And they always tell me that, "You're always smiling, and you're always cheerful. How can you be?" Even my sisters, my niece, when they came to the house after Katrina, they wanted to know. I said, "Well, God gave me this smile, and I ain't gonna let the devil steal it."

Like any personal narrative, Katrina stories are crafted stories. Personal narratives are not simply catalogues of events; they are framed in particular ways, emphasizing particular lessons. The ways in which a person crafts her story can itself be a source of personal resilience. For example, Lydia framed her story in such a way that Katrina, even with all the devastation, sorrow, and hardship it inflicted, was (in the end) a blessing.

I have been very fortunate. I talk to people who wish they could've come back every day, and I feel very fortunate and I have nothing to complain about. I've got a brand-new house here, and it wasn't this nice I can tell you, and I didn't have these nice hardwood floors and all that. I'm making memories now. I won't have a lot of stuff anymore, but I'm gonna have me some really nice memories. When the smoke clears, I'll be able to talk about all of the wonderful people that I met and the times that I shared in the restoration of my house, and it'll be good stuff. And God has done allowed me to cook up a whole bunch of good memories with friends, and I'm not worried anymore. At first I was worried, but God builds my confidence up with every time something looks like it's not happening, God says, "Oh, yeah, I got that." Or send somebody along to say, "I'm gonna take care of that for you." It's been amazing. I almost could say Katrina was a good thing for some of us. It really was.

Many of the people we interviewed crafted their stories in ways that made New Orleans, and the return to and restoration of New Orleans, an imperative. The role of place in these stories ranged from the practical ("in Texas, [my father] felt like he was a handicap person, that he was disabled") to the emotional ("New Orleans is a beautiful place, even in a storm").

Some narratives cast New Orleans as a leading character in their story, a character that was noble, but beaten down and in need of rescue.[9] Again, Lydia provides an apt example.

I am tied to New Orleans. I grew up with the culture. I grew up living across the street from the graveyard. I saw the second lines. I knew what that was about. We do funerals here like nobody else, here in New Orleans. We can start a parade for anything. But back when I was a child, it was a sad occasion to see the horn players going to the graveyard. Over when they came out, they would be playing—going in they'd be playing "Just a Closer Walk with Thee," moving real slow and sad, and they'd come out playing "Oh When the Saints Go Marching In." I grew up on Washington Avenue when the Jewish people had all these little dry goods stores, and our predominant shopping

area was Treme Street, not Canal. The blacks went to Treme.
And that's when New Orleans was a real small community,
and I think that can happen again. The beauty of the city, the
houses and the porches and the neutral grounds. You don't go
anywhere else and see that, and I think it would be a shame
for us to lose that, all those beautiful old houses up and down
Esplanade Avenue. I love that. I still like to go and walk down
Esplanade just to look at the beauty in the city.

And recall Saundra, for whom the city of New Orleans is inti-
mately woven into the story of her extended, close-knit family.

I say all of this so that I can explain to you that there are six
generations of us on my maternal side that have lived in this
city. [. . .] It was in a very black kind of way, Ozzie and Harriet.
It was that kind of a familial familiar-ness that bonded us and
made us really, really comfortable about being together. [. . .]
[New Orleans] is the city that I love and the reason that I don't
want to live nowhere else [. . .] There is so much oldness that
informs today, like the music and like the food and like the traditions that every New Orleans commercial or public view puts
forward in a very one-dimensional kind of way. When we were
away from the city for a long, long time and were able to come
back just for an evening, something that was going on at the
Ashe Cultural Arts Center. [. . .] The drums were there, and it
was like the heartbeat had got started again, and I didn't realize
how much of that I missed or that how it was missing in my life.
I guess what I didn't realize was how important it was for me
to hear that—to kind of enliven my spirit, to quicken my heart.
[. . .] Rebuilding is not somebody else's job. We have to own it
ourselves. [I get asked,] "How do you balance all of that with
family and yourself and the need to get this done?" [. . .] We
have to own it as almost the same thing and by doing that we
have to include our children and our families in the explaining of
how important it is and charging them to be responsible.

Sometimes the stories that people craft are stories of their community's identity. And sometimes these stories have direct rel-
evance for post-disaster recovery. As Father Vien observed,

"We've been through it before, worse than this. Again, [Katrina] is a minor inconvenience. We are unified." Father Vien articulated this community narrative over and over again, from the pulpit, through the media, at cultural events, and in casual conversations. This narrative—the narrative of "this is who we are"—resonated with members of the community, and they repeated it to themselves and to others. As Kim observed,

> See, the history of our community is that our elderly traveled from Vietnam to America and so they stay close together. They had gone through years of being refugees and evacuating and leaving and all that. So they have survival skills. So, if it will happen again, we're prepared. We are always ready.

Katrina stories, like those gathered here, are important to us because each is a thread that helps us weave a collective memory of this critical moment in American history. Such stories are important because they allow us to bear witness to the suffering experienced and courage displayed by ordinary people caught in extraordinary times. Finally, these stories are important because they give us essential clues as to how individuals and communities are able to rebound in the face of catastrophic disaster. The power of personal and community narratives to serve as sources of resilience is best captured and conveyed when we hear those stories directly from the people who craft them. With these lessons in mind, we offer this collection to those attempting to gain a deeper understanding of this chapter in the American experience.

Notes

INTRODUCTION

1. See, for instance, the following studies: Emily Chamlee-Wright, *The Cultural and Political Economy of Recovery: Social Learning in a Post-disaster Environment* (New York: Routledge, 2010); Emily Chamlee-Wright and Virgil Henry Storr, eds., *The Political Economy of Hurricane Katrina and Community Rebound* (Cheltenham, UK, and Northampton, MA: Edward Elgar, 2010); Emily Chamlee-Wright and Virgil Henry Storr, "'There's No Place Like New Orleans': Sense of Place and Community Recovery in the Ninth Ward after Hurricane Katrina," *Journal of Urban Affairs* 31, no. 5 (2009): 615–34; Emily Chamlee-Wright and Virgil Henry Storr, "Club Goods and Post-disaster Community Return," *Rationality and Society* 21, no. 4 (2009): 429–58; Emily Chamlee-Wright and Virgil Henry Storr, "The Role of Social Entrepreneurship in Post-disaster Recovery," *International Journey of Innovation and Regional Development* 2, no. 1–2 (2010): 150–64; and Emily Chamlee-Wright and Virgil H. Storr, "Expectations of Government's Response to Disaster," *Public Choice* 144, no. 1–2 (2010): 253–74.

2. Chamlee-Wright and Storr, "'There's No Place Like New Orleans.'"

3. See Emily Chamlee-Wright, "Signaling Effects of Commercial and Civil Society," *International Journal of Social Economics* 35, no. 8 (2008): 615–26.

1. NINTH WARD

1. James M. Dessauer and Avery Armstrong, "Physical, Economic and Social Attributes of the New Orleans Ninth Ward," Cornell University New Orleans Planning Initiative, January 18, 2006, 6.

2. "This house type is one room wide, one story tall and several rooms deep (usually three or more) and has its primary entrance in the gable end. Its perpendicular alignment breaks with the usual Euro-American pattern, in which the gables are on the sides and the entrance is on the facade or long side. Although gable-entry houses occur in some parts of central Africa, the shotgun house is a New World hybrid that developed in the West Indies and entered the United States via New Orleans in the early 19th century." John Michael Vlach, "Afro-Americans," in *America's Architectural Roots: Ethnic Groups That Built America*, ed. Dell Upton (New York: Preservation Press, 1987), 43.

3. Sarah Searight, *New Orleans* (New York: Stein and Day, 1973), 30.

4. *New Orleans Times-Picayune*, November 9, 1955, quoted in Juliette Landphair, "Sewerage, Sidewalks and Schools: The New Orleans Ninth Ward and Public School Desegregation," *Louisiana History: The Journal of Louisiana Historical Association* 40, no. 1 (1999): 35–62.

5. See Greater New Orleans Community Data Center, Pre-Katrina Orleans Parish Data and Information, accessed January 1, 2015, http://www.datacenterresearch.org/pre-katrina/orleans/index.html.

6. Frank Etheridge, "Last of the Ninth," *New Orleans Gambit Weekly*, November 22, 2005, quoted in Juliette Landphair, "'The Forgotten People of New Orleans': Community, Vulnerability, and the Lower Ninth Ward," *Journal of American History* 94, no. 3 (2007): 837–45.

7. Thomas J. Campanella, "Urban Resilience and the Recovery of New Orleans," *Journal of the American Planning Association* 72, no. 2 (2006): 141–46, 145.

8. James M. Dessauer and Avery Armstrong, "Physical, Economic and Social Attributes of the New Orleans Ninth Ward," 6.

9. Ibid.

10. Chamlee-Wright and Storr argue that the reason behind this tenacious drive to return and rebuild is tied to the ninth-warders' particular sense of place. They contend that "by focusing on the meanings that the returnees attach to their neighborhoods we can learn a great deal about Ninth Ward residents' sense of place. Specifically . . . that the narratives of Ninth Ward residents reflect a particularly strong sense of place, perhaps because of the surprisingly high levels of homeownership in some of these communities." What they learn through the narratives of returning residents "suggest[s] high levels place attachment, identity and dependence even though outsiders have emphasized the supposed negative characteristics and vulnerabilities of these neighborhoods." Once again the residents of the Ninth Ward see their community through a different lens than do outsiders; it is a place in which they can find identity; it is a place in which they can be an activist; it is the place where they can sit on the porch and know the name and family connection of everyone that passes by; a place where many feel comfortable leaving their doors unlocked. They see the place as home. Katrina, as we will learn, did not change that, at least for those who chose to return. Chamlee-Wright and Storr, "'There's No Place Like New Orleans,'" 619.

11. Many people moved out to St. Bernard and Plaquemines Parish to avoid desegregation. Searight, *New Orleans*, 118.

12. "Eighty-one people died, and damage in southeast Louisiana totaled $1.4 billion. After the overtopping of the levees, it took nearly eight hours to get the pumping systems back to normal. . . . The Orleans Levee Board responded by raising the levee height to 12 feet." Barbara McCarragher, "Hurricanes: History," *New Orleans Hurricane History*, Massachusetts Institute of Technology, accessed January 1, 2015, http://web.mit.edu/12.000/www/m2010/teams/neworleans1/hurricane%20history.htm.

13. "Also known as the 'Captain's Houses' and 'Pilot Houses,' these two nearly identical structures with their green tile concave roofs date back to 1910 when Paul Doullut, a steamboat captain, had them built at Egania and Douglas Streets." Historic Green, "Lower Ninth Ward History: Landmarks in the Lower Ninth," accessed January 1, 2015, http://historicgreen.org/2007/12/lower-ninth-ward-history/.

14. Interview with Sheila J.

15. Ibid.

16. A *po'boy* is a submarine sandwich in which the essential ingredients are fried seafood served on a baguette. A *huckabuck* is a frozen lemonade, Kool-Aid, or other syrupy beverage, traditionally served in a Styrofoam or paper cup. Both are traditional Louisiana fare.

17. Landphair, "'The Forgotten People of New Orleans,'" 837.

18. Ibid.

19. Ceci Connolly, "9th Ward: History, Yes, but a Future? Race and Class Frame Debate on Rebuilding New Orleans District," *Washington Post*, October 3, 2005.

20. Some homes were damaged to the point that not enough house was left for which to issue a demolition permit.

21. Marline Otte, "The Mourning After: Languages of Loss and Grief in Post-Katrina New Orleans," *Journal of American History* 94, no. 3 (2007): 828–36.

22. Bruce Nolan, "Katrina Takes Aim," *Times-Picayune*, August 28, 2005.

23. Bruce Nolan, "Lakeview Levee Breach Threatens to Inundate City," *Times-Picayune*, August 30, 2005.

24. nola.com, The Katrina Files, "Timeline," accessed January 1, 2015, http://www.nola.com/katrina/timeline/.

25. Nolan, "Lakeview Levee Breach Threatens to Inundate City."

26. Interview with Rita.

27. See Data Center, Data Resources, "Neighborhood Statistical Area Data Profiles," accessed December 31, 2014, http://www.datacenterresearch.org/data-resources/neighborhood-data/. Also see New, who reports, "Four and a half years after Hurricane Katrina submerged most of New Orleans, the city has regained nearly 75 percent of its pre-Katrina population. The one notable exception is the Lower Ninth Ward. This traditionally poor neighborhood has seen less than 20 percent of its 14,000 residents return." Brian New, "Pride of the Lower Ninth Ward Makes Most of New Start in S.A.," *KENS 5 Eyewitness News San Antonio*, November 9, 2013.

28. From both the social harms and deviance-based definitional approaches, governmental failures in the context of Hurricane Katrina have been conceptualized as a state crime of omission. See Kelly L. Faust and David Kauzlarich, "Hurricane Katrina Victimization as a State Crime of Omission," *Critical Criminology* 16, no. 2 (2008): 85–103. See also Chamlee-Wright and Storr, "Expectations of Government's Response to Disaster."

29. See Emily Chamlee-Wright and Virgil H. Storr, "Filling the Civil-Society Vacuum: Post-disaster Policy and Community Response" (Policy Comment No. 22, Mercatus Center at George Mason University, Arlington, VA, February 2009).

30. Interview with Pastor Willis.

31. See Kristin E. Henkel, John F. Dovidio, and Samuel L. Gaertner, "Institutional Discrimination, Individual Racism, and Hurricane Katrina," *Analyses of Social Issues and Public Policy* 6, no. 1 (2006): 99–124, 107.

32. When New Orleans came under US control in 1805, the city was divided for ease of governance, eventually evolving into 17 official wards by the time Katrina hit. The distinction between Upper and Lower Ninth Ward neighborhoods likely came about in the 1920s when the Industrial Canal bisected the ward.

33. See Keith Elder, Sudha Xirasagar, Nancy Miller, Shelly Ann Bowen, Saundra Glover, and Crystal Piper, "African Americans' Decisions Not to Evacuate New Orleans before Hurricane Katrina: A Qualitative Study," *American Journal of Public Health* 97 (Suppl. 1) (2007): S124–29.

34. See Cheryl Corley, "New Orleans Endures New Floods in Rita's Wake," *NPR Weekend Edition Sunday*, September 25, 2005.

35. See Chamlee-Wright and Storr, "'There's No Place Like New Orleans.'"

36. Following a disaster, the return of businesses, small and large, sends a critical signal to displaced residents that the neighborhood is rebounding, that life is returning to normal, and that the community is likely to be viable long term. See Chamlee-Wright, "Signaling Effects of Commercial and Civil Society in Post-Katrina Reconstruction."

37. See Danielle Furfaro, "Enterprising Thieves Turn Metal to Money: Jump in Prices Has Led to Thefts of Nearly Anything That Can Be Sold as Scrap," *Times Union* (Albany, NY), February 20, 2007 (accessed via EBSCOhost).

38. In the New Orleans East community, particularly the Vietnamese community, many residents relied on savings to rebuild. In many other communities, residents did not have savings sufficient to rebuild.

39. Studies have shown that the image of citywide looting is often overblown. See Kathleen Tierney, Christine Bevc, and Erica Kuligowski, "Metaphors Matter: Disaster Myths, Media Frames, and Their Consequences in Hurricane Katrina," *ANNALS of the American Academy of Political and Social Science* 604, no. 1 (2006): 57–81. See also Lauren E. Barsky, "Disaster Realities Following Katrina: Revisiting the Looting Myth," in Learning from Catastrophe: Quick Response Research in the Wake of Hurricane Katrina (Boulder: Natural Hazards Center, University of Colorado at Boulder, 2006), 215–34.

40. Airline Highway runs from northwest New Orleans to Baton Rouge.

41. Chamlee-Wight has described the regime uncertainty that characterized the days and months following Katrina. See Emily Chamlee-Wright, "The Long Road Back: Signal Noise in the Post-Katrina Context," *The Independent Review* 12, no. 2 (2007): 235–59. Similarly, in their work, Clara Irazábal and Jason Neville explain that many residents were shocked to see green dots where their neighborhoods once stood in the Bring New Orleans Back and Urban Land Institute redevelopment plan, which signified that the neighborhood would not be allowed to rebuild. Such plans confirmed for many that the government did not want poor communities to return and rebuild. See Clara Irazábal and Jason Neville, "Neighborhoods in the Lead: Grassroots Planning for Social Transformation in Post-Katrina New Orleans?," *Planning Practice & Research* 22, no. 2 (2007): 131–53.

42. The SBA provides low-interest disaster loans to homeowners to repair or replace property that has been damaged or destroyed in a declared disaster. See the SBA website, http://www.sba.gov/services/disasterassistance/.

43. "Common Ground Relief is a state and federally registered 501(c)(3) non-profit organization providing short term relief for victims of hurricane disasters in the gulf coast region, and long term support in rebuilding the communities affected in the New Orleans area." Common Ground Relief, accessed January 1, 2015, http://www.commongroundrelief.org.

44. In New Orleans, porch or stoop sitting is an important part of the culture. "It is a city of kindness and hospitality, where walking down the block can take two hours because you stop and talk to someone on every porch." Philip E. Steinberg and Rob Shields, *What Is a City? Rethinking the Urban after Hurricane Katrina* (Athens: University of Georgia Press, 2008), 35.

45. That is a total of six children.

46. As Donald DeVore notes, "When Hurricane Katrina made landfall in August 2005, African American churches in New Orleans were both heirs of and con-tributors to the community-building tradition of the black church. The black church had been the organizational entity that gave meaning to the lives of many black New Orleanians and was the vehicle for their religious beliefs, expressions, and practices. In the churches they exercised leadership, worked for and attained status, and earned the admiration and respect of their fellow members." See Donald E. DeVore, "Water in Sacred Places: Rebuilding New Orleans Black Churches as Sites of Community Empowerment," *Journal of American History* 94, no. 3 (2007): 762–69.

47. There are four state correctional institutions within a 150-mile radius of New Orleans. The largest and most infamous of those is the Louisiana State Penitentiary (also known as Angola). It is the largest maximum security prison in the United States. It is about 135 miles northwest of New Orleans.

48. Landphair describes changes that took place between Hurricanes Betsy and Katrina. See Landphair, "'The Forgotten People of New Orleans.'"

49. In their analysis of New Orleanians still living in Houston three years after the storm, Chamlee-Wright and Storr find that half the respondents preferred life in Houston over their lives in New Orleans. The other 50 percent who would have preferred to resume their lives in New Orleans faced some logisti-cal challenge that made their return difficult or impossible. See "'There's No Place Like New Orleans.'"

50. These may have been undocumented workers. See Elizabeth Fussell, "Latino Immigrants in Post-Katrina New Orleans" (paper presented to the Regional Seminar on Labor Rights, New Orleans, LA, October 19–22, 2006).

51. The low rates of homeownership may have been a factor in the slow rate of return in some neighborhoods but cannot explain the slow rates of return in parts of the Ninth Ward where homeownership rates are surprisingly high. Pre-Katrina Ninth Ward rates of homeownership ranged from 45 percent in parts of the Upper Ninth Ward to 59 percent in the Lower Ninth Ward. See Greater New Orleans Data Center, Pre-Katrina Archive, Orleans Parish Data and Information, accessed January 1, 2015, http://www.datacenterresearch.org/pre-katrina/orleans/index.html.

52. See Chamlee-Wright and Storr, "'There's No Place Like New Orleans.'"

53. Brad Pitt founded the Make It Right project to build 150 green, storm-resistant houses in the Lower Ninth Ward. See the Make It Right website, accessed January 1, 2015, http://www.makeitrightnola.org.

54. Pontchartrain Park was a subdivision built for middle-class African Americans.

55. See Chamlee-Wright and Storr, "Expectations of Government's Response to Disaster."

56. Bandit, Miss Sandra, and Melvin are featured in a film, *MINE*, about the relationship between people and their animal companions during natural disasters. See the film trailer, Erin Essenmacher and Geralyn Pezanoski, *MINE, the Movie* (2009), http://minemovie.squarespace.com/trailer.

2. CENTRAL CITY

1. *Living with History in New Orleans' Neighborhoods: Central City* (New Orleans, LA: Preservation Resource Center of New Orleans), 1–2, accessed June 9, 2010, http://www.prcno.org/neighborhoods/brochures /CentralCity.pdf.

2. "New Orleans," in American-Israeli Cooperative Enterprise, *Jewish Virtual Library* (2013), accessed June 9, 2010, http://www.jewishvirtuallibrary. org/jsource/judaica/ejud_0002_0015_0_14797.html, citing Greater New Orleans Archivist, *Jews of New Orleans, an Archival Guide*, Irwin Lachoff and Catherine C. Kahn, *The Jewish Community of New Orleans* (Mount Pleasant, SC: Arcadia Publishing, 2005).

3. William R. Mitchell Jr., *Classic New Orleans* (Savannah, GA: Golden Coast Books, 1993), 227.

4. Shotgun houses are typically 12 feet wide with a door at the front and the rear. The rooms are laid out in a row, rather than the box pattern typical of a colonial-style house. Although these houses have African and Haitian influences and can be found in Chicago and Key West, the style is commonly associated with the city of New Orleans. See Virginia McAlester and Lee McAlester, *A Field Guide to American Houses* (New York: Knopf, 1997), 90.

5. According to Campanella and Campanella, "in much of New Orleans, a neighborhood's quantity of tree coverage is correlated with its prosperity." This, thus, set these Central City homes apart from those in their more prosperous adjacent neighborhoods. Richard Campanella and Marina Campanella, *New Orleans: Then and Now* (Gretna, LA: Pelican Publishing, 1999), 336.

6. Mitchell, *Classic New Orleans*, 227.

7. *Daily Picayune*, 1849, quoted in Keith Weldon Medley, "Dryades Street/ Oretha Castle Haley Boulevard Remembrance and Reclamation," *New Orleans Tribune*, April 2001.

8. Ibid.

9. Ibid.

10. Plater Robinson, *A House Divided: A Study Guide on the History of Civil Rights in Louisiana* (New Orleans: Southern Institute for Education and Research, 1995), 46.

11. Dryades Street would be renamed Oretha Castle Haley in honor of this civil rights leader. Kim Lacy Rogers, "Memory, Struggle, and Power: On Interviewing Political Activists," *Oral History Review* 15, no. 1 (Spring, 1987): 165–84.

12. Robinson, *House Divided*.

13. Associated Press, "Mostly Black New Orleans Could Pick White Mayor," *New Orleans City Business*, January 8, 2010.

14. In a 1979 article, William H. Frey posits that there are both racial and non-racial causes of "white flight" into the suburbs away from the city center. "Central City White Flight: Racial and Nonracial Causes," *American Sociological Review* 44, no. 3 [1979]: 425–48. Mickey Lauria of the University of New Orleans argues that it was a particularly nonracial reason for the demographic change in the New Orleans East section of New Orleans: "Middle-income professional whites employed in businesses impacted by recession who had recently bought housing with high loan-to-value ratios were forced to sell or have their houses foreclosed upon. The depressed market, in turn, made such housing affordable to middle-class blacks interested in homeownership. Thus, black economic opportunity, rather than white flight, dramatically transformed the racial composition of many New Orleans East neighborhoods." Lauria, "A New Model of Neighborhood Change: Reconsidering the Role of White Flight," *Housing Policy Debate* 9, no. 2 (1998): 395–424, 395.

15. Kevin Fox Gotham, "Tourism Gentrification: The Case of New Orleans' Vieux Carre (French Quarter)," *Urban Studies* 42, no. 7 (2005): 1099–1121, 1103.

16. See Nicole Gelinas, "Baghdad on the Bayou," Manhattan Institute for Policy Research, New York, May 26, 2007, http://www.manhattan-institute.org /html/miarticle.htm?id=3944 (originally published in *RealClearPolitics*).

17. Deep South Center for Environmental Justice, "Central City, Orleans Parish," in *Community Profiles*, June 4, 2009.

18. Metropolitan Policy Program at Brookings and Greater New Orleans Community Data Center, *The New Orleans Index: Tracking the Recovery of New Orleans and the Metro Area*, August 2009, 20–21, http://www .brookings.edu/~/media/Research/Files/Reports/2011/8/29-new-orleans -index/200908_Katrina_Index.PDF.

19. "CCRA grew out of a community planning initiative commissioned in 2002 by the City of New Orleans and the Ford Foundation. . . . With additional support from other local and national philanthropic partners, more than 200 residents, stakeholders and municipal partners worked together for 18 months in an authentic dialogue that involved sharing ideas, concerns and strategies to develop the Central City Community Plan." "Mission/History," Central City Renaissance Alliance website, accessed June 9, 2010, http://www.myccra .org/#/about-ccra/4530391365.

20. Jews 4 New Orleans, accessed June 9, 2010 (no longer accessible).

21. Central City Artist Project, accessed January 1, 2015, https://www.facebook. com/pages/Central-City-Artist-Project/118834906161?sk=info&tab=page_info.

22. Greater New Orleans Foundation, Community Revitalization Fund, August 2009 Report, *Learning in Two Directions: The Community Revitalization*

Fund, http://www.gnof.org/receive/economic-opportunity/ (accessed January 1, 2015).

23. New Hope Baptist Church, http://www.newhopeno.org/pray/.

24. Chamlee-Wright and Storr discuss the key role that churches and church leaders played in helping their congregants evacuate and also in helping them to return and rebound. See "The Role of Social Entrepreneurship in Post-disaster Recovery." See also Emily Chamlee-Wright, "Pastor's Response in Post-Katrina New Orleans: Navigating the Cultural Economic Landscape," in *Culture and Economic Action*, ed. Laura Grube and Virgil H. Storr (London: Edward Elgar, 2015).

25. Chamlee-Wright has discussed this chicken-and-egg game that has complicated recovery. See "Signaling Effects of Commercial and Civil Society in Post-Katrina Reconstruction."

26. See Chamlee-Wright and Storr, *The Political Economy of Hurricane Katrina and Community Rebound*.

27. For a theoretical discussion of such social coordination problems, see Mancur Olson Jr., *The Logic of Collective Action* (Cambridge, MA: Harvard University Press, 1965).

28. She was not the only educator who was without a job after Hurricane Katrina. A quarter of the New Orleans' teachers were displaced by the storm: 12,000 teachers in total. The Department of Education took out a full-page advertisement in the newspapers, instructing teachers to apply for jobs in other districts. "Katrina Hits Louisiana Schools Hard: Teachers Told to Apply for Jobs in Other Districts," *CNN.com*, September 10, 2005, http://www.cnn.com/2005/US/09/10/katrina.la.schools/index.html.

29. See Sarah Jane Gilbert, "HBS Cases: Reforming New Orleans Schools after Katrina," Working Knowledge, Harvard Business School, July 14, 2008, http://hbswk.hbs.edu/item/5826.html; and Erin Marie Agemy, "Improving Academics in the Aftermath: A Case Study of New Orleans' Experiment with Charter Schools," in *The Political Economy of Hurricane Katrina and Community Rebound*, ed. Emily Chamlee-Wright and Virgil Henry Storr (Cheltenham, UK: Edward Elgar, 2010), 106–28.

30. See Jeb Bleckley and Joshua Hall, "School Choice and Post-Katrina New Orleans: An Analysis," and Agemy, "Improving Academics in the Aftermath," in *The Political Economy of Hurricane Katrina and Community Rebound*, ed. Chamlee-Wright and Storr, 90–105 and 10–128.

31. Defying police orders, school administrators, community activists, and other stakeholders cleaned up the school and eventually facilitated its reopening, well beyond the target date the district had set. See Chamlee-Wright and Storr, "The Role of Social Entrepreneurship in Post-disaster Recovery."

32. Ben Franklin High School is a charter school located on the campus of the University of New Orleans. See Benjamin Franklin High School, http://www.edline.net/pages/bfhsla.

33. As Agemy explains, the badly damaged New Orleans public schools were "slower to reopen, in part because the city owned them. . . . Chartering, however, proved critical to these schools being able to open their doors. Previous magnet (selective admissions) school leaders, for instance, drew up individual charters to sidestep the district, which could not seem to coor-

dinate or organize the daunting task of reopening so many schools. They used their networks of teachers and strong ties with parents to alleviate the delay of reopening." See Agemy, "Improving Academics in the Aftermath," in *The Political Economy of Hurricane Katrina and Community Rebound*, ed. Chamlee-Wright and Storr, 232.

34. See Chamlee-Wright, "Long Road Back."

35. "At road junctions, forests of advertising signs have also sprouted, promoting house-gutting crews, roofers, mould removal and disinfecting experts, tree-removal teams, carpenters, flooring specialists, demolition and reconstruction firms with names such as Masters of Disasters and American Dream Construction. 'We Buy Houses', 'We Gut Houses', 'We Demolish', they read." Jacqui Goddard, "No People, No Power, No Money—A City Struggling to Live Again: 11 Weeks after Katrina, New Orleans Is Working Flat Out to Drag Itself from the Mud, but It Has a Long Way to Go," *The Times* (London), November 12, 2005.

36. See Chamlee-Wright and Storr, "'There's No Place Like New Orleans.'"

37. Ibid.

38. She is not alone in this. Many insureds took the insurance companies to court. See Brant McLaughlin, "All State Accused of Bad Faith Payout," *Associate Content*, August 6, 2007.

39. As Norcross and Skriba note, "Road Home was designed to serve as more than a disaster compensation program; it was designed to function as both planning and housing policy. The program aimed to simultaneously compensate victims, to recreate existing neighborhoods by awarding larger sums to those choosing to stay in Louisiana and to develop affordable housing options.... The program's efficacy has been widely criticized. By August 2007, only 23 percent of applicants had received grants. Applicants have expressed frustration at the program's complex application process, inequitable design, confusing policies, erroneous calculations and slow payout rates. Recovery authorities and state legislators blame overly rigid federal regulations, insufficient Congressional allocations, mismanagement by ICF International and miscommunication with the federal government." See Eileen Norcross and Anthony Skriba, "The Road Home: Helping Homeowners in the Gulf after Katrina?," in *The Political Economy of Hurricane Katrina and Community Rebound*, ed. Chamlee-Wright and Storr, 185.

40. As King notes, "When insurance adjustors and damage experts assessed the properties damaged by the 2005 storms, they were faced with the issue of allocating damages between wind (a covered loss) and flood (an excluded loss). The delays and economic uncertainty that this activity has engendered have raised financial and legal issues for insurers, as well as homeowners and businesses along the Gulf Coast region." See Rawle O. King, *Post-Katrina Insurance Issues Surrounding Water Damage Exclusions in Homeowners' Insurance Policies*, CRS Report for Congress (Washington, DC: Congressional Research Service, 2007), CRS-11.

41. Although the Road Home website (https://www.road2la.org) no longer reports these figures, as the program was being implemented, those visiting the site were told, "Eligible homeowners affected by Hurricanes Katrina or Rita may receive up to $150,000 in compensation for their losses to get back into their homes. The exact amount of funding that homeowners are eligible

for is determined by a number of factors, including the level of damage to their homes, any FEMA assistance that has been received and insurance settlements that have been provided."

42. Section 8 is another name for the US Department of Housing and Urban Development's housing choice voucher program. This program allows participants (low-income families, the elderly, and the disabled) "to afford decent, safe, and sanitary housing in the private market. Since housing assistance is provided on behalf of the family or individual, participants are able to find their own housing, including single-family homes, townhouses and apartments." Perhaps most important, "The participant is free to choose any housing that meets the requirements of the program and is not limited to units located in subsidized housing projects." Department of Housing and Urban Development, "Housing Choice Vouchers Fact Sheet," accessed July 8, 2010, http://www.hud.gov/offices/pih/programs/hcv/about/fact_sheet.cfm.

43. There is good reason to be skeptical that rent controls will accomplish what she hopes, but her frustration with rising prices and the potential distortions in the home rental market that result from the Section 8 program is understandable.

44. See Eloisa Rodriguez-Dod and Olympia Dunhart, "Evaluating Katrina: A Snapshot of Renters' Rights Following Disasters," *Nova Law Review* 31, no. 3 (2012): 467.

45. See Chamlee-Wright and Storr, "'There's No Place Like New Orleans.'"

46. For a discussion of why activism and demands for public support are so common in post-Katrina New Orleans, see Chamlee-Wright and Storr, "Expectations of Government's Response to Disaster."

3. GENTILLY WOODS, GENTILLY TERRACE, AND PONTCHARTRAIN PARK

1. John Law was a Scottish speculator and financial advisor to the Duc d'Orleans (regent for the young Louis XV) who founded the ill-fated Mississippi Company and convinced Frenchmen to invest in and settle the Louisiana-Mississippi area.

2. John Churchill Chase, *Frenchmen, Desire, Good Children: And Other Streets of New Orleans!* (Gretna, LA: Pelican Publishing Company, 2001), 54.

3. Carol McMichael Reese and Jane Wolf, "Ecological Crisis and the Modernist Residential Landscape: Pontchartrain Park, New Orleans, Louisiana," in *The Challenge of Change: Dealing with the Legacy of the Modern Movement*, ed. Dirk Van den Heuvel, Maarten Mesman, Wido Quist, and Bert Lemmens (Amsterdam: IOS Press, 2008), 191–96, 191.

4. Ibid.

5. Ibid., 193.

6. Craig E. Colten, *The Unnatural Metropolis: Wresting New Orleans from Nature* (Baton Rouge, LA: LSU Press, 2006), 99.

7. New Orleans Conveyance Office, COB 340/FOL 446, 1921, quoted in Colten, *Unnatural Metropolis*, 99.

8. Jonathan and Donna Fricker, *Louisiana Architecture: 1945–1965, Post-War Subdivisions and the Ranch House* (Baton Rouge: Louisiana Division of Historic Preservation, 2010), 16.

9. Lolis Elie, "Pontchartrain Park's Trailblazing Spirit Is Being Rekindled," *Times-Picayune*, May 23, 2009.

10. The architectural disconnection with the rest of the city played a part in the Katrina catastrophe, according to Reese and Wolf. "The infrastructure made it possible to forget the fundamentally soggy characteristics of the ground. The community never developed a flood culture and the explanation for today's crisis among the neighborhood residents, like that offered by so many New Orleanians, is that the Corps of Engineers failed in its responsibility to maintain levees that were, in fact, doomed from the beginning." Reese and Wolf, "Ecological Crisis and the Modernist Residential Landscape," in *The Challenge of Change*, 194.

11. Ibid., 193.

12. Wendell Pierce is also a leader in the Pontchartrain Park revival efforts.

13. Reese and Wolf, "Ecological Crisis and the Modernist Residential Landscape," in *The Challenge of Change*, 196n3.

14. Greater New Orleans Data Center, Pre-Katrina Data Archive, Orleans Parish, accessed January 1, 2015, http://www.datacenterresearch.org/pre-katrina /orleans/index.html.

15. Ibid.

16. Steven Gray, "Will Louisiana's Levees Hold?," *Time*, September 1, 2008.

17. Reese and Wolf, "Ecological Crisis and the Modernist Residential Landscape," in *The Challenge of Change*, 192.

18. Colley Charpentier, "Survey Shows Gentilly on the Rebound," *Times-Picayune*, April 26, 2007.

19. Amy Liu and Allison Plyer, *The New Orleans Index, January 2009*, Brookings Institution and Greater New Orleans Community Data Center, January 27, 2009, 18.

20. R. Stephanie Bruno, "Gentilly Woods Shopping Center Redevelopment Proposals Weighed," *Times-Picayune*, July 1, 2011.

21. Jill Hezeau, "Greater Gentilly High School Latest Sign of Progress Post Katrina," WWLTV, February 11, 2010.

22. Pontchartrain Park was established in 1954 and marketed as New Orleans' first black middle-class subdivision. See Farrah D. Gafford, *Life in the Park: Community Solidarity, Culture and the Case of a Black Middle Class Neighborhood* (New Orleans: Tulane University, 2008).

23. "To some degree the [city's black] neighborhoods are class-defined: London Avenue, certain sections of the Uptown area, Pontchartrain Park, and the vicinity of Dillard University might be considered upper or middle class. Many of them are homogeneous by class but racially mixed." Forrest E. LaViolette, "The Negro in New Orleans," in *Studies in Housing and Minority Groups*, ed. Nathan Glazer and Davis McIntire (Berkeley: University of California Press, 1960), 117.

24. For an alternative view of price gouging and a discussion of why such a practice was not part of the box stores' post-disaster business strategy, see Dreda Culpepper and Walter Block, "Price Gouging in the Katrina Aftermath: Free Markets at Work," *International Journal of Social Economics* 35, no. 7 (2008): 512–20. Also see Steve Horwitz, "Wal-Mart to the Rescue: Private Enterprise's Response to Hurricane Katrina," *Independent Review* 13, no. 4 (2009): 511–28; and David Skarbek, "Market Failure and Natural Disasters: A Reexamination of Anti-gouging Laws," *Public Contract Law Journal* 37, no. 4 (2008): 771–80.

25. Chamlee-Wright and Storr, "Expectations of Government's Response to Disaster."

26. She moved into this area after whites began moving out. Blacks settled in Pontchartrain Park in the mid-1950s and began moving into Gentilly Woods after segregation ended. This transformation of the area "led, in the 1970s and 1980s, to the departure of many whites from Gentilly, opening up more fine housing stock for middle-class black families." Richard Campanella, "An Ethnic Geography of New Orleans," *Journal of American History* 94 (December 2007): 704–15.

27. Hurricane Betsy affected the Gentilly neighborhood because the storm surges caused Lake Pontchartrain to flood its borders.

28. Her husband's nickname.

29. See David Skarbek, "Occupational Licensing and Asymmetric Information: Post-hurricane Evidence from Florida," *Cato Journal* 28, no. 1 (2008): 71–80; and David Skarbek, "Restricting Reconstruction: Occupational Licensing and Natural Disasters," in *The Political Economy of Hurricane Katrina and Community Rebound*, chapter 5, for a discussion of regulatory licensing in the post-disaster environment.

30. "With a high homeownership rate, many residents of Gentilly have since returned to their homes, restoring, rebuilding, and in some cases raising houses on piers to protect them against future flood damage." Rebuilding Together New Orleans, "Gentilly," 2009, http://www.rtno.org /neighborhoods/gentilly/.

31. For more information on Ferrara Supermarket, see Amy Ferrara-Smith's story, "I Just Need to Get These Old Bones Home," in *Voices Rising: Stories from the Katrina Narrative Project*, ed. Rebeca Antoine (New Orleans: University of New Orleans Press, 2008).

32. Easton refers to Chase and Bank One interchangeably. In 2004, JPMorgan *Chase* merged with *Bank One* Corp.

33. Like many New Orleans residents, Easton reserves the phrase "I own my house" for when the mortgage is paid in full.

34. Easton is likely talking about Sunday night. He had said earlier in the interview that he worked at the Daiquiri shop on Sunday evenings, and this would also fit with the timeline of Katrina's landing.

35. Again, Easton likely means Monday morning.

36. The National Weather Service had issued a Flash Flood Warning for Orleans Parish and St. Bernard Parish at 8:14 a.m., citing a levee breach at the Industrial Canal.

37. Chamlee-Wright and Storr describe the "social contract" that Katrina victims often expressed that they had with the federal government. See "Expectations of Government's Response to Disaster."

38. This canal has also been termed "The Ditch or . . . the 'DMZ'—a drainage ditch that once cut a line separating white from black." Soledad O'Brien, "Rebuilding after Katrina Honors a Generation," *CNN.com*, August 20, 2010.

39. Michael tells us in another part of the interview that Chip has been on CNN: "Chip have been everywhere."

40. The John C. Stennis Space Center is located on the Louisiana–Mississippi border in Hancock County, Mississippi.

41. Indeed, the New Orleans Police Department did experience a shortage of officers. "The NOPD is shrinking, in terms of both the budget for police officers and the actual number of officers on the street. In the first 14 months after Katrina (from August 2005 to October 2006), the budgeted commissioned police force was cut about 15 percent, from 1,885 to 1,600. During the same period, the actual on-board strength declined by an even larger amount: 321 officers—from 1,742 to 1,421—or about 18 percent." RAND Gulf States Policy Institute, "Improving Recruitment and Retention in the New Orleans Police Department," RAND Research Brief, 1, accessed January 2, 2015, http://www.rand.org/pubs/research_briefs/2007/RAND_RB9243-1.pdf.

42. Neighborhoods in the Uptown/Carrollton area in the 17th Ward.

43. In 2007, the *Times-Picayune* reported that "The number of copper-related thefts in New Orleans this year is through the roof, especially in the city's flood-ravaged regions." Brendan McCarthy, "Police Struggle to Stop Post-Katrina Copper Looters," *Times-Picayune*, October 1, 2007.

44. Greensburg is a small town outside Baton Rouge.

4. THE MARY QUEEN OF VIETNAM COMMUNITY IN VILLAGE DE L'EST

1. Greater New Orleans Community Data Center, Pre-Katrina Archive, "Village de l'Est Neighborhood Snapshot," last modified July 25, 2006, http://www .gnocdc.org/orleans/10/56/snapshot.html.

2. Robert L. Reid, "Defending New Orleans," *Civil Engineering*, November 2013.

3. Nolan, "Katrina Takes Aim."

4. *New Orleans, Louisiana: A Strategy for Rebuilding, November 12–18, 2005,* Advisory Services Program Report (Washington, DC: Urban Land Institute, 2006), 43.

5. Stephanie Stokes, "Vitality Returns to Homes in Village de L'Est," *Times-Picayune*, December 27, 2008.

6. Although MQVN's lead pastor, Father Vien, estimates that the Vietnamese population immediately surrounding the church was 95 percent just before Katrina, the 1990 US Census placed it at 87 percent. See Carl L. Bankston and Min Zhou, "De Facto Congregationalism and Socioeconomic Mobility in Laotian and Vietnamese Immigrant Communities: A Study of Religious

Institutions and Economic Change," *Review of Religious Research* 41, no. 4 (2000): 453–70.

7. Emily Chamlee-Wright and Virgil Henry Storr, "Club Goods and Post-disaster Community Return," *Rationality and Society* 21, no. 4 (2009): 429–58.

8. Kathleen Carlin and Cam-Thanh Tran, "Tet, the Vietnamese New Year, in the New Orleans Vietnamese Community," in *Folklife in Louisiana: Louisiana Living Traditions*, accessed January 2, 2015, http://www.louisianafolklife.org/LT/Articles_Essays/VietnameseNewYear.html.

9. Min Zhou and Carl Bankston, "Social Capital and the Adaptation of the Second Generation: The Case of Vietnamese Youth in New Orleans," *International Migration Review* 28, no. 4 (1994): 821–45.

10. Chamlee-Wright and Storr note that this was a grassroots effort with the funds coming from Vietnamese Catholics and local community, pointing out that this is another example of how active the community is in banding together to create change. See "Club Goods and Post-disaster Community Return."

11. Casey Sanchez, "Communities Rebuild in the Aftermath of Hurricanes Katrina, Rita, and Ike," *American Prospect*, March 17, 2009.

12. Bankston and Min Zhou, "De Facto Congregationalism and Socioeconomic Mobility."

13. Chamlee-Wright and Storr, "Club Goods and Post-disaster Community Return." This would change after Katrina. The first Vietnamese American elected to congress (Anh "Joseph" Cao, elected in 2008) was one of those who fled South Vietnam and made a home in New Orleans, an active member of the MQVN community.

14. Interview with Father Luke, April 6, 2006.

15. Interview with Mary T.

16. Interview with Quang N.

17. MQVN residents were not the only New Orleanians who expressed an appreciation for the transportation system, and frustration with public transportation in other cities was cited among the reasons why people returned to New Orleans after Katrina.

18. Interview with Bill D.

19. Interview with Lai N.

20. See NBC, "Postcard from New Orleans," *Dateline*, aired June 15, 2007, http://www.nbcnews.com/video/dateline/19292199#19292199.

21. Interview with Lynn N.

22. Ibid.

23. Interview with Samantha N.

24. We see this type of entrepreneurship across New Orleans following Katrina.

25. Interview with Bill D.

26. Ibid.

27. "Entergy Corporation is an integrated energy company engaged primarily in electric power production and retail distribution operations. It is the second-

largest nuclear generator in the United States. It delivers electricity to 2.7 million utility customers in Arkansas, Louisiana, Mississippi and Texas." "About Entergy," accessed January 2, 2015, http://www.entergy.com/about_entergy/.

28. Bring New Orleans Back was a planning commission appointed by the mayor of New Orleans. It was a parallel and competing planning organization to the state-organized Louisiana Recovery Authority "and included features that were similar to the city plans developed by the Urban Land Institute with proposals for category 5 flood protection; light rail, parks, and playgrounds; and selective neighborhood rebuilding." Urban Land Institute, *New Orleans, Louisiana: A Strategy for Rebuilding*, "Executive Summary of Key Recommendations." After considerable controversy over the prospective use of eminent domain, the Bring New Orleans Back planning process was effectively abandoned by May 2006.

29. Bayou Sauvage National Wildlife Refuge is "24,000 acres of fresh and brackish marshes and coastal hardwood forests, all within the city limits of New Orleans, making it the nation's largest urban National Wildlife Refuge." "Bayou Sauvage National Wildlife Refuge," US Fish and Wildlife Service, last updated July 14, 2014, http://www.fws.gov/bayousauvage/.

30. "Vietnamese communities in the New Orleans area often have extensive gardens behind the houses. These urban gardens are an important link with Vietnam and traditional life, especially for older people who may speak no English. The choice of plants . . . , the layout of the gardens, and gardening techniques all reflect culturally meaningful ways of doing things, although these too are changing in America." Kathy Kilbourne, "Vietnamese Folklife in New Orleans," in *Folklife in Louisiana: Louisiana's Living Traditions*, accessed January 2, 2015, http://www.louisianafolklife.org/LT/Articles_Essays/creole_art_vietnamese_folk.html.

31. In July 2008, the Mary Queen of Viet Nam Community Development Corporation Inc., in partnership with Children's Hospital, opened a children's clinic in the New Orleans East community. Mary Queen of Viet Nam Community Development Corporation, "Health Care Services," accessed January 2, 2015, http://mqvncdc.org/page.php?id=16.

32. Chamlee-Wright and Storr, "Club Goods and Post-disaster Community Return."

33. NAVASA's mission is "to improve social and economic justice in the Vietnamese communities throughout the country . . . by implementing three key strategies: (1) Building organizational capacity of Vietnamese-led community-based organizations (CBOs) and faith-based organizations (FBOs), (2) Developing a new generation of non-profit leaders, and (3) Increasing funding support for Vietnamese CBOs and FBOs." National Alliance of Vietnamese American Service Agencies, accessed March 1, 2015, https://www.facebook.com/pages/NAVASA-National-Alliance-of-Vietnamese-American-Service-Agencies/20512712875?sk=info&tab=page_info.

34. Providence Community Housing works to foster "healthy, diverse and vibrant communities by developing, operating and advocating for affordable, mixed-income housing, supportive services and employment opportunities for individuals, families, seniors and people with special needs." Providence Community Housing, accessed January 2, 2015, http://www.providencecommunityhousing.org.

CONCLUSION

1. See Joel Kotkin, "America's Fastest Growing Cities since the Recession," *Forbes*, June 18, 2013.

2. See Greater New Orleans Data Center, Pre-Katrina Archive, Orleans Parish Data & Information, accessed January 1, 2015, http://www.data centerresearch.org/pre-katrina/orleans/index.html.

3. See Vicki Mack and Allison Plyer, "Neighborhood Growth Rates: Growth Continues through 2014 in New Orleans Neighborhoods," August 6, 2014, Data Center, https://s3.amazonaws.com/gnocdc/reports/TheDataCenter _NeighborhoodGrowthRates.pdf.

4. Ibid.

5. Ibid.

6. See Doug MacCash, "The Changing Face of St. Claude Ave. Neighborhood in Flux," *Times-Picayune*, January 29, 2013. See also Richard Rainey, "St. Roch Market's $3.7 Million Renovation Under Way," *Times-Picayune*, December 9, 2014.

7. See Jared Green, "In New Orleans, a Vietnamese Community Bounces Back with Urban Agriculture," *Grist*, June 23, 2013.

8. See Katy Reckdahl, "New Orleans Children Still Likely to Live in High-Poverty Neighborhoods," *Times-Picayune*, March 6, 2012. As Reckdahl reports, "nearly four out of ten children in New Orleans live in high-poverty neighborhoods" as opposed to one out of ten in neighboring Jefferson Parish. See also Nathaniel Rich, "Jungleland: The Lower Ninth Ward in New Orleans Gives New Meaning to Urban Growth," *New York Times Magazine*, March 21, 2012.

9. See Emily Chamlee-Wright and Virgil H. Storr, "Between *Gemeinschaft* and *Gesellschaft*: The Stories We Tell," in *Commerce and Community: Ecologies of Social Cooperation*, ed. Robert F. Garnett Jr., Paul Lewis, and Lenore T. Ealy (New York: Routledge, 2015), 157–76.

Further Reading

Boettke, Peter, Emily Chamlee-Wright, Peter Gordon, Sanford Ikeda, Peter Leeson, and Russell Sobel. "The Political, Economic, and Social Aspects of Katrina." *Southern Economic Journal* 74, no. 2 (2007): 363–76.

Boettke, Peter, and Daniel Smith. "Self-reliance and Social Resilience." In *The Economics of Natural and Unnatural Disasters*, edited by William Kern, 87–102. Kalamazoo, MI: University of Michigan Press, 2010.

Chamlee-Wright, Emily. "The Long Road Back: Signal Noise in the Post-Katrina Context." *Independent Review* 12, no. 2 (2007): 235–59.

———. "Signaling Effects of Commercial and Civil Society in Post-Katrina Reconstruction." *International Journal of Social Economics* 35, no. 8 (2008): 615–26.

———. *The Cultural and Political Economy of Recovery: Social Learning in a Post-Disaster Environment*. New York: Routledge, 2010.

———. "Reflections on Methodology, Disasters, and Social Learning." *Studies in Emergent Order* 4 (2011): 87–104.

———. "Pastor's Response in Post-Katrina New Orleans: Navigating the Cultural Economic Landscape." In *Culture and Economic Action*, edited by Laura Grube and Virgil Storr. Cheltenham, UK: Edward Elgar, 2015.

Chamlee-Wright, Emily, and Daniel Rothschild. "Disastrous Uncertainty: How Government Disaster Policy Undermines

Community Rebound." Mercatus Policy Series, Policy Comment 9, Mercatus Center at George Mason University, Arlington, VA, 2007.

———. "Hosting a Disaster: Tips for Host Cities." Mercatus on Policy 23, Mercatus Center at George Mason University, Arlington, VA, 2008.

Chamlee-Wright, Emily, and Virgil Storr. "The Entrepreneur's Role in Post-disaster Community Recovery: Implications for Post-disaster Recovery Policy." Mercatus Policy Series, Policy Primer 6, Mercatus Center at George Mason University, Arlington, VA, 2008.

———. "Club Goods and Post-disaster Community Return." *Rationality and Society* 21, no. 4 (2009): 429–58.

———. "Filling the Civil Society Vacuum: Post-disaster Policy and Community Response." Mercatus Policy Series, Policy Comment 22, Mercatus Center at George Mason University, Arlington, VA, 2009.

———. "'There's No Place Like New Orleans': Sense of Place and Community Recovery in the Ninth Ward after Hurricane Katrina." *Journal of Urban Affairs* 31, no. 5 (2009): 615–34.

———. "Community Resilience in New Orleans East: Deploying the Cultural Toolkit within a Vietnamese-American Community." In *Community Disaster Recovery and Resiliency: Exploring Global Opportunities and Challenges*, edited by DeMond S. Miller and Jason David Rivera, 99–122. New York: Taylor & Francis, 2010.

———. "Expectations of Government's Response to Disaster." *Public Choice* 144, no. 1–2 (2010): 253–74.

———, eds. *The Political Economy of Hurricane Katrina and Community Rebound*. Cheltenham, UK: Edward Elgar, 2010.

———. "The Role of Social Entrepreneurship in Post-Katrina Community Recovery." *International Journal of Innovation and Regional Development* 2, no. 1 (2010): 149–64.

———. "Social Capital as Collective Narratives and Post-disaster Community Recovery." *Sociological Review* 59, no. 2 (2011): 266–82.

———. "Commercial Relationships and Spaces after Disaster." *Society* 51, no. 6 (2014): 656–64.

Coyne, Christopher, Peter Leeson, and Russell Sobel. "The Impact of FEMA Reorganization: Implications for Policy." Mercatus Policy Series, Policy Comment 24, Mercatus Center at George Mason University, Arlington, VA, 2009.

Coyne, Christopher, and Jayme Lemke. "Lessons from 'The Cultural and Political Economy of Recovery.'" *American Journal of Economics and Sociology* 71, no. 1 (2012): 215–28.

Gordon, Peter, and Sanford Ikeda. "Power to the Neighborhoods: The Devolution of Authority in Post-Katrina New Orleans." Mercatus Policy Series, Policy Comment 12, Mercatus Center at George Mason University, Arlington, VA, 2007.

Gordon, Peter, and Richard Little. "Building Walls against Bad Infrastructure Policy in New Orleans." Mercatus Policy Series, Policy Primer 10, Mercatus Center at George Mason University, Arlington, VA, 2009.

Horwitz, Steven. "Making Hurricane Response More Effective: Lessons from the Private Sector and the Coast Guard during Katrina." Mercatus Policy Series, Policy Comment 17, Mercatus Center at George Mason University, Arlington, VA, 2008.

———. "Best Responders: Post-Katrina Innovation and Improvisation by Wal-Mart and the US Coast Guard." *Innovations* 4, no. 2 (2009): 93–99.

———. "Wal-Mart to the Rescue: Private Enterprise's Response to Hurricane Katrina." *Independent Review* 13, no. 4 (2009): 511–28.

———. "Doing the Right Things: The Private Sector Response to Hurricane Katrina as a Case Study in the Bourgeois Virtues." In *Accepting the Invisible Hand: Market-Based Approaches to*

Social Economic Problems, edited by Mark D. White, 169–90. London: Palgrave Macmillan, 2010.

Leeson, Peter, and Daniel Smith. "Private Solutions to Public Disasters: Self-Reliance and Social Resilience." In *The Economics of Natural and Unnatural Disasters,* edited by William Kern, 87–102. Kalamazoo, MI: Western Michigan University Press, 2010.

Leeson, Peter, and Russell Sobel. "Flirting with Disaster: The Inherent Problems with FEMA." Cato Policy Analysis 573, Cato Institute, Washington, DC, 2006.

——— . "Government's Response to Hurricane Katrina: A Public Choice Analysis." *Public Choice* 127, no. 1-2 (2006): 55–73.

——— . "The Use of Knowledge in Natural Disaster Relief Management." *Independent Review* 11, no. 4 (2007): 519–32.

——— . "Centralization Proves Inadequate to Disaster Aid." *Journal of International Peace Operations* 3, no. 4 (2008): 11–12.

——— . "Weathering Corruption." *Journal of Law and Economics* 51, no. 4 (2008): 667–81.

——— . "Blame the Weather? Natural Disasters, FEMA, and Corruption in America." *Administrative and Regulatory Law News* 36, no. 4 (2011): 10–11.

Marlett, David. "The Potential Impact of an Optional Federal Charter on the Social Resiliency of Hazard-Prone Regions." Mercatus Policy Series, Policy Comment 27, Mercatus Center at George Mason University, Arlington, VA, 2010.

Schaeffer, Emily. "The Housing Voucher Choice Program: More Than Just a Lagniappe for New Orleans." Mercatus Policy Series, Policy Comment 13, Mercatus Center at George Mason University, Arlington, VA, 2007.

Sobel, Russell, Christopher Coyne, and Peter Leeson. "The Political Economy of FEMA: Did Reorganization Matter?" *Journal of Public Finance and Public Choice* 17, no. 2-3 (2009): 49–65.

Sobel, Russell, and Peter Leeson. "The Use of Knowledge in Natural Disaster Relief Management." *Independent Review* 11, no. 4 (2007): 519–32.

Storr, Virgil, and Laura Grube. "The Capacity for Self-governance and Post-disaster Resiliency." *Review of Austrian Economics* 27, no. 3 (2014): 301–24.

Storr, Virgil, and Stefanie Haeffele-Balch. "Post-disaster Community Recovery in Heterogeneous, Loosely-Connected Communities." *Review of Social Economy* 70, no. 3 (2012): 295–314.

Storr, Virgil, Stefanie Haeffele-Balch, and Laura Grube. *Community Revival in the Wake of Disaster*. New York: Palgrave Macmillan, 2015.

Sutter, Daniel. "Building a Safe Port in the Storm: Private vs. Public Choices in Hurricane Mitigation." Mercatus Policy Series, Policy Comment 21, Mercatus Center at George Mason University, Arlington, VA, 2008.

Yandle, Bruce, and Mark Adams. "Regulatory Flexibility: How to Mitigate the Effects of Katrina and Other Disasters." Mercatus Policy Series, Policy Comment 28, Mercatus Center at George Mason University, Arlington, VA, 2010.

ABOUT THE AUTHORS

Nona Martin Storr is an affiliated scholar at the Mercatus Center at George Mason University. Her work has focused on the political and social histories of disadvantaged communities. She holds a PhD in history from George Mason University and a MA in public history (with an emphasis in oral history) from Loyola University Chicago.

Emily Chamlee-Wright is a senior research scholar and board member at the Mercatus Center. She is provost and dean of the college at Washington College in Chestertown, Maryland. Her scholarly work examines the intersection between cultural and economic processes, and includes a groundbreaking body of work on community resilience in New Orleans following Hurricane Katrina, ethnographic research on female entrepreneurship in sub-Saharan Africa, and theoretical work on cultural economy. Chamlee-Wright is the editor of *Liberal Learning and the Art of Self-Governance* (Routledge 2015), which investigates the role institutions of liberal learning play in fostering habits of engaged citizenship and robust civil society.

Virgil Henry Storr is a senior research fellow and director of Graduate Student Programs at the Mercatus Center. He is also a research associate professor in the department of economics at George Mason University. His scholarly work has focused on the relationship between culture and economic action, including research on the role of entrepreneurship in promoting community rebound after disasters. Storr is a coauthor of the forthcoming *Community Revival in the Wake of Disaster: Lessons in Local Entrepreneurship* (Palgrave 2015) with Stefanie Haeffele-Balch and Laura E. Grube.

ABOUT THE MERCATUS CENTER AT GEORGE MASON UNIVERSITY

The Mercatus Center at George Mason University is the world's premier university source for market-oriented ideas—bridging the gap between academic ideas and real-world problems.

A university-based research center, Mercatus advances knowledge about how markets work to improve people's lives by training graduate students, conducting research, and applying economics to offer solutions to society's most pressing problems.

Our mission is to generate knowledge and understanding of the institutions that affect the freedom to prosper and to find sustainable solutions that overcome the barriers preventing individuals from living free, prosperous, and peaceful lives.

Founded in 1980, the Mercatus Center is located on George Mason University's Arlington campus.

www.mercatus.org

45406246R00154

Made in the USA
Middletown, DE
03 July 2017